The House of Hades

Studies in Religion • 2

Edited by:
Per Bilde, Armin W. Geertz,
Lars Kruse-Blinkenberg, Ole Riis and
Erik Reenberg Sand

For Bebi

The House of Hades

Studies in Ancient Greek Eschatology

Lars Albinus

AARHUS UNIVERSITY PRESS

Cover: The Tomb of Agamemnon (Treasury of Atreus), at Mycenae, Greece
Cover photograph: Tønnes Bekker-Nielsen
Colour separation: Ploug Repro, Aarhus
Printed in the UK by the Alden Press, Oxford
ISBN 87 7288 833 4

Published with financial support from the Danish Research Council for the Humanities and Aarhus University Research Foundation

AARHUS UNIVERSITY PRESS
Langelandsgade 177
DK-8200 Aarhus N
Fax (+ 45) 8942 5380
www.unipress.dk

73 Lime Walk
Headington, Oxford OX3 7AD
Fax (+ 44) 1865 750 079

Box 511
Oakville, Conn. 06779
Fax (+ 1) 860 945 9468

ANSI/NISO
Z39.48-1992

Preface

What happens, when we die?

If we are looking for answers in the field of *religion*, we may find that *death* is rarely, if ever, represented as the complete end of individual existence. But what does individual existence really mean? By investigating interrelated meanings of life and death in different contexts in ancient Greece, we shall try to characterize one historical and religiously significant answer to this question, the trans-historical dimension of which is not, therefore, to articulate what death could be when we are dead, but rather what death can be taken to mean when we are alive.

When we pose a question to the unknown, our gaze confronts a mirror. Even the total *otherness* presupposes something *familiar*; the *different* somehow always implies the *same*. In the mirror that death raises to our gaze, the life of the individual is provided with a reference to something else, and still it seems to be nothing but this life in its own living totality that is stamped on the image of death. In the following, we are not going to spot the mirror of death as a clue to what death means as an independent phenomenon. The meanings that we are looking for are those of the ancient Greeks. What does Greek death say about Greek life? That is what we will be looking for in the mirror, which is also the mirror of history of ourselves as a result of former deaths. Futhermore, we shall strive to make visible what is indeed invisible in itself, namely, the mirror as such, the process of reflection.

The following text is itself a reflection of the combined process of learning, making a theoretical choice, and communicating the results. I am therefore thankful to the editorial board of the series *Studies in Religion* for suggesting that I turn this work, which was originally presented as a university dissertation, into a book.

In the course of completing this project I have enjoyed a great deal of help from many people and institutions. In this regard I wish to thank the Aarhus University Research Foundation and the Danish Research Council for the Humanities for their financial support; Neil Stanford for language revision; Inge Albinus, Per Bilde, Armin Geertz and Giuseppe Torresin for reading the manuscript at various stages and for providing helpful advice; Mary Lund and Liselotte Bülow of Aarhus University Press, for kind assistance in the editiorial work.

Lars Albinus
Aarhus, June 2000

Contents

Introduction

This book presents studies of ancient Greek eschatology in a pre-Christian context. It should be noted at the outset that eschatology is used as an observer's category from the perspective of phenomenology of religion. The eponymous Greek word ἔσχατος carried no specifically religious connotations until the Christian notion of ἐσχατολογία was used to designate 'the last times', 'the end of the world'. Yet, before the introduction of Christianity, the Greeks seemed more or less unconcerned with the general fate of mankind.[1] What mattered was the fate of the individual mortal being. In this respect, however, it is worth noticing that ἔσχατος was implicitly associated with the invisible realm of immortality and afterlife by denoting extremes of space and time (meaning, e.g., "furthest", "uttermost" or "last"). Thus, the phrase τὰ ἔσχατα παθεῖν, which means "to suffer the fate of death", can be translated literally as "to experience the last things". Specifically, then, I shall use the word eschatology in this study *as referring to human afterlife within a perspective of what is generally beyond space and time in the world of mortals.*[2] The purpose of this definition is to single out a field of statements and ritual practice that concern death as a religious phenomenon. It is not my objective to relate this complex of 'attitudes' or 'ideas' to any trans-historical question of truth, but simply to discover some basic, traditional responses to the condition of mortality within the complex of ancient Greek religion. In order to do so, I shall attempt to render visible the dominant traits of semantic organization, while pointing to contesting frameworks of representation and interpretation that seem constitutive in this respect. The notion of discourse is provided to guide this line of investigation[3] and is understood to mean *an order of rules that organizes certain conditions of communicating experience and belief*. Hence, it will be the phenomena of religious communication, rather than religious experience as such, that specify the object of investigation. The point here is rather banal, i.e., it is not the thing thought, but the thing said or done which is immediately approachable to the historian.

1. Hesiod's reference to the five races of mankind can be taken as an exception, cf. *Op.*109 ff., but does not strictly represent an eschatological issue.
2. In an attempt to define eschatology as different from the context of apocalyptic writings, Geo Widengren holds that "Die Eschatologie umfaßt [...] sowohl die individuelle Eschatologie als auch die allgemeine Eschatologie, umfaßt das Los sowohl den einzelnen Menschen als auch der ganzen Menscheit nach dem Tode", 1969, 440.
3. For the specific implications of the concept of discourse as I use it and understand it in the context of ancient history, see Albinus, 1994; 1997a.

Somewhere along the line, religious experience may inevitably come into the picture; all I am saying is that by trying to grasp it as the real and original object of study, one may, if perhaps unwittingly, take the texts hostage in attempt to bridge what seems for various reasons to be fractures and distortions of an underlying world-view or just, say, an integrated but unwarranted conception of afterlife. It will not only be the surviving texts, for that matter, but the missing ones as well which then come to satisfy the expectation of continuity. Seen from another angle we may ask: what if various inconsistencies, differences and omissions that one may stumble upon in the investigation of ancient textual traditions point more than anything else to different restrictions of discourse? Take, for instance, the tradition of Homer. Why is it that "he" represents the deceased as mere shadows when we know from other texts as well as from various archaeological findings that the Greeks actually had a cult of the dead? True, the Homeric characters can appear *post mortem* in the form of an image that is capable of communicating with the living, but this motif is far from indicating that various kinds of hero-cult formed the back-bone of local religion, as other sources seem to suggest they did.[4] What is the reason for this inconsistency? Is it that the songs of Homer are not genuinely religious, but rather a work of art having other interests than "living" beliefs at its centre, as has been suggested, for example by Nilsson (1955, 360 f.) and Harrison (1912, 334 f.)? Or is it that Homer is merely one of many voices of representation, with "his" silence being strategic and significant on that account? What makes a difference here is the notion of *religion as belief*. If detached from this criterion, Homer may be as genuinely religious as any other source speaking of the gods or other supernatural referents. The fact that on several points, Homer is difficult to reconcile with other testimonies to Greek religion may not be something to be explained away, but rather the crux of the matter.

Following that line of thought, it should be additionally noted that not only is Homer remarkably silent about a cult of the dead, but the firm distinction between "the immortals" (ἀθάνατοι) and "the mortals" (θνητοί), which is constitutive of the epic relationship between gods and human beings, is in conflict with the representations in Classical texts of an immortal human soul. Is it that a universal experience of a *second* soul connects the different representations of ψυχή in Homer and Pindar, as Rohde suggests (1925, 6)? Or is it that the meaning of ψυχή simply changes from one discourse to another? One thing is certain: the sources of ancient Greek religion are full of discrepancies in terms of a supposed, overall belief-system. Not only are the

4. See, for example, Snodgrass, 1979, 31 ff.

various statements rooted in different periods, they also carry specific meanings in different contexts. How are we to come to grips with such a heterogeneous field of information? The historian of Greek religion, Karóly Kerényi, put it this way:

> Nicht, wie muss das Phänomen gewendet, gedreht, vereinseitigt oder verkümmert werden, um aus Grundsätzen, die wir uns einmal vorgesetzt, nicht zu überschreiten, noch allenfalls erklärbar zu sein, sondern: wohin müssen unsere Gedanken sich erweitern, um mit dem Phänomen in Verhältnis zu stehen. (1941, 214)

Perhaps this is easier said than done.[5] Still, it will count as a prescription for our present approach. The phenomenon to be apprehended is a phenomenon of ancient discourse, not of ancient minds, not of the history that leads from them to us (although somewhere along the line of interpretation this history is implicit), but the texts themselves in their specific historical and intertextual contexts.

From a point of view of hermeneutics, Paul Ricoeur speaks about textual fixation as an exteriorization of discourse.[6] What happens in the process of writing is that the author's meaning is transformed into a semantic autonomy of the text (1976, 26-30). The writer disappears from the horizon which is produced by the text itself, and although the author's original intention *with* the text may still be a traceable part of its *context*, it is being irrevocably detached from the mind that produced it. "What the text means now matters more than what the author meant when he wrote it," as Ricoeur states (op.cit. 30). From a perspective of discourse analysis, one might be inclined to ask whether this bracketing of an access to the original author is sufficiently critical. If the human subject took the place of God in idealistic anthropology, creating the final resort of reference, then the text may perform a similar function in hermeneutics, even in the very radicalization of hermeneutics which can be said to be the position taken, for example, by Derrida (see Foucault, 1977, 119). Could it be that we need a double bracketing of meaning, so that not only the subject of the author, but also the text is reduced to the discourse that, as the very condition of their existence, allows for a specific expression of 'subject' and 'text' (Foucault, 1969, 44 ff.; Dreyfus & Rabinow, 1982, 48 ff.)? And if so, is there a point of view, beyond the level of meaningful apprehension, from which we would be able to detect, let alone

5. As formulated by Foucault: 'L'analyse de la pensée est toujours *allégorique* par rapport au discours qu'elle utilise', 1969, 40. So, although the object of investigation will be "Gedanken", rather than "Vorstellungen" (according to the distinction made by Frege, 1891-92, 44 ff.), these 'thoughts' will still *have* to be transformed into those other thoughts that our discourse allows them to be.
6. Discourse is here being understood as language use, the event of speaking, cf. 1976, 7 f.

describe, such a discourse? How would we be able to recognize structures or systems of discourse other than those which already delimit the vantage point from which we are looking? At least it seems to me that in so far as *meanings* are to be identified, even the tiniest process of such identification creates, in the depth of its appearance, a bond between ourselves and the past that transcends the category of formal analysis. For better or worse, it seems to me that we cannot escape the field of interpretation,[7] and every discourse, including a discourse behind the unity of the text, remains tied to former texts. Even the systems of thought which form the analytical perspective of Foucault's historical descriptions are not purely formal or more basic than the texts themselves. The encounter between text and reader is rooted in a discourse that is neither totally the *same*, nor totally *other*. The limit of the text may always be a mirror of its reading, but every reading is, at the same time, a reflection of the text. We may say that they die and live together. If the reading reproduces nothing more than purely structural properties, reflecting only the very process of reflection, then this formality counts *as* meaningful, imbued with the prospect that it perhaps strove to transcend in the first place. Thus, I will have to admit that Scylla and Charybdis may lurk on the horizon of the textual investigations at hand, namely as far as these will be carried out from a point of view that pretends to be neither full-blooded structuralist nor full-blooded hermeneutical but yet something of both at one and the same time.[8] The perspective may be called *genealogical* in the sense that I shall concentrate on how textual frames of meaning provide the grounds for other frames to appear or disappear, and how discursive limits border on each other by referring to other limits being the limits of eschatology.

Throughout this investigation, I will remain sceptical towards prefigured concepts such as the supposed "Lebender Leichnam" in the cult of the dead (cf. *Chapter II*) and the "Freiseele" of primitive, Archaic thought, connected as the latter is to the misleading category of "Greek Shamanism" (cf. *Chapter III*). Not only may such concepts be forced on scarce availability of source material, but they are also appreciated as meta-discursive which is unfortunate for the attempt to recognize what goes on, not behind, but between the events and orders of discourse. I shall try to release the order of the Homeric epics from primitivist stereotypes, while at the same time, I shall take the surrendered texts seriously as the verbal expression of a religious discourse. I shall refrain from asking

7. See Fabian, 1979, 4 ff.; *HDA* III, 3; Pêcheux, 1988, 643, who make this point in relation to the Foucault-inspired field of discourse analysis, within which the scope and purpose of analysis is often defined as basically incompatible with the hermeneutic pretension to *understand*.
8. See further, Albinus, 1994; 1997a, 205-10.

questions about ultimate origins, as the phenomenologists of religion did at the turn of the century. On the one hand, I shall not use the all-too-convenient category of folk-religion to explain away disturbing difficulties in the epics (cf. *Chapter V*), but on the other hand, I would not want to turn a blind eye to possible interpolations, editions and reinterpretations of the textual tradition. Indeed, it is precisely the smallest instances of alteration in the midst of the work of preservation that are of interest from a genealogical perspective. Not the origin of a proper meaning, but traces of relative origins, i.e., the descent and transformation of meaning in discourse, is what I shall be looking for.[9] So, in this context, Homeric discourse is not to be regarded merely as a survival from an Archaic mentality, but as a living source of religious orientation all through the period of ancient Greek culture. The other dominating strand of a religious, epic tradition, namely the songs of Orpheus, may be relatively younger than the songs of Homer, but it was precisely as living traditions that both discourses were, presumably interactively, influential at the beginning of Classical times. Hence, the perspective of this book is primarily synchronic, not just because of the difficulty we may have in resolving the genetic relations of a diachronic perspective, but also - and even more so - because the research that I am about to undertake is not a search for origins, but for relations of meaning within discursive formations, tied to the field of interaction between them.

Tradition is understood, in this perspective, as the practice of repetition. This includes verbal repetition as well as the prescribed performance of other communicative acts. If we consider Homer, not as an author in any historical sense, but as the authorizer of an oral tradition, we notice that the crucial act consists of *recitation*. Likewise, if we consider Orpheus, not solely as a mythical character, but also as a similar authorizer of a tradition, we notice that the crucial act, in this respect, consists of *initiation*. This "rite of passage" may, or may not, have been immediately joined by a recitation of what were later delivered as the "sacred tales" (ἱεροὶ λόγοι) of Orpheus. Still, the crucial discursive act was the act of performing the ritual. Hence, the main difference between Homeric and Orphic tradition, apart from the names of identification, was that they formed different arrangements of ritual communication. Yet the semantic and the

9. As I read Foucault's reception of Nietzsche's *Genealogy*, 1977, 139 ff., I largely subscribe to his view on "effective" or "genealogical" history, see especially, op.cit. 153 ff.; see also Albinus, 1997b, 216. The only reservation is that I find his ultimate suspicion of *recognition* somehow self-refuting. Foucault seems to argue that we do not exactly recognize systems of thought, since they only appear negatively, as formalized by the limits that once rejected them. This is still an act of recognition, though, and what one must be aware of is rather the precise character of this act.

pragmatic dimension were also interrelated insofar as Homeric recitation may have been a kind of initiation on the part of the listeners, while Orphic initiation may have been structured as a kind of narrative. More importantly, however, both traditions recognized the original author as the authority of tradition (Homer and Orpheus respectively), while the current performer, the singer or the mystagogue, was only supposed to perform the anonymous role of repetition. To deliver this discourse by inspiration from the Muses and thus to re-perform verbal or dramatic imitation of the past was installed, once and for all, in the name of the first performer. Maintaining the decisive authority of discourse, this performer authored a tradition within a system of communication that can be held as being specifically religious. Without attempting to define "religion" in any adequate phenomenological extension of the term, I shall thus consider *religious discourse* as this practice of "referring to someone" (τὸ ἀναφέρειν εἴς τινα) who authorizes a formation of statements by having special access to the realm of the beyond. Homer and Orpheus were such authorities since, on the one hand, they had an extraordinary contact with the divine, be it the voice of the Muses or the daemons from the cave, and since, on the other hand, they were themselves transcendent beings in the tradition of performing certain communicative acts in their names. The struggle for exclusive authority associated with these poets of the past, being "creators" (ποιηταί) of the past as well,[10] was also introduced as the line of demarcation between them, as we see, for instance, in the polemical suggestion that Orpheus was really the forefather of Homer (see p.109).

No doubt, the implication was that he was the first of the two to receive the divine gift of song. Thus, by reference to the authorities of 'Homer' and 'Orpheus' two orders of religious discourse established themselves in opposition to each other.[11]

In reality neither the Homeric nor the Orphic discourse survived as repetition pure and simple. Every performance risked the fate of being altered, of being the legitimation of changes. Perhaps no complex tradition ever remains totally un-

10. Cf. the Greek word for "poet", ποιητής, the literal meaning of which is a "maker".
11. It goes without saying that there were many religious *agones* other than that between Homer and Orpheus, the most important one perhaps being the rivalization between the dictions of Homer and Hesiod, as represented in the 4th Century BC by Alcidamas, cf. *Hom.Hes. Gen.Ag*. Furthermore, there were other configurations of rivalization than the one authorized by reference to the name of an initiator. The use of genres, the formation of concepts, the introduction of a new kind of referentiality, among other things, all played decisive roles. The purpose of this book, however, is to focus primarily on relationships between Homeric and Orphic discourse, this focus being central for estimating transformations in the complex of eschatology from Archaic to Classical times.

changed during the period of its authorized existence. Some elements may, in the continuous work of actualization, pass unchanged, while others may be transformed. Often we speak loosely of tradition as a single world-view, a consistent, and perhaps even constant, set of beliefs and practices. In ancient Greece, there was no such thing as one single religion in this sense. Rather there was a grid of discursive struggles. The rivalization, however, was a productive one. New rules of communication, new frames of authority, were created as the result of conflict and competition. Instead of *one* tradition, eventually passing away as superstition, we see several *traits* of tradition, differently combined, and differently connected to changing and interacting rules of discourse.[12] Rather than a paradigm of μῦθος changing into a paradigm of λόγος, we recognize a complex system of semantic transportation and transformation that certainly had more than *one* crucial limit. What was indeed pivotal in making a single tradition survive as a tradition within this crucible of changes was that the main feature of identification persisted. Even if the Homeric singer did not succeed in reproducing a verbatim repetition of the last performance (which he, presumably, never did), he was still supposed to repeat what Homer had originally heard from the Muse. And even though the context of meaning-attributions to the texts of Orpheus differed, as, for example, between the Derveni-commentary of the 4th Century BC and that of the early Church fathers, Orpheus himself remained at the core of the referential system being immutably the originator of initiations incorporated in the framework of his own poems. Accordingly, we shall apprehend 'tradition' principally as *a complex of continuity and discontinuity*[13] and fundamentally as a matter of discourse. However, although tradition thus regarded may in fact be recognizable as a synchronic network of interrelations on the level of semantic analysis, we should not forget that there was always *someone* to use the means of communication and to use them in certain *situations*. Hence, when speaking of discourse, or rather of several discourses, and accordingly of several traditions such as the Homeric and the Orphic ones, we shall not only be dealing with them as autonomous and static systems, but also as interrelated, historical processes. Therefore the method will be neither purely structural nor purely historical. The intention has been to

12. As in the words of Foucault: "[L]e problème n'est plus de la tradition et de la trace, mais de la découpe et de la limite; ce n'est plus celui du fondement qui se perpétue, c'est celui des transformations qui valent comme fondation et renouvellement des fondations", 1969, 12.
13. I do not hereby propose a definition, but merely a certain point of view. For a more detailed discussion on the concept of 'tradition', see Albinus, 1997a, 213- ff.; 1997b, 239-243.

appreciate formations and transformations of eschatological motives in a dense context of semantic as well as pragmatic preconditions.

In very broad terms, the overall frameworks of meaning, and the historical processes between them, seem clear enough. The Archaic attitude towards death was confined to remembrance and adoration of the dead through hero-cult and epic song. Under the sway of Homeric discourse, the fate of mortals was regarded, with only a few exceptions, as a departure for the House of Hades, inhabited by the ghost-like images of former lives. However, a specific interest in the *hereafter*, representing a continuation of individual existence in its own right, developed from Archaic to Classical times, much under the influence of Orphic discourse, and accompanied by extensive changes in social life. In Homeric discourse the individual was surrendered, by dying, to collective memory, while in Orphic discourse the individual was in some sense trained to surrender on his own. The final end became an ultimate beginning. The representation of life and death was metaphorically inverted, reflected as if by a mirror. By way of ritual manipulation the limits of time and space moved into the reach of living human beings. Immortality was no longer the monopoly of the gods who failed to remain therefore those totally other-worldly and unquestioned powers they once were. Eventually, the tradition of religious discourse became involved in a mystery of silence as was the case, even quite literally, in the Eleusinian mystery cult in honour of Demeter and her daughter. In this complex of secret initiation the discrepancies between those traditions which represented and influenced them lost some of their significance due to the rule of non-representation. Yet the *Eleusiniai* grew to be a highly influential discourse in its own right, and, thankfully, ancient lore has not completely prevented us envisaging the frame as well as the basic content of its religious orientation. There are indeed many sources left to be considered, and if approached with the requisite care they may be of great help to our study of eschatology. The main question in this respect will be in what way, or rather in what *ways*, the Mysteries of Eleusis addressed the relationship between life and death and, specifically, how they addressed the matter of human afterlife.

Throughout, we shall bear in mind such questions as: What were the connections between shifting representations of life and death? What bearings did they have on matters of legitimization? What were the reasons and the preconditions for bringing the *other*, the world of the dead, into focus? What were the relations between former identities, as represented in the dead, and the formation of new identities, aiming at the fate of the living?

Insofar as the question is not only *why*, but also *how* semantic changes such as these came about, my initial search for the answers is in the complex work of traditional renewal. What the ancient Greeks show us with exceptional clarity, I think, is that this work is by itself a vehicle of authorization as well as of resistance, and that the flexibility of preservation as well as the force of innovation seem to draw on a common strategy of imitation, inversion and opposition. From this perspective, interaction of discursive practices pushes itself to the forefront of investigation. Furthermore, I suggest that the representation of death, significant as a transformation into the invisible, was of the highest priority on the battleground of legitimization. Controlling the frame of the mirror, the reflection of death in its relation to life, was concomitant with gaining a profound discursive power over religious discourse. Apart from the authorial authorizations of tradition, the organization of discursive limits was thus defined by the formation of central concepts such as 'soul', 'immortality', 'death' and 'afterlife'. As for the tradition of Homer and Orpheus, however, different formations of eschatology were so closely associated with the power of each of their names that we shall permit ourselves, for the sake of clarity, to use the designations of *Homeric* and *Orphic discourse* as headings for our study, referring not only to the *works* that have survived as Homeric and Orphic, but also to the contexts of orientations and practices of which they are still the visible result. As initiators of the dominating systems of tradition (all through the period from Archaic to Classical times) they identified continuous models of meaning that accounted for almost every aspect of Greek life and death. Hence, in the Platonic words of Ion:

> One poet is suspended from one Muse, another from another: the word we use for it is "possessed" (κατέχεται), but it is much the same thing, for he is held (ἔχεται). And from these first rings[14] - the poets - are suspended various others, which are thus inspired, some by Orpheus and others by Musaeus;[15] but the majority are possessed and held by Homer (Pl. *Ion* 536b).

Finally, the suggestion is that along these sketched-out lines of approach, the study of ancient eschatology will intrinsically lead us to the interrelated limits and frontiers of the Homeric and the Orphic discourse, as well as *vice versa*. The perspective of Homeric eschatology, basically negative as it ascribes all true value to the presence and image of life, is rivalled by the perspective of Orphic eschatology, which is, in turn, basically positive as it ascribes all true value to the immortality of the soul and the world beyond. While not striving to extract any single eschatology from the heterogeneous complex of Greek religion, we shall attempt to estimate those different attitudes towards death that may, at the same time, be essential to the overall framing of religious discourse.

14. This refers to rings of magnetism mentioned earlier, *R*.533d-e.
15. Musaeus was being closely associated with Orpheus, see, for example, Pl.*R*.364e.

Part One

Homeric Discourse

I. The Homeric Tradition

Socrates: And so you act as interpreters of interpreters?
Pl. *Ion* 535a

The Mycenaean world (from about 1500 until about 1200 BC), or "the age of the heroes", is separated from the Archaic world (from the 9th Century until the 6th Century BC) by the so-called 'Dark Age'.[1] This name alludes to the poor amount of source-material available from that period, a gap of silence which has thus fostered a burden of missing links between Mycenaean civilization and what seems to be a representation of it in the epic tradition of Homer. It is quite reasonable to suggest that this tradition may have some kind of prehistoric roots.[2] What escapes us is the precise nature of the connection between the world, as presented in the epics, and the world in which this description grew into a traditional framework of diction. The question is, in the present chapter, whether it is possible to say anything about the bonds between the introduction of this tradition and the form of it that is known to us through the written epics.

The singer himself is significantly imprecise. He invokes the Olympic Muses, whose inspiration enables him to sing of the past:

for ye are goddesses and are at hand (πάρεστε) and know all things,
whereas we hear but a rumour (κλέος) and know not anything. (*Il.*2.485-86)

Although the singer admits to living several lifetimes after the events and generations to which he refers, he nevertheless explicitly assumes the position of one who delivers the truth about the past rather than a mere "rumour" (κλέος).[3] His words show a concern for what really happened, and who was actually there.

Yet who was *he*, we might ask. Did his voice belong to a real person called Homer or did it belong to the succession of singers deputized to speak on his behalf? This problem has divided philologists as long as they have been trying to establish the identity of Homer. The *unitarians* (and to some degree also the *neo-analytics*) claimed that the psychological consistency of the described

1. See especially Snodgrass, 1971.
2. Cf. Bengtson, 1960, 61; Heubeck, 1974, 203 f.; Finley, 1979, 165 ff.
3. Normally, however, the content of κλέος does not stand in any immediate opposition to what actually happened, see however, Ford, 1992, 59.

characters and the narrative consistency of the plot had to originate from a single and genius author.[4] The *analytics*, on the other hand, took more critical notice of stylistic incompatibilities and various other sorts of inconsistencies. Their conclusion was that the epics, as we know them, originated from the contributions of many poets. Most analytical studies, however, still referred to traces of an original author.[5] The neo-analytics actually delivered the studies to modify the perspective of this identification. They showed that not only did the narrative frames of the *Iliad* and the *Odyssey* obviously belong to an older correlative to the *Epic Cycle* (the summary of which we find in the *Chrestomathia* reported by Proclus, cf. Procl. *Chr.*), but that this relationship was itself a constitutive element of the Homeric style.[6] So, even if Homer existed as an original composer, the roots of his work ran deep into the dark of collective tradition.[7] The question as to the origin of Homer became a new one. What were the elements of tradition, and how were they integrated into the work that was, at some point in time, written down under the name of Homer? In the late twenties Milman Parry presented some theoretical reflections that, although they were passed over in silence for several decades, supplied the outlines of a probable answer. Parry argued that the abundance of identical or analogical verse-makings in the epics came from a mnemonic reservoir of *formulae*. These formulae covered every need for the description of situations and personal characters.[8] A principle of *economy* (no more formulae than necessary) and a

4. For example, Hölscher, 1939; P. Krarup, 1945, 233; K. Reinhardt, 1961, 11 ff.; U. Heubeck still supports such a view in certain respects, 1974. D.L. Page sides with the neo-analytics, claiming that different layers of narrative elements do not necessarily imply different poets, 1963a, 16 ff.
5. Ulrik von Wilamowitz-Moellendorf, whose attitude was basically analytical, suggested that Homer was perhaps the author of one original poem, to which several layers had been added in the course of time, 1884, 227 ff. Other analytic positions are taken by Merkelbach, 1951, 199 ff.; Mühl, 1952.
6. See especially Schadewaldt, the first, perhaps, to cross the line between analytics and unitarians, 1959, 345 ff.; compare Hölscher, 1972, 388 ff.
7. See Finley, 1979, 33 ff.; Nagy, 1990b, 72 ff. As Nagy points out, the poems of the *Epic Cycle* were often ascribed to Homer, simply because he was "the central figure of textual fixation", op.cit. 78. Still, they were also ascribed to other poets such as Arctinus and Lesches, while the *Iliad* and the *Odyssey* were systematically, and exclusively, associated with the authority of Homer as a part of the process Panhellenic canonization, op.cit. 70 ff.
8. A *formula* is thus defined as "a group of words [originally in French: *une expression*] which is regularly employed under the same metrical conditions to express a given essential idea", 1971 (1930), 272. Take, for instance, the third verse of the *Iliad*, which is a set of formulae consisting of two unchanging word-groups, πολλὰς δ'ἰφθίμους and

principle of *extension* (knowledge of all necessary formulae) enabled the singer to recite comprehensive, pre-figured, compositions of narrative and diction by heart. "It is obvious", as Parry puts it, "that one poet never could have created this entire series of formulae" (1971 (1928), 18). Hence, Parry's demonstration of the pervasive, structural properties of Homeric verse-making challenged the unitarian argument of authorial consistency as well as the equally psychological perspective of most of the analytical arguments. The originating principle was not to be found in any authorial subject, but in the system of oral tradition. The object of Parry's analysis was not the *meaning* of sentences but the metrical *rules* of constructing them. We may, however, object to the reductionism of this approach, if it is actually used to explain *away* the option of individual creations and interpretations of meaning.[9] Confining the mode of expression to the frames of traditional story-telling is not the same as exhausting actual meanings beforehand. As long as the singer followed the rules of composition, nothing would necessarily have prevented him from making his own variations, however small they might have been (insofar as originality was not regarded as a virtue). What is important to remember is that it was always optional within oral tradition to make such contributions of meaning. Oral poetry was never just a self-identical system of repetition;[10] it was a property of various performances in various places. As it is today a property of *our* reading, we must grasp it like any other text, while of course adjusting our interpretation to the knowledge of relevant historical preconditions. Nothing, on the other hand, obliges us to take a historical Homer into account as the agent who brings about psychological coherence.

Parry's theory of the epics as an oral tradition does not solve the problem of their age, but it turns the identity of Homer into the identity of tradition. In consequence, the date of origin also loses some of its significance.[11] In principle, the first steps of textual fixation could have taken place together with the actual introduction and vocalization of the Phoenician alphabet, that is, as early as in the latter part of the 8th Century BC.[12] The full elaboration of style, exhibited in

Ἄιδι προΐαψεν, surrounding a paradigm of a certain type of words (or expressions), where the word ψυχή is chosen in this case (instead of, e.g., θυμός, which appear synonymously in other similar expressions), Parry, op.cit. 301.

9. See, for example, Parry, 1971 (1928), 68; Lord, 1968, 1 ff.
10. See especially Hainsworth's study of the flexibility of formulaic regulation (1968, 110 ff.), and Lowenstam, 1981, 9.
11. See Nagy, 1996, 9 ff.
12. Contrary to earlier assumptions, Carpenter suggested that the alphabet was probably not introduced before the second part of the 8th Century BC, 1933, 8 ff.; likewise Page, 1963b, 119 ff., who argues for regarding the epic tradition as predating Archilochus; see however Wade-Gery, 1952, 13.

the *Iliad* and the *Odyssey* as *we* know these poems, belongs, I suggest, to a later period. Be that as it may, the basic oral form must have stabilized well before the appearance of epic motives on archaic vase-paintings,[13] at latest in the Geometric Period, from which we have some archaeological evidence for supposing that a Panhellenic hero-cult in commemoration of the epic characters was already developing.[14] None of this proves anything as to the origin of epic poetry, but only makes it probable that it consolidated its Panhellenic dimension as early as in the 8th Century BC. Indeed, this is interesting on its own account, but the question remains whether there is any reason to suggest that the introduction of the poems in a written form had anything to do with it. Skafte Jensen does not think so and argues for the middle of the 6th Century as a probable date for the production of the first textual editions. The demand for written versions of the narratives could very well have been promoted by the festival of Panathenaia where a formal competition was held between professional 'rhapsodes'; thus, the option of consulting written accounts yielded the basis of artistic evaluation (Skafte Jensen, 1968, 84 f.).[15] A further conjecture is that the labour of turning the oral tradition into writing was introduced by the famous four editors under the sway of Pisistratos.[16]That the tradition of Homer went through the hands of this editorial board in Athens has been known since antiquity,[17] but to regard it as the very birthplace of written Homeric poems expresses a radically new understanding of Homer, and the suggestion begs the question why it took so long after the introduction of the alphabet before written versions were actually

13. Wilamowitz, 1916, 356 ff.; Friis Johansen, 1934, 17 ff.; Schadewaldt, 1944, 94 f. See, however, Nagy who holds that Archaic Greek iconographical evidence indicates 'that the earliest identifiable pictorial responses to epic concern are predominantly the themes of the *Cycle*, not those of the *Iliad* or *Odyssey*', 1990b, 72, n.104.
14. Some have argued that the reopening of abandoned Mycenaean graves for commemorative use in the Geometric period was occasioned by the spreading of the epic tradition to the mainland (cf. Farnell, 1921, 280 ff.; 340 ff.; Coldstream, 1976, 8 ff.; 1977, 341-356), while others have held that hero-cult and epic poetry developed as contemporary, interacting traditions through the Dark Age, or Iron Age (Price, 1979, 221 ff.; Calligas, 1986, 232 ff.; Schmitt-Pantel, 1982, 185). See, however, Snodgrass, 1988, 19 ff., who basically argues for regarding the cult traditions of Mycenae as independent of the epics.
15. See also Allen, 1924, 226 f.
16. For a more detailed elaboration of the view, see Merkelbach, 1951, 239 ff.; Skafte Jensen, 1992, 13.
17. See also Carpenter, 1956, 12.

produced.[18] On the other hand, it is perhaps not of such great importance for the understanding of Homer as a *tradition*. Whatever the precise date of textual fixation, we will have to take into account the possibility of incessant variations, not merely as a matter of editorial interference by way of which they become interpolations in the proper sense, but also, if maybe on a smaller scale, as a matter of individual oral repetition. We have no access to the exact utterance in the exact ritualized act of recitation. What we have is a very late version of the written corpus that went through the hands of Alexandrian editors. Yet, however significant this situation may be for the perspective of our interpretation,[19] the object of our interpretation will be something more than just the written tradition, namely, insofar as a text is not the exhaustion of discourse, as I have stated earlier, but rather a regulation of it. Moreover, the division of the Panhellenic Homer, into the *Iliad* and the *Odyssey*, may point in the direction of two, not entirely parallel, traditions. Actually, the *Odyssey* is often regarded as one or more generations younger than the *Iliad* (Nilsson, 1935, 55 f.; Kirk, 1962, 282; Bengtson, 1960, 63), and viewing the epics as oral traditions does not necessarily modify this suggestion (cf. Marzullo, 1952, 32 ff.). Hence, it is not impossible that the *Odyssey* reflects a new orientation, in relation to the *Iliad*, within the shared frame of Homeric discourse. And then there are the hymns. Not only are they of an even more recent date, composed for the most part within the span of the next centuries, they also present a new genre, and partly a new diction. Yet they share the dactylic hexameter with the epics, and Homer was still recognized as their author, thus the grouping of them together in the discrete formation of Homeric discourse.[20]

18. That the use of writing was certainly very restricted even until the mid-fifth Century, cf. Havelock, 1963, 38 ff., cannot immediately be taken to defend the thesis, insofar as the singers of epic poetry, belonging to a rather small elite, might still have been motivated, for whatever reason, to produce a written version. While Lord yields in principal to the view of 'Homer' as a figure of tradition participating in the city-state festivals, he does not, however, find any reason to connect it with the need for a written version, nor does he find the festival to be a likely opportunity to produce one, 1960, 152 f. Rather, the dictation of a final, developed version was, according to Lord, inspired by the Eastern literary traditions, most prominently those of the *Creation Epic*, and the *Gilgamesh Epic*, op.cit. 156 f. I see no reason why Lord's and Skafte Jensen's suggestions should irreconcilably exclude one another. At any rate, the exact nature of motivation behind textual fixation is something we will never *know*.
19. See especially Finley, 1979, 30 f. and Lesky, 1971, 73. Against their view, see Skafte Jensen, 1980, 28 ff.; Nagy, 1990b, 17 f.
20. See Foucault, 1997, 123.

As for the epics, we assume that the bards[21] travelled about, reciting their poems in different places of Hellas. Hence they encountered different audiences, and they must have been prepared, to a certain degree, to oblige different expectations.[22] Thus, it should not surprise us, after all, to find various kinds of inconsistencies in the epic texts.

However, I do not wish the supposed influence of compromises between individual singers and their local audiences to bear the whole burden of explanation in this respect. It goes without saying that the process of collecting and editing different contributions to the overall epic formation may also have exerted its influence. In any case, the heterogenous nature of the resulting text may only have enlarged the scope of appeal as long as it did not disturb the 'balance' of Panhellenism.[23] The discordance between the mythologems of 'Hades' and '*Ēlusion*', for instance, can be seen as a controlled representation of different traditions (cf. *Chapter IV*). The way in which they were adjusted to each other was, however, significantly Homeric. By reading Homer as a source for the history of Archaic Greek religion, we will not attempt, therefore, to dissolve a complex of religious themes into 'Einzelheiten religiöser Vorstellungen', as Nilsson did (1955, 360),[24] but rather try to grasp its internal organization, that is, the present frame of its discourse.

21. See Schadewaldt, 1944, 379, and Nagy, 1990b, 21-30, concerning the difference between the role of the 'singer' (ἀοιδός) and that of the later 'rhapsode' (ῥαψῳδός).
22. See Skafte Jensen, 1992, 51 ff., and Dowden, 1989, 49 ff.
23. As seems to be the case in Hdt.5.67, where we read that after his campaign against Argos, Clisthenes 'stopped the rhapsodists' competitions in reciting from Homer's poems in Sicyon, because they were full of praise for Argos and the Argives'. Translation taken from Sélincourt, *Text ed.* (p.205).
24. Compare also Kakridis, 1949, 11 ff., and Page, 1955, 13 ff.

II. The Funeral Rites of Patroclus

For to dead corpses should no man grudge,
when once they are dead, the speedy consolation of fire.

Il. 7.409-410

It seems that the Greeks of the Mycenaean age had a continuous cult of the dead in addition to a tradition of inhumation. Archaeological evidence from shaft-, tholos- and chamber-tombs (originating already in the Middle Helladic period) tells us that people buried in such graves were often equipped with clothes, jewellery, articles of food and other items for everyday use.[1] Grave gifts are a common phenomenon in prehistory and in 'primitive' societies in general and have often been ascribed to the thought that the deceased were to continue some sort of life in the tomb. It is doubtful, however, if the presence of equipment does in itself indicate a belief in life after death.[2] Furthermore, the dead do certainly not lead an active life in the Homeric underworld. On the contrary, they are frozen pictures of the persons they once were in life. The deceased rower Elpenor, for example, does not ask Odysseus to bury him together with his oar, but to place this on top of his grave (*Od.*11.77). At the same time he wishes to be buried according to the custom of cremation. Thus, although the world of the epics has ancient roots, the Homeric tradition presents us with death rituals which are radically different from those of Mycenaean times. The question is whether there are any traces left at all, in the epics, of the Mycenaean practice of tending the dead body, and if so, whether or not such traces carried any eschatological meanings with them in the context of Homeric discourse.

The evidence of grave cults in Mycenaean times has actually led to the generally accepted opinion that the Greeks had a long tradition of belief in the *living dead* - or *Lebender Leichnam* as the phenomenon has been labelled (Nilsson, 1955, 41; Schnaufer, 1970, 8; W.F. Otto, 1927, 55). The first step in substantiating this suggestion may be to demonstrate that at least the 'tendance'[3] of the corpse in Mycenaean grave cults expressed such a belief. The suggestion, on behalf of

1. For a general introduction, see Taylour, 1983, 65-84; Dickinson, 1994, 208-233.
2. Thus questioned by Bremmer, 1983, 95; Nock, 1972, I, 277 ff.; cf. also the subtle argument of Wilamowitz writing that: 'Von einer Seele darf nicht geredet werden; Seelen essen nicht', 1959, I, 304.
3. See Farnell, 1921, 4 f., as for the invented concept of 'tendance'.

the prehistoric Greeks, seems to have been that the dead continued to be present among the living as long as they *looked* like the living. Thus, only after the process of natural decomposition, when the corpse had lost its human likeness, did the remaining bones cease to inspire fear. But is it really possible, one might ask, to take the piles of human bones, which have been found put aside in the Mycenaean graves, as a proof of this,[4] or do they merely reveal a practical way of creating new burial space? Another thing, which has been held in favour of the *Lebender Leichnam*-hypothesis, is the regular offerings of food and libations, which seem to have taken place from very early times.[5] However, such traces of a continuous cult of the dead are also found, and mentioned, in connection with the practice of cremation, which was introduced in Proto-Geometric times.[6] If one is justified in claiming, as I think one is, that the precise form of funeral does not necessarily reflect any specific belief in the destiny of the dead,[7] this change of tradition from pre-Homeric to Homeric source-material need not disturb us. But then again, the suggestion that the gifts and offerings are evidence for the belief in *living corpses* is hardly credible. Whether we see the gesture of grave offerings as honouring the dead, or we see it as an apotropaic ritual of appeasing their potential wrath, or even as part of a 'Totenmahl', i.e., a meal of communion between the living and the dead, the argument in all instances seems to be that the type of offerings defines the type of the recipients, so that they were 'living

4. See especially Mylonas, 1948, 70; Schnaufer, 1970, 10 f.; Nilsson, 1955, 12; 30 ff. Occasional finds of outstretched skeletons have been explained as due to the commonly agreed fact that the graves were generally abandoned at some point in time (during the Dark Age). While Mylonas speaks of a royal cult tradition only, Nilsson (1949, 618) and Persson (1931, 109) are inclined to describe the same belief and practice as a more general phenomenon in the Mycenaean age.
5. Apart from Schliemann's more conjectural views, 1878, 247 f., see Rohde, 1925, I, 231 ff.; Wiesner, 1938, 168; Mylonas, 1957, 134 ff.; Thönges-Stringaris, 1965, 1-13; 48-68; Andronikos, 1968, 106 f.; Vermeule, 1979, 87. As for the archaic περίδειπνον, see immediately below.
6. Schnaufer tries to demonstrate that, although votive offerings are found in relation to the practice of inhumation as well as to the practice of cremation, testimony to the former far exceeds that to the latter, 1970, 38 ff. The reason, according to Schnaufer, must be that the fire destroys the visible basis for fear of the corpse as a living entity, op.cit. 46. Along the same lines of argument, he sees the reason for not cremating child-corpses as due to a wish to keep them amongst the living, op.cit. 50; compare Rohde, 1925, I, 30 ff. Against the premise of Schnaufer's thesis, Kurtz and Boardman state that 'There is no apparant difference in either the rites or offerings which have been associated with the grave, and the predominance of one method over the other varies from place to place', 1971, 96.
7. See Hack, 1929, 69; W.F. Otto, 1927, 53 f.; Nilsson, 1955, 377; Bremmer, 1983, 94 f.

corpses' because of the fact that they were in need of the same articles as living beings. This may not hold, though, for the simple reason that the gods were also offered various articles for 'human' use, one such example being the *peplos* (robe), brought to Athena at her festival. No one would argue that this made her human, at most it applied to her anthropomorphic representation in myth and iconography. In other words, the very concept of *Lebender Leichnam* is born from a loose interpretation of 'primitive thought'. We cannot know whether the Mycenaeans feared the corpse as a kind of zombie. What we actually do have reason to believe is that the corpse was tabooed through a certain period of time until its decomposition. That, however, is an entirely different matter.

Studies of funeral rites in Indonesia encouraged Robert Hertz, a student of Durkheim, to make the general claim that in primitive societies a funeral always takes place twice. The intervening period may vary from a few days to several years (for example until all the flesh has decayed, leaving the bare skeleton). Also the type of a second burial may differ. Nevertheless, the very organization of a double ritual is the same in all cases (1905-6, 49).[8] Another model for analysing the structure of funeral rites in general, and specifically of the double burial, is provided by the more inclusive category of *rites of passage*, as originally defined by Arnold van Gennep (1909). The category analytically encompasses rites which conduct a transition of initiates from one social status to another.[9] Any such passage is introduced by a rite of separation followed by a period of marginality and brought to an end by a rite of reintegration (van Gennep, op.cit. 210-213). This seems to apply to Hertz' model if we regard the first burial as an instance of separation and the second burial as an instance of reintegration. According to Victor Turner, the intervening period of liminality (*la periode de marge* in Van Gennep's terms), is an interval of anti-structure, where all normal relations are

8. See the comment on Hertz' model in Huntington & Metcalf, 1979, 61 ff. It seems reasonable to regard the piles of bones, which are found in Mycenaean graves, as a testimony of such a second, and final act of 'burial', cf. Hertz, 1905-6, 53. More importantly, Hertz takes Indonesian and ancient Indian traditions of cremation as examples of a first burial (the act of burning the corpse on the pyre), followed by the interment of the urn as the second burial, op.cit. 69 ff. For obvious similarities in the Greek custom of cremation, he refers to Rohde, 1925, I, 71, n.3; see also Garland, 1985, 38 f., and further below. As a modern, equivalent example, Danforth describes the Greek ceremony of the exhumation of the bones as 'a second funeral', 1982, 16, drawing explicitly on Hertz, op.cit. 36-38. See also Howard's description of a second funeral ceremony among the Polynesians to 'end the death taboos', 1996, 129; likewise among the Japanese, Plath, 1964, 308.
9. Cf. also Durkheim, 1912, 576 ff.; Leach, 1976, 77-79.

either dissolved or inverted (1969, 94 ff.).[10] It is a time for bringing the departed from the world of the living to the world of the dead; in other words, it is a ritualized period of contact and of preparing oneself to take a final and proper farewell.

Classical sources tell us of different meals which demarcate the transition of relations between the living and the dead.[11] Having returned from the funeral, the relatives prepare the so-called περίδειπνον, which seems to have been a communal meal. A month later the final meal, τριακοστία, takes place at the grave and may have closed the ritual period of grief.[12] This meal was probably not a communal meal, since the accompanying offerings to the dead, ἐναγίσματα, were, according to their name, polluted and thus appropriate for demarcating the *division* between the living and the dead. Hence we may, after all, assume that between the event of death and this final rite of leave-taking the deceased *was* in some sense dangerously present among the living, not because of any visual similarity, but simply because the transition has not yet been ritually secured. This explains why the corpse is typically represented as contagious, not for hygienic reasons, but simply as a matter of categorical definition. That the deceased is indeed often associated with evil powers follows rather from this inter-categorical state of its being than from any imaginative fear which may supply it. The newly defunct is not precisely a *Lebender Leichnam*, but a creature *between* life and death.[13] The attitude of the living towards this creature is first of all understandable in terms of social relations, namely the crisis of their temporary rupture.[14]

As Rohde rightly points out, the characters of the Homeric world want to get this situation over with as quickly as possible. That the living should not hesitate to bring the corpse to the pyre in order to let the fire do its work (*Il*.7.409-10) is even related to us by the ψυχή of the deceased himself (*Il*.23.71). But who - or what - is this ψυχή? Is it a relic of a belief in the dead as a *Lebender Leichnam*, as has been suggested by Rohde (1925, I, 32), Nilsson (1955, 100) and Schnaufer

10. For a review of the uses of Van Gennep's model, see J.P. Schjødt, 1992, 5 ff.
11. See Garland, 1985, 39 f.; 110 f.
12. Structurally the final meal can of course be seen, if not as a second burial, then as a concluding rite of reintegration, see also further below. See, however, Garland, who is not certain that it also concludes the rites of mourning, 1985, 41.
13. See Turner, 1967, 93 ff.
14. Radcliffe-Brown thus suggests that the society reacts upon death as if it was 'partly a destruction of social cohesion', 1933, 285. However, to consider death rituals as socially significant does not necessarily imply the functionalist view of a basic equilibrium, cf. Danforth, 1982, 27; see also Humphreys, 1983, 146 ff.

(1970, 75; 125 f.) Surely, they are all aware that the Homeric concept of ψυχή is hardly compatible with the fear of the corpse as a living entity. As a rule the ψυχή goes immediately to Hades at the moment of death. In the case of Patroclus, however, his ψυχή explicitly states that 'he' is not yet allowed entrance to the realm of the dead (*Il.*23.71-74).[15] Only through a proper burial, which should be undertaken without delay, will he gain this entrance. Otherwise, the living will draw down the wrath of the gods on their own heads (*Od.*11.73). Again, we learn that the ritual process of transition is indeed considered to be important, but what do we hear about a living corpse? It is the gods, who should be feared, Elpenor seems to say, not the dead themselves. Still, the presence of the voice of Elpenor and of Patroclus, who are both dead, but not yet amongst the inhabitants of Hades, makes us wonder. Could it be that we do after all see a belief in the dead as some kind of ghost?

Schnaufer argues that the corpse *is* actually feared by the Homeric characters as far as there is a custom, μασχαλισμός, of cutting it into pieces (1970, 138 f.; 156).[16] Even if we accept this interpretation, the act of μασχαλισμός is also, and more explicitly, represented by Homer as a defamation, and it is the obligation of the *living* - friends or relatives - to avenge it.[17] Again, the dead are not explicitly feared in themselves, i.e., as living corpses, but feared indeed are various other characters who may react on their behalf. There is no reason to doubt, however, that the corpse was in fact, more generally, a religious object of awe, presumably by way of being a transitional entity as well as a ghost, perhaps even a potential vampire.[18] The problem is that *Homer* does not state any of this, and as long as we are trying to interpret the frames of 'his' discourse, we must keep within the range of 'his' own words. As we shall see in *Chapter III*, we will

15. Compare the ψυχή of Elpenor, *Od.*11.72-73.
16. See also Nilsson, 1955, 99 ff.; Garland, 1985, 94; Chantraine, 1968, ad loc. μασχάλη, and compare, for example, A.*Ch.* 439 and S.*El.* 445, compare *Od.*22.474 ff.. The Slavonic folk tradition of apotropaic rites against vampires seems to represent a similar practice, cf. Moszyński, 1976, 180 ff.
17. The same applies to the other testimony mentioned by Schnaufer, namely the practice of stripping the corpse of the armour. Even if this *might* express a fear of the dead person, as Schnaufer suggests, op.cit., it certainly *will* promote the wrath of a living avenger, as, for example, when Achilles gets back at Hector, not only for having killed Patroclus, but also for having stolen his armour, *Il.*22.331 f. Likewise, we must assume that his own hesitation in stripping Eëtion of his armour, *Il.*6.417-19, is primarily caused by fear of a similar revenge. After having killed Hypsenor, Deïphobus proclaims that he has thus avenged the fallen Asius, *Il.*13.414-16. It might be opposed that since the Homeric characters are in the middle of a war, the immediate threat comes from those who are still alive and thirsty for blood.
18. See above, *n.16*.

have to make a distinction, at any rate, between the word, σῶμα, for 'corpse', and the word ψυχή, which seems to mean something like 'a shadow of the one who is no longer amongst the living'. Hence, the conclusion must be that the presence of the dead is divided between himself, as a corpse, and his representation in the form of an image which appears to be some kind of *ghost* or *spirit*. This much we can say. For the presence of a *Lebender Leichnam*, however, we have still not found any support.

It seems to be customarily prescribed that the cremation takes place as quickly as possible in order to let the deceased vanish from the sight of the living (cf. *Il*.7.409-10; 23.52); and it is likely that this prescription is associated with an attempt to preserve the honour and glory of the person. By lying too long before the eyes of the living, the corpse might generate an undesirable impression. It is true that the body of a defunct hero is typically described as beautiful and awe-inspiring, but the vital strength and activity has nevertheless disappeared from it,[19] and the danger of μασχαλισμός is inevitably at hand. Obviously then, the importance of a hurried funeral was to prevent anything from disturbing the impression of glory, and to make the body of the dead invisible[20] by relocating him or her from *this* world to the *other* world. Actually, Hades, the realm of the dead, was, at least from Classical times, associated with the *invisible*,[21] a fact that may thus have bearings on a little more than just Sophistic interests in constructing etymologies.

However, since the funeral process is not to be delayed, it begs the question why the πρόθεσις (*lite de parade*) of Achilles lasts a full 17 days (*Od*.24.63). It has been explained by the fact that Thetis, Achilles' divine mother, takes care of her son's corpse, as she took care of Patroclus (*Il*.19.30 ff.),[22] and as Apollo protected

19. See, for example, Achilles' scornful remarks about the corpse of Hector, *Il*.22.73 f., as well as his anxiety concerning the corpse of Patroclus, *Il*.19.24-28.
20. Cf. *Od*.11.219-221; *Il*.2.455, where it is expressed that *fire makes things invisible*.Thus, it seems that one ritual significance of fire is to establish a demarcation between phenomena which are visible and accessible to the senses, on the one hand, and phenomena which are invisible and only accessible to the memory, on the other. If we accept this, we actually do imply that the practice of cremation *is* symbolically linked to the meaning potential of Hades, cf. above p. 28, n.7. The question is, whether this connection tells us anything about the fate of the dead, or if it just reveals how fire is interpreted.
21. Cf. Pl.*Grg*. 493a; *Phd*.80d, where Ἅιδης is etymologized as ἀϊδής ('invisible'). Schulze refers to 'the helmet of Hades', *Il*.5.845, which makes the one who carries it invisible, 1892, 468, compare Hes.*Sc*.227; see also, and especially, *LFE*, s.v. Ἄϊδος; Vernant, 1965, 335, and Burkert, 1985, 196.
22. See Petzl, 1969, 58 f.

Hector against the defamation perpetrated by Achilles (*Il.*24.18). The delay is thus justified, and even glorified, through the intervention of gods who make the dead hero immune to the normal vulnerability of a corpse.[23] Still, it is the religious duty of man to carry out the ritual promptly. In order to understand this seeming ambivalence on the part of Homer, we shall take a closer look at the funeral rites of Patroclus in the 23rd song of the *Iliad*.

The whole funeral is represented in terms of myth, that is, within the frame of inspired story-telling, concerning a remote past. Although there might be in this representation some historic survivals of the Mycenaean period, not to mention the Dark Age, it recreates the past as, first and foremost, a mythical event.[24] The poets seem either to have been ignorant or merely indifferent, when they referred to the practice of cremation as if it were indeed a tradition of the heroes at Troy, whereas we know that it did not start to replace the Mycenaean custom of inhumation earlier than the 11th BC. The way in which funeral rites were actually practised in Archaic times must have created the general background for appreciating the epic description, yet epic description may not, in turn, have been rigorously committed to any exact correspondence with contemporary practice. Why should it have been? Its concern was the past world of heroes. Still, the Homeric representation of funeral rites is clearly related somehow to a real practice, and we shall regard it accordingly, not so much in respect of eclectically clustered elements, but primarily in respect of the tripartite structure that may be generally characteristic, according to Van Gennep, of *rites of passage*.

As a part of the preparations for the funeral, the wounded body of Patroclus is washed, rubbed with ointment and oil and covered with linen and a robe (*Il.*18.345-353). Finally, Thetis, the goddess, puts nectar and ambrosia in his nose (*Il.*19.38). Nectar and ambrosia are idiomatically the materials which grant the immortality of the gods, and Thetis' intervention, presumably corresponding to

23. It is explicitly stated, however, that Patroclus and Achilles are embalmed, *Il.*18.350-51, *Od.*24.67-68, and if Humphreys is right (1983, 149) that cremation and embalming are alternative practices of avoiding decomposition (even though the two practices are part of the same ritual in Homer), we are perhaps not in need of a special explanation for the delay. It is plausible that embalming is doing the job of preservation until the circumstances permit a proper funeral, compare Hertz, 1905-6, 66 f. Still, the delay cannot but create a poetic 'tension' in relation to the customary rule.
24. Although Chantraine points to the anachronism of the epic description, 1964, 3; 25 f., he still argues, contrary to the perspective of the present investigation, that the Homeric funeral should be appreciated from the testimonies of Mycenaean grave-findings, op.cit. 4 ff. Compare Coldstream, 1977, 341 ff., and Calligas, 1986, 229 ff.

the practice of embalming with honey,[25] may therefore be seen as a kind of immortalisation.[26] This seems to be consistent with the cult of the dead, of which we know from other, albeit later, testimonies that the departed were honoured - and feared - for their 'power' (δύναμις), but it does not immediately agree with the meaning complex of the epics, in which they are generally doomed to exist as mere shadows in the realm of Hades. As for the epic representation, then, the act of Thetis does not necessarily aim at anything but a preservation of the body until the fire shall make it invisible for evermore.

Among the introductory rites of the πρόϑεσις—or *lit de parade* (being the first part of the funeral proper), we hear of mounted warriors circling the corpse thrice (*Il.*23.13-14). This is probably reflected later, at the end of the funeral, by the circular demarcation of Patroclus' barrow (*Il.*23.255),[27] and further, beyond the scope of ritual obligations, by Achilles's relentless act of dragging Hector's body thrice around the tomb (*Il.*24.14 ff.). The purpose of ritual circling has been defined as *apotropaic*, i.e., to ward off evil influence, as well as *therapeutic*, i.e., to convert the power to one's own advantage.[28] This interpretation, however, draws heavily on the knowledge of the hero-cult, where the δύναμις of the hero can prove either beneficial or harmful.[29] Regarded as a significant part of the *rites de passage* the circling seems rather to point, before anything else, to a ritual isolation of the corpse. Such a demarcation is typical in rites of *separation* as well as rites of *integration*,[30] establishing, as it seems, both the spatial and the temporal

25. See E.*Ba.*143. Burial embalming with honey is mentioned, for example, as a custom among the Spartans, cf. Plut. *Age.* 40.3, as well as among the Babylonians, Hdt. 1.198; compare *Il.*16.678-83.
26. Thus the word ἀμβροσία denies the state of being 'mortal' (βροτός), and νέκταρ can be etymologized, according to Nagy (1983, 205-9), as a victory (cf. *ταρ) over 'death' (νεκύς). In the *Epic Cycle* Achilles is even translocated to the 'White island' (Λευκὴ νῆσος, Procl.*Chr.* 106, 12 f.) instead of going to Hades.
27. Cf. *Od.*24.69; Paus. 10.31.6; as for comparison, E.B. Tylor refers to a Caucasian ritual, where the widow and the horse of the deceased are being carried thrice around his corpse, 1873, 1, 463 f. See also *Od.*9.65, where Odysseus calls thrice on his dead comrades before leaving them behind. See also Richardson, 1993, ad loc. 255.
28. See especially Focke, 1941, 34, and likewise Schnaufer's concept of a 'Bannkreis' (1970, 165), which he even parallels with the Mycenaean grave circles A and B (op.cit. 19).
29. See Rohde, 1925, I, 173 f.; Focke, 1941, 37; Dietrich, 1967, 45; Kirk, 1974, 226.
30. Apart from Van Gennep and Hertz, op.cit., see Eliade, 1955, 13, who mentions, for example, that 'The Yuin, the Wiradjuri, the Kamilaroi, and some of the Queensland tribes prepare a circular ring of earth, in which preliminary ceremonies will later take place', op.cit. 5. Likewise, we hear of the Attic feast by the name of Amphidromia, that '[a]m fünften Tag der Geburt trug man den Säugling um den Hausalter und nahm ihn so in die Familie auf. Auf dieselbe Art und Weise—durch dreimahlige Umgebung des

limits of ritual transformation. This means that the ritual transition to the realm of Hades is, at one and the same time, a separation from the world of the living and an integration into the world of the dead.

The γόος ('lamentation') of *prothesis* (e.g., *Il*.23.10; 14; 17) is not just to be seen as private outbursts of grief, but also, as Achilles puts it, as a gift of honour for the dead, which forms a part of the ritual obligations (cf. *Il*.23.9 ≈ *Il*.16.457; 675).[31] Schnaufer takes the ritual expression of grief as evidencing the belief in a living corpse (1970, 160), whereas Rohde takes it to be a reaction to the loss of ψυχή (1925, I, 222 f.).[32] The latter is also supported by Reiner, who connects it, however, with the former by stating that 'nicht nur jenen Klagen Achills um Patroklos, sondern auch allen übrigen homerischen γόοι liegt ein Glaube an die Macht der Psyche des Toten zugrunde' (1938, 23). What is this power, of which we hear nothing from the lips of the Homeric singer, but only from the much later sources of the hero-cult (see above, n.29). The lamentation does not by itself tell us anything about the presence of a power, a soul or a spirit. Grief was indeed communicated, but not necessarily to anyone other than the living partakers themselves. Lamentation may simply have told people that they were not to be forgotten, when they died. Personal grief was, of course, a natural part of it, but the frame of expression was predominantly collective and ritual. Yet it

Hausalters —verband sich die Neuvermählte der Familie des Mannes', Andronikos, 1968, 15; see also Focke, 1941, 34 f.

31. Also denoted as κομμός, which may have been associated with a Persian custom, Reiner, 1938, 44 ff.; 60; Andronikos, 1968, 9; Alexiou, 1974, 102 ff.; against this view, however, Wilamowitz, 1959, I, 301, n.1. The same rites apply to the Trojans, *Il*.24.724; 741; 747. The lamentation could even take the form of self-mutilation, for which we have references as late as in the Classical times, even though it was then prohibited by law, see especially E.*Alc*.98; *Hel*.1088. See also *plate 1*.
32. That the loss of life *as such* may be ritually comparable to the loss of life *as a child*, or *as an unmarried person*, namely as being instances of state-transitions, is indicated by the custom of hair-sacrifice in each case, cf. *Il*.23.46; 134, compare, for example, Paus.8.41.3, and specifically Paus.1.37.3 with *Il*.23.141 f., in which Achilles transfers his ritual obligation in the homeland with a similar, or corresponding, obligation while being abroad; see further Richardson, 1993, 181-83; Andronikos, 1968, 18-20; and for comparison, Thomsen, 1992, 80; 88 ff. A difference, however, is that while it is the dead that receives a *timē* of hair in the funeral process, it is otherwise living persons in-between-states that sacrifice the lock of hair, typically to nymphs or gods, as the river-god, Spercheüs, cf. *Il*.23.141 f. Thus, one might be tempted to suggest that Patroclus takes up the place of a god, or at least is being treated like one. I would not make too much of this seeming correspondence, though. Rather than Patroclus assuming the state of divinity, locks of hair might be sacrificed on behalf of Patroclus who is no longer himself capable of doing so. The earlier view that the sacrifice of hair was a substitution of human sacrifice has been generally discredited, cf. Andronikos, op.cit. 20.

is precisely this point which is blurred by the epic representation insofar as it features the mourning of Achilles who is not just acting as an ordinary, ritual participant, but also as an individual who, contrary to his religious obligation, tries to postpone the actual funeral because of his close relationship with the deceased. The epic description thus presents us with a paradox. As far as the implementation of the funeral is concerned, Achilles is the one who temporarily hinders the ceremony as well as the one who brings it to its proper conclusion. To put it differently, the personal relationship between Achilles and Patroclus interferes with the impersonal perspective of the ritual. Achilles is the only one who actually addresses his dead friend, namely with the words: 'Rejoice, I bid you, O Patroclus, even in the House of Hades' (χαῖρέ μοι, ὦ Πάτροκλε, καὶ εἰν 'Αΐδαο δόμοισι, *Il*.23.19; 179), and the ψυχή of Patroclus later appears before Achilles in his sleep, asking him not to put off the act of cremation any longer (cf. *Il*.23.69-71). The deceased is *present* somehow, by virtue of his name, and by his psyche. The two friends communicate across the limits of life and death. This seems to be due to the very situation of liminality, which characterizes *la periode de marge*. The deceased does not yet belong properly to the world of the dead. Although the contact between Achilles and Patroclus is thus explainable, perhaps even to be expected, within the scheme of the ritual structure itself, it is not thematically explained *by* the ritual alone. The reason for Achilles' 'belief' in the existence of a 'spirit' is not borne out of the ritual acts themselves, but rather in the controlled space between them. Before reaching a closer understanding of this epic double, we shall therefore try to detach, as far as possible, the collective dimension of the funeral rites from the personal drama between Achilles and Patroclus.

Sacrifices of bulls, sheep, goats and swine are undertaken as a preparation for the *funeral meal* (*Il*.23.29 ff.). The Achaeans gather, probably around the bier, to drink and eat (23.56 f.), and so the meal has been seen as a communion between the deceased and the living, the dead being summoned by the blood of the sacrificed animals. In fact, we read that 'everywhere about the corpse of the dead the blood ran so that one might dip cups therein' (πάντῃ δ'ἀμφὶ νέκυν[33] κοτυλήρυτον[34] ἔρρεεν αἷμα, *Il*.23.34), a description that may remind us of certain sacrificial rites, the νέκυιαι, where libations of warm blood were offered to the dead, as the *Odyssey* describes it, for example, in the Eleventh Song (*Od*.11.36 ff.), which was even called νέκυια ('evocation of the dead', alternating with

33. In the *Iliad*, the word, νέκυς, refers to a dead person in close relation to the corpse, cf. *LS*, s.v. νέκυς, and thus justifies Murray's translation, 'the corpse of the dead'.

34. For κοτυλήρυτος, see the note immediately below.

νεκυομαντεία, 'oracle of the dead'). Here, Homer seems to tell us that the dead regain a momentary power of life by the drinking of blood. The immediate context, however, is one of divination, not one of funeral rites. The dead are not just summoned for the sake of their presence, but for their ability to speak the truth. First of all, the Odyssean sacrifice invokes an oracle. The context of a funeral meal is obviously a different one, and we cannot necessarily agree with Rohde (1925, I, 25), Mylonas (1948, 57) and Schnaufer (1970, 173) in that the sacrificial blood secures any communal participation of the dead.[35] If the deceased is somehow thought to be present at the feast, this must be due to tacit meanings of ritual discourse; it is not, in any case, poetically represented as emotionally significant in the same way as the personal ties between Patroclus and Achilles are. Granted, Achilles' act of pouring wine on the ground (*Il*.23.220-21, later to be repeated on the burning pyre, 238) is related to his calling upon Patroclus, but nothing is said of any contact between the two in this situation. Although Schnaufer is correct in his assertion that wine-offerings were generally a substitute for offerings of blood, he is mistaken in seeking to base a comparison between the ritual performances by Odysseus (cf. *Od*.11.27-37) and Achilles (cf. *Il*.23.220 ff.) on this fact alone (1970, 171). As for the two types of libation, the latter cannot be automatically interpreted in terms of the former only because both are simultaneously present in the epic universe of Homer. More importantly, Patroclus is not mentioned as a recipient of the libation, even though Achilles addresses his ψυχή in the very act of pouring the wine; and as for the corpse, it is in a state of being burned until nothing but the bones remain. The *Lebender Leichnam*-hypothesis of funeral-related eschatology still remains to be proved.

Achilles does, in fact, react directly in relation to a *corpse*, namely the corpse of Hector, which he drags about, shamefully, in the dust before placing it beside Patroclus' bier (23.25). Perhaps this act is even related to his refusal to have himself cleansed of dust and blood before the ritual is performed (23.41-44). In avenging his comrade, Achilles seems to emphasize the most gruesome aspect of death by maltreating the corpse of Hector and, furthermore, by assuming a

35. Thus, granted that Cunliffe is right in taking κοτυλήρυτος of *Il*.23.34 to mean '(caught in cups and) poured out from them on the ground', it might refer to an act of honouring, rather than communicating with, the dead, see also Richardson, 1993, ad.loc., who further allows for interpreting the verse as simply indicating a huge quantity of blood. If actually designating a rite of communion, 'one might expect', with Richardson, 'the ritual to be more explicitly described in this case', ibid. It is possible that we should even compare the funeral meal in honour of Patroclus with the ἐπικυδέα δαῖτα for Hector, *Il*.24.802, which does not seem to refer to a meal of communion.

similar appearance himself. Patroclus, on the other hand, has been embalmed and lies on the bier as beautiful and awe-inspiring as ever, surrounded by various items of funerary equipment, which only make him look even more 'alive'. It is as if Achilles tries to transfer some of the power of life to the corpse of his friend by covering himself with dirt and blood.[36] This does not make the corpse living, of course, but rather inverts the meanings and attributes of life and death on a symbolic level. One factor is that the ritual participants may not fear the pollution, being a potential consequence of such an inversion, as long as they find themselves within the confines of the ritual, i.e. within the 'ritualized transitions between states' (Turner, 1968, 97),[37] another point is that Achilles does not unambiguously meet his ritual obligations. He commits an 'unseemly deed' (ἀεικέα ἔργα, *Il.*23.24) toward Hector, he hesitates to go when sent for by Agamemnon, he refuses to wash himself, and, most importantly, he is reproached by the shadow of Patroclus for delaying the funeral. In the final case we are present at a personal encounter between the living and the dead.

After Achilles has fallen asleep, he is approached by Patroclus' ψυχή, equal in all to the hero himself (23.66). It stands above the head of Achilles, hence idiomatically resembling a dream (see later p. 48), and bids him hesitate no longer. Instead, it says, 'bury me with all speed, that I pass within the gates of Hades' (23.71). Then, the 'ghost' offers Achilles his hand as a last expression of intimacy in 'life'. However, this token of their friendship seems to be a pact of death as well, since the psyche of Patroclus continues by foretelling that the two shall never again meet in life but soon enough in death (23.82). Perhaps at that precise moment, Achilles understands the finality of death since from now on he changes his attitude towards the funeral, by even trying to speed up the act of cremation (cf. 23.128-129; 208-210). But why did he hesitate in the first place? Probably, the aim was not merely to make Patroclus look as brilliant as possible, but also to prolong the marginal state of contact and to emphasize it by conflating signs of life and death. This is exactly what the period of liminality allows, however, opening a controlled and temporary space, as it seems, for the categorical exchangeability of life and death. Hence, the act of negligence (i.e., the postponement of cremation), which explains, or runs parallel to, Achilles' other initial actions, is itself ritually-structured. Moreover, Homer takes us even further along the lines of ritual thematization, for in trying to hold onto his dead

36. Achilles' refusal to wash his body is connected with the ritual cleansing of Patroclus' body by the same formula, *Il.*23.41 ≈ 18.345. Thus, Achilles seems to embody the look of a dead corpse as it appears prior to the ritual tendance.
37. See also Douglas, 1966, 159 f.

companion, Achilles himself seems to conduct a kind of ritual on a personal level within the overall social level of the funeral. Resting on the beach, he is surrounded by his comrades in arms as if separated from them by means of a ritual encirclement (23.60). It is as if Achilles is preparing himself for an *incubation* (ritual of oracular dreaming), and indeed the actual dream, which 'takes place' in the demarcated space, can be viewed as such an incubation. Later, we shall delve into other examples of ritual dreaming, which orders the incubant to act in a certain way. Till then, let us simply note that ψυχή, the dream-object in the likeness of Patroclus, reveals to Achilles that it is nothing but a 'phantom' (εἴδωλον) itself, disappearing like vapour when he tries to embrace it (23.99-100), and furthermore that death is, therefore, final. For this reason there is nothing left for Achilles to do but to accomplish the funeral as quickly as possible. Hence, the relationship between Achilles and Patroclus is not only described in terms of their affection for each other, but also in terms of a ritual process and of a ritualized knowledge. Homer shows that emotional bonds may indeed make a person strive to overcome the gap between life and death by symbolic means, thereby endangering the whole stability of categorical demarcations, but also that the general category-shifting as well as the temporary manifestation of its exception has to be ritualized. Achilles' initial actions are against the workings of ritual by trying to keep life and death in a state of confusion, but by his subsequent counter action all he accomplishes in the end only confirms these very workings all the more forcefully.

The second part of the ritual is the funeral proper, introduced with the bringing of the corpse to the funeral pyre (23.134)[38] and followed by a final preparation (of both the corpse and the pyre) in what becomes, in the hands of Achilles, a demonstrative act of honour. He furnishes the bier and pyre with jars of honey and oil as well as with the sacrificed bodies of 4 horses, 2 dogs, and 12 young Trojan boys, and he covers his dead friend with fat from the corpses of sheep and oxen placed at the side of the pyre (166-76).[39] Apparently, there is no need for separate *rites of passage* on behalf of the slaughtered Trojans, allegedly because they have no immediate bearings on the community of the Achaeans. The ritual is not directed towards death as a rupture of individual life as such,

38. This part correlates with the domestic custom of 'carrying out' (ἐκφορά) the bier (from the house to the funeral), cf. Th.2.34; A.*Th*.1029; *Ch*.9; 430, as also denoted by ἐξέφερον (*Il*.24.786) in Homer. See further, Andronikos, 1968, 18.

39. As Kübler shows, the art and proportions of offerings underline the social status of the dead, 1959, 87; the question is whether the slaughter of Trojan prisoners represents a relic of an earlier custom of human sacrifice, cf. Chantraine, 1964, 5, or if it points, first of all, to the wrath and grief of Achilles. I personally believe the latter.

but towards the impact that death makes on social relations. The ritual now takes a crucial turn. After the act of cremation, the bones of Patroclus are collected and wrapped in a layer of fat, whereupon they are placed in an urn covered with a linen cloth (*Il*.23.252-54). The subsequent burial of this urn[40] can be seen, of course, as the second and concluding part of a ritual double, as Hertz suggested (see above p. 29). Patroclus is to be separated from the world of the living as well as from the realm of visibility, but only for a new integration to take place, namely a transition to Hades, the realm of invisibility and memory. Although we do not have the exact testimony in the specific case of Patroclus, we may suggest from the *formula* 'τύμβῳ τε στήλῃ τε'[41] that the 'gravemound' (τύμβος, *Il*.23.245; σῆμα, 255; 24.16), which is piled up around the pyre, carries a memorial in the form of a 'post' or a 'tombstone' (στήλη). The deceased, who shall never again be seen alive, is replaced by a 'sign' (σῆμα),[42] which display the '[p]résence insolite et ambiguë qui est aussi le signe d'une absence', as Vernant puts it (1965, 327). In this way, Patroclus is, in the end, reintegrated in the community of the living, namely as an object of recollection (as also reflected by the poetic κλέος, see later, p. 59).

Before dispersing the funeral gathering, the Acheans engage in various contests (chariot-racing, boxing, wrestling, armed combat, archery, and other track and field events) ordered by Achilles. That he actually hinders his people from leaving (cf. *Il*.23.257),[43] may imply that the games did not form an expected part of the funeral rites themselves. Other funerals, however, are mentioned together with similar competitions (*Il*.23.629-32; 678-80; 22.162-64), and we even find motifs of horses and chariots on tombstones from Mycenaean times.[44] We should be allowed therefore to assume that there was some connection between the funeral rites and these rites of contest.[45] The fact that the important feature in the description of the games is the honour of the dead together with the

40. The exact resting-place of the urn ἐν κλισίῃσι, 254, cannot be determined with certainty from the text itself. See Richardson, 1993, ad loc.23.254, who suggests, with some reservation, that κλισίαι could perhaps refer to the tomb itself and not Achilles' hut as is usually supposed.
41. *Il*.16.457 = 675; 17.434; 11.371; *Od*.12.14.
42. Cf. IG 12.fasc.8.398.
43. See, however, Richardson, 1993, ad loc.
44. Cf. Mylonas, 1948, 66. It is also worth noticing that Nestor encourages Achilles to hold 'funeral rites with contests' (ἀέθλοισι κτερέϊζε) for his comrade, *Il*.23.646, thus suggesting one composite custom.
45. See, however, Wilamowitz, who is not inclined to regard the competitions as forming a part of the cult of the dead, but rather as belonging to "dem Feste, das der Erbe zu Ehren des Toten gibt", 1959, I, 303; see also Price, 1979, 224.

vitality of the living,[46] makes it even seem likely that the contests were nothing but the final rite of reintegration.[47] Disproportionately long as it may seem, the concluding part of the 23rd Book emphasizes the community of surviving warriors in remembrance of their fallen comrade.

Hence, we may find that every act in this Book does, some way or another, belong to the frame of ritual, the purpose of which is expressed, on several interrelated levels, as establishing the proper relation between the living and the dead. Underlined as one of the major themes is the honour of the dead and the contrast, in this respect, between the way Patroclus is treated and the way Hector and the Trojan boys are mistreated. Moreover, this theme integrates the ritual obligations with the personal actions of Achilles. In these actions Homer takes us beyond the mere implementation of ritual to the tragic account of a personal loss. As Patroclus' sworn brother and closest friend, Achilles stands out as the natural master of the funeral, and although there is no fundamental contradiction between the formal obligation of his orders and the ambivalence and passion with which they are given, we understand that it must have been the emotional character of the sequence that constituted its immediate appeal to the audience. This interpersonal drama between separated friends thus introduced a particular Homeric dimension in the representation of funeral rites. Achilles does indeed only exhibit resistance towards their implementation within the scope of ritual control itself, but nevertheless at the expense of playing down the significance of other ritual distinctions as, for instance, that between the *pure* and the *impure* (probably involving, among other things, apotropaic rites of appeasing the dead). The workings of ritual are present in every line, but only to serve the orientation of Homeric discourse. That the epic description of Archaic funeral practice is ideologically selective is, at the same time, the closest we get to the possibility of accepting the *Lebender Leichnam*-hypothesis. Whether Homer's silence proves significant in this respect, we shall discuss in due course.

Having followed the stages of Patroclus' funeral we must admit that it has not provided us with much knowledge about beliefs in the afterlife. The 'tendance' of the corpse, the embalming, and the cremation, aim primarily, if not entirely, at a *transition* to the other world. For the *future* existence in this other

46. See *Il*.23.748 for an explicit act of honouring Patroclus, and 822-23 for the fear that an accidental death should befall a competitor.
47. Segal regards the funeral rites as restoring stabilization on the narrative level insofar as they 'restore an atmosphere of orderly and reasonable social procedures' which stands in stark contrast to the barbarity of Achilles' wrath in Books 21-22, cf. Segal, 1971, 53.

world no salient concern is expressed,[48] and no further obligations are mentioned on behalf of the living.[49] Although we should not forget that the Greeks were abroad on a mission of war (and therefore unable to engage in a continuous cult practice), nothing would preclude a reference to such practices at home, had it been required. Instead, we are left with the impression that it is not the individual situation *post mortem* that matters, but rather the perpetuation of heroic fame and honour together with the group of living people who remember. Mycenaean cult practice seems to be quite absent from the perspective.

48. A.D. Nock states that '[f]unerary ritual is associated with the tomb and not with afterlife as theoretically conceived', 1972, I, 277 ff.
49. See, however, *Il.*24.595, where Achilles addresses Patroclus with the words: 'And unto thee shall I render even of this [ransom] all that is thy due' (σοὶ δ'αὖ ἐγὼ καὶ τῶνδ'ἀποδάσσομαι ὅσσ'ἐπέοικεν), which may imply that Achilles thinks of carrying out new sacrifices in honour of the deceased. Uncertain as the concrete meaning of the verse may be, it does not intelligibly transcend the level of a personal relationship.

III. The Concept of ψυχή

Even as he thus spake the end of death enfolded him;
and his psuchē fleeting from his limbs was gone to Hades,
bewailing her fate, leaving manliness and youth.[M]

*Il.*16.855 -57; 22.361-6

To get a clearer picture of the *post mortem* fate of human beings in the epics, we will have to take a closer look at the concept of ψυχή (psyche), which was explicitly used with an eschatological reference. It is crucial to make clear from the start, however, that the Homeric language does not inhabit a one-word equivalent to the modern concept of *soul* or *mind*, even though the ancient word has long since been borrowed to denote it. It seems that ψυχή actually was, as early as in the Classical times, attributed to a meaning potential, which may in some respects resemble the modern notion. As for Homeric discourse, however, we will have to bracket this similarity as much as possible. This is important to mention because of the huge impact that Erwin Rohde's monumental work *Psyche* from 1893 has had on the general understanding of ancient Greek eschatology. It was not that Rohde was unaware of the dissimilarity between the modern and the ancient meanings of 'soul', but he tried, nevertheless, under the influence of the contemporary theory of animism, to trace what he understood to be a 'Seelenkult und Unsterblichkeitsglaube der Griechen' back to the earliest stages of Greek religion. Presented as a subtitle to his work, this classification had in fact already provided a definition of the phenomenon of investigation, namely the ancient concept of psyche. On page 3 Rhode boldly goes as far as to state that 'Ihr Name bezeichnet sie, wie in den Sprachen vieler anderer Völker die Benennungen der 'Seele', als ein Luftartiges, Hauchartiges, im Athem des Lebenden sich Kundgebendes' (1925, I, 3). Despite Rohde's own reservations such a definition is unfortunate, if not completely misguided, for reasons that shall be given below.

The modern meaning of psyche, or soul, is basically conceived in terms of *self* or *identity*. With regards to the concept of ψυχή, the opposite is actually stated in the beginning of the *Iliad*, where we hear of Achilles' wrath that it

> sent forth to Hades many valiant psuchai
> of heroes, and made themselves (αὐτούς) to be a spoil for dogs
> and all manner of birds [...] (*Il.*1.3-5[M])

Here, the deceased is clearly identified with the 'corpse' (σῶμα) and not with the psyche, which flies off to the invisible realm of memory.[1] Another passage tells us, however, that the sons of Antenor have been sent to their deaths by Agamemnon (*Il.*11.262-63). In this case nothing suggests that it is anything but the sons *themselves* who have gone to Hades. Thus, if one poses the question, as Rohde does, 'welches [...] der 'eigentliche Mensch' sei', namely the body or the soul, 'so gibt Homer freilich widerspruchsvolle Antworten' (1925, I, 5). He concludes that the problem of identification is not solved with an *either/or* and that 'Der Mensch ist nach homerischer Auffassung zweimal da, in seiner wahrnehmbaren Erscheinung und in seinem unsichtbaren Abbild, welches frei Wird erst im Tode. Dies und nicht Anderes ist seine Psyche' (op.cit. 6). Rohde also calls 'das Abbild' 'einer Zweiten Ich', since it does at least partly identify the dead person. From Rohde's theoretical point of view this archaic 'Annahme des Doppellebens im Menschen' is due to 'die phantastische Logik' of primitive thinking. Obviously, Rohde's claim is itself due to the logic of contemporary theories of animism, as were developed, for example, by E. B. Tylor in his theoretical fiction of an 'ancient savage philosopher'.

Put briefly, Tylor's typological construction drew on the possibility of recognizing a deceased person in a dream as if he or she were alive. Such an experience, according to Tylor, probably inclined the primitive mind to postulate a division between the *life* and the *phantom* of a human being. Tylor further stated that '[t]hese two are evidently in close connexion with the body, the life as enabling it to feel and think and act, the phantom as being its image or *second self*' (1873, 1, 428 f.), and his conclusion sounds: 'The second step [...] is merely to combine the life and the phantom. As both belong to the body, why should they not also belong to one another, and be manifestations of one and the same soul?' (ibid.). Rohde seems to follow this theoretical suggestion, when he speaks of a 'Zweiten Ich', which is not just an 'Abbild des Leiches', but also an active part of the living person. 'Es lebt also in [den Mensch] ein zweites Ich', Rohde says (1925, I, 6), 'das im Traume thätig ist'. For this he may find justification in Pindar's *Fr.* 131 (cf. ibid., see later p. 47), but surely he does not find it in Homer,[2]

1. Compare *Il.* 23.105 (cf. 66), and *Od.*11.53 with *Od.*11.72. It can be held that ψυχή is identical with ἐγώ from 11.51 on to 71, but ἐγώ in 72 clearly refers to σῶμα in 53 and thus confirms *Il.*1.3 f. 23.244, 15.251; and 14.456 can be understood in the same way. See also, Moore, 1916, 24; Otto, 1927, 36. Further, ψυχάς is exchanged with κεφαλάς in *Il.*11.55, with no apparent shift in meaning, cf. Warden, 1971, 97, the latter being thus merely a metrically determined synecdoche for the persons in question.
2. This point has been held against Rohde's view, e.g., in W.F.Otto, 1927, 17 f.; Ehnmark, 1948, 12; Kessels, 1978, 5; 162.

where ψυχή never plays an active role in a person who is alive and conscious. Rohde is referring to a semantic representation that is either of a later date (as various Classical sources may lead us to believe) or embedded in discursive frameworks other than those which have survived to come down to us from the Archaic period. Conclusively, Rohde does not sufficiently substantiate his generalized claim that ψυχή defines an *alter ego* 'in dem Innern des täglich sichtbaren Ich' (cf. op.cit. 6), and unfortunately, this is the main premise on which he builds his thesis that ψυχή originally and basically denoted a hidden, immortal soul, which releases itself from the body at the moment of death. This confronts us with two problems. First, we may have to pursue the question, if only very briefly, whether the generalized psyche-as-soul-thesis could possibly find any other phenomenological support (other than that which underlies Rohde's study). Secondly, how are we to understand the Homeric psyche on its own terms ? The aim of this particular examination will be to provide us with a supposedly very important element in the semantic constellation of what we want to isolate, phenomenologically and historically, as a semantic field of *eschatology*.

The understanding of ψυχή as a soul-conception is not in any determinate way bound to a theory of animism. One example can be found in the comparative studies of primitive soul-conceptions by the Swiss ethnologist of religion, Ernst Arbman, who criticizes Tylor's concept of soul for being unjustifiedly monistic 'in ihrer verführerischen Einfachkeit' and 'weit mehr ein Reflex des unter den abendländischen Völkern erebten Seelenbegriffes' (1926, 87).[3] Another example is Wilhelm Wundt, who, as far back as in his 'Völkerpsychologie' from 1910, reproached Tylor for dismissing an obvious duality in primitive soul-representations. Instead, Wundt introduced a distinction that should prove very influential, namely that between what he called a 'Freiseele', on the one hand, and a plurality of 'Körperseelen' on the other (1910, 24; 78 f.).[4] *Freiseele* he understood to be an 'Atemseele', which had developed into an independent soul from being one of the powers of the body, i.e., from the 'Körperseelen' (op.cit. 79). Although Arbman appropriated this conceptual distinction, he found that the way in which Wundt explained it did not sufficiently escape the monism of a modern soul-conception. Insofar as primitive soul-conceptions might be basically dual, Arbman found it unwarranted to speak of a free-soul as derived from the

3. See also similar opinions expressed by Arbman's students and close colleagues Hultkrantz, 1953, 21, and Paulson, 1958, 17 f. Likewise, Otto, 1927, 15 f.; Nilsson, 1955, 192.
4. See also Ankermann, 1918, 102.

body-souls.[5] It should be clear, though, that the very use of the notion 'soul', which interconnects all the studies from Tylor to Arbman, is itself unavoidably monistic and perhaps problematically modern. Arbman's attempt to *split* the concept without *dissolving* it does not protect him from falling into the epistemological trap, he addressed himself. In trying to estimate the importance of this problem for the purpose of our specific study, we will therefore have to compare the matter of *identity* and *consciousness*, which, as I take it, basically determines the soul-concept in question, with the way in which these 'phenomena' are, or are not, represented in relation to the Homeric man.

First of all, Homeric characters certainly have an *I* (ἐγώ), which is aware of itself (cf. *Il.*11.407 ≈ 22.122). However, this 'I' often seems to reflect upon its own activity by recognizing certain bodily abilities, which are activated in certain ways by certain situations.[6] Not unlike our own modes of expression, emotions are, in the epic language, closely associated with the 'heart' (ἦτορ, κῆρ, καρδία), and words like ϑυμός and μένος, which primarily denote the power of life (often specified as *anger* and *courage* respectively), are at the same time imbued with organic connotations (cf. *Il.*1.193; 9.496). The word φρήν seems to have a meaning potential that is especially polyvalent in this respect, since it can refer (often in the plural) to the *heart*, the *breast*, the *lungs*, and the *midriff*, as well as to the presence of a conscious and even reasoning *mind*.[7] While today we may be inclined to speak *either* of mental or physical phenomena, Homeric tradition thus seemed to name a kind of psycho-physical instances as located through the dominant features of experienced activity. Νόος, which is perhaps best translated as 'wit', takes up a special position in this respect, since it does not refer to anything corporeal.[8] However, not even νόος is identical with the ἐγώ. In fact, none of the above mentioned concepts are.[9] The act of consciousness in a

5. With regard to a general, cross-cultural level of primitive religion, Arbman states that 'Körperseele, oder Körperseelen, und Psycheseele [Freiseele] stellen also voneinander ganz unabhängige Vorstellungen dar, sie sind von verschiedenen Wesen und Ursprung und haben verschiedene Aufgaben und Tätigkeitsgebiete', Arbman, 1926, 183; likewise Paulson, who speaks about a dualistic pluralism of soul-concepts, 1958, 18; similarly Paasonen, 1909, 3, with respect to a Finno-Ugrian field of investigation.
6. See, e.g., *Il.*13.281 f.; 16.280; 19.37; 202; 319 f., and the formula 'and the heart roused in his breast'[M] (τῇ δ'ἄρα ϑυμὸν ἐνὶ στήϑεσσιν ὄρινε, *Il.*4.208 ≈ 11.803 ≈ 13.468).
7. See Chantraine, 1968, ad loc. φρήν.
8. In contrast to the other concepts, νόος is never used for animals. *Il.*23.880 and *Od.*14.426 exemplifies that, e.g., both ψυχή and ϑυμός can be used to describe the death of an animal.
9. See Böhme, 1929, 50. The matter is not unambiguously clear, though, as φρένες, for example, not only mediate a sense-perception to the 'I' but also, occasionally, take the

Homeric character only seems to be the recognition of internal 'powers', which make him or her act in certain ways. As Böhme puts it:

Der homerischen Seelenvorstellung ist deshalb jeder einheitliche Seelenbegriff und ebenso jedes System von verschiedenen gegen einander abgegrenzten Begriffen fremd. (1929, 88)[10]

Accordingly, Böhme disagrees with Bickel (1926, 281) that the epics should possess any idea of 'das ganzen inneren Menschen' (Böhme, 1929, 90). The following verse, 'For of a surety know I this in heart and soul' (εὖ γὰρ ἐγὼ τόδε οἶδα κατὰ φρένα καὶ κατὰ θυμόν, *Il.*6.447), does not, according to Böhme, express the abstract thought of an all-encompassing 'I', but may simply be the verbal reflection of an immediate experience (op.cit. 92). The emphasis of the ἐγώ probably depends only on the particular person in question, i.e., Hector, and not to some autonomy of the 'I's ability to *know*. 'Knowing' happens through the activity of, e.g., φρήν and θυμός, which thus exemplifies Wundt's category of *Körperseelen*.

Thus far, Arbman agrees with Wundt (cf. Arbman,1926, 94), but contrary to Wundt, Arbman holds ψυχή to be an independent expression of individual personality (op.cit.100; 106; 132) and therefore intrinsically different from any of the *Körperseelen* (op.cit. 92 ff.; 131; 185, 190 ff.).[11] Unfortunately, Arbman also refers to *Fr.*131 by Pindar (cf. p. 44) in trying to validate this definition of ψυχή as a *Freiseele* of the living human being (1926, 94).[12] The free-soul is active, so the argument goes, only in sleep and in the absence of 'consciousness', whereas the body-souls are active in normal, daily life (op.cit. ff.; cf. Pi.*Fr.*131). Along the same lines of argument, Jan Bremmer, who seems to affiliate himself with Arbman's view, has recently stated that

although we do not find in Homer the activities of a dream soul, its absence does not necessarily presuppose its nonexistence. [...] The Greeks, like many other peoples, considered the soul of the dead to be a continuation of the free soul of the living. (1983, 123)

I cannot know what has made Arbman and his supporters so sure, but the burden of proof remains on their hands. Surely, E.R. Dodds seemed to be on a much safer ground, when he stated that

position of direct consciousness (or self-reflection), op.cit. 50-52.

10. That the 'soul'-concepts are not even clearly distinguished from one another, see also Nilsson, 1955, 193, and Torresin as for the concept of θυμός, 1989, 47.
11. In the second volume of his work, Arbman is primarily concerned with Vedic material and here he claims that *prana*, *atman* and *manas* are expressions of body-souls, 1927, 3 ff., while *asu* represents the eschatological soul, corresponding to ψυχή in the Greek context, op.cit. 20. G. Nagy, on the other hand, finds that *asu* as well as *manas* in the Vedic tradition, corresponding to εὖ and μένος and the epic Greek tradition, bears the meaning of psycho-physical power in a basic Indo-European eschatology, 1980, 183 ff.
12. As might be expected, Böhme objects to this suggestion, 1935, 469, n.2.

> Homer, indeed, ascribes to the ψυχή no function in the living man, except to leave him, its 'esse' appears to be 'superesse' and nothing more. (1951, 138)

Whatever exactly we take that to mean, the concept of 'free-soul' may not be the first to choose for explanation. Whereas it is possible to reconstruct the concept of body-souls from the Homeric concepts alone, it is only possible to understand the Homeric ψυχή as a free-soul by referring to non-Homeric descriptions. For this reason we shall from now on abandon the concept of free-soul and look at the epic 'I' from another angle.

As Walter F. Otto has pointed out, it actually seems to be the dream itself, not the 'I' of the dreamer, that is active while a Homeric character is asleep (1927, 18).[13] In this respect, we may notice a striking similarity between the 'dream' (ὄνειρος) and the psyche, which are both said, as a matter of formula, to approach the sleeper by standing above his head (cf. *Il.*2.20; 23.68). Moreover, the same verb, πέτομαι ('to fly'), qualifies both concepts.[14] This does not make ψυχή a free dream-soul, though. If the psyche of *Il.*23.68 were the soul of anything, it would have to be the soul of Patroclus, but certainly not of Achilles.[15] How are we then to assess the obvious similarity between the dream and the psyche? Otto's answer lies in supposing a different dualism.

By referring to the comparative investigations of Preusz (1914, 18) and Kruyt (1906, 166; 235 ff.; 325),[16] he claims that primitive people characteristically distinguish sharply between the living and the dead person. Hence, in a Greek

13. Cf. *Il.*2.22 ff.; 23.68 ff.; Likewise, Dodds claims that the dream was seen as an 'objective fact', 1951, 104 f. For a similar definition, see Kessels (1978, 161 f.) who disregards Onians' suggestion that the dream as subject in the formula 'stood above the head' (στῆ δ'ἄρ'ὕπερ κεφαλῆς) should be addressing the psyche of the sleeper, since Onians also seems to claim that the psyche leaves a person who is asleep, cf. Onians, 1951, 102, n.7. As for a description of mental activity in sleep, Otto refers to the *Eumenides* of Aeschylus, where Clytemnestra is making her appeal to the φρένες of the sleeping Erinyes, 1927, 19, cf. A.Eu.103-5. This contradicts Arbman's description of ψυχή as being the active dream-soul in the dualistic relationship between ψυχή and φρήν. Thus, Böhme is convinced that Arbman could not have known Otto's studies, when he first proposed the theory of ψυχή as a *Freiseele*, 1935, 469.
14. Cf. ὄνειρος: *Il.*2.71; ψυχή: *Il.*16.856; *Od.*23.7; both: *Od.*11.222.
15. See Kessels, 1978, 55.
16. Otto sympathizes with the distinction, made by Kruyt, between 'Zielestof', which denotes the vital principle, and 'Ziele', which is a 'Totengeist', 1927, 39. However, the animistic, or dynamistic, perspective, within which Kruyt's terminology is to be evaluated, cf. Van Baal & Van Beek, 1985, 72 f., does not harmonize with Otto's own view, cf. 1927, 14. Hence, it is his own study rather than that of Kruyt, which is really in oppositions to the suggestions of Tylor and Spencer, op.cit. 46.

context Otto understands θυμός to be a *Lebenseele* and ψυχή to be a *Totengeist*, i.e.,

> zwei verschiedene 'Seelen', eine für das Leben, die andere für den Tod, wenn man das Εἴδωλον den materielosen Körper überhaupt 'Seele' nennen will. (1927, 37)

The Homeric ψυχή — or psyche — leaves man at the moment of death, not as his immortal soul, as Rohde and Arbman would have it, but simply, according to Otto, as *life* itself.[17] This interpretation offers an explanation as to why the corpse occasionally identifies the 'owner'of the psyche, which, as being a concept of life, has just left it (1927, 36). Otto further claims that what is subsequently called εἴδωλον or ψυχή refers to a *Totengeist*, i.e., the corpse itself as a ghost or zombie.[18] Although this classification may remind us of the *Lebender Leichnam*-type,[19] Otto takes pains to limit his definition to the concept of εἴδωλον, meaning merely an 'image' or a 'shadow' of the person it represents. In this sense the *Totengeist* is comparable to the 'dream' (ὄνειρος), which is also an instance of ghost-like representation (as, for instance, by way of disguising a god). On the one hand, Otto writes that

> Das εἴδωλον des Verstorbenen gleicht dem Körper an Grösse, Gestalt und Stimme vollkommen [...] *Sie* [ψυχή/εἴδωλον] ist gewissermassen ein ausgehöhlter Körper, der nun bildhaft wirken kann, also ein 'entmaterialisierter' Leib, mit allen Vorzügen und Nachteilen einer solchen Beschaffenheit. (1927, 32)

On the other hand, he states that, just as a dream seems to act on its own, the psyche

> ist unzweifelhaft ein selbständiges Wesen, das erscheinen und handeln kann, das mit anderen seinesgleichen zusammen an einem besondern Ort, dem Hades, seine Wohnstätte hat. (Ibid.)

Once the 'dead' (νεκροί) are integrated in Hades they generally seem to be 'senseless' (ἀφραδέες, *Od*.11.476), but they are also ghosts in the ritual sense of

17. Otto admits that ψυχή may also be associated with 'respiration' (and, accordingly, the last breath at the moment of death), as have often been proposed, cf. Otto, 1927, 28, but he still finds this meaning reducible to the more basic meaning of 'life', op.cit. 25 ff., cf. *Il*.21.568; 9.401; 22.161; *Od*. 22.245; 9.423 (and the passage of *Od*.9.523 in relation to which Warden agrees that 'ψυχή means nothing more than life', 1971, 95); see also Torresin, 1989, 48.
18. The two words, ψυχή and εἴδωλον, are often used synonymously as in *Od*.24.14, and *Il*.24.72, where the dead are described as ψυχαί as well as being εἴδωλα καμόντων, or as in *Od*.11, where Elpenor is called a ψυχή (51) and later an εἴδωλον (83). See also Nilsson, who agrees with Otto's distinction, 1955, 195, and Warden, who recognizes 'a marked semantic distinction between usage [of ψυχή] in death-descriptions and what one might call *Totengeist* usage', 1971, 95.
19. See Kerényi's objection to Otto's formulations in this respect, 1941, 176, n.2.

being able, for a short while, to regain the life-faculties through the drinking of blood (op.cit. 34 f.).[20] What about the ψυχαί of Elpenor and Patroclus, however, who exhibit the power of speech before having acquired the proper status of being inhabitants of Hades? Whether they have been enjoying the sacrificial blood or not (it is neither directly stated nor precluded), they are ψυχαί, as we have seen, who are neither living nor dead in the ritual sense of the word. If the epic distinction between life and death is somewhat ambiguous, or at least variably conditioned by the immediate context of meaning, the discrimination that Otto wants to make between the human entities of life and death may be exaggerated at a general level. Furthermore, it begs the question how one word, ψυχή, can have the meaning of *life* as well as the almost opposite meaning of 'ghost', even if the immediate context should account for the specific use. In order to gain some clarity regarding this issue, we will have to look more thoroughly at some of the sequences in which the word occurs.

Ψυχή is most frequently used in descriptions of the moment of death, where it leaves behind the 'limbs' (ῥέθεα) in order to go to Hades (e.g., *Il.*16.856 ≃ 22.362; 14.518). Similarly, Elpenor's own psyche tells us that it went down there (*Od.*11.65), when the neck became disconnected from the spine. It seems a little strange that the psyche thus speaks of itself in the third person, but this may actually be an example of a collision between two different contexts of meaning, the one being that Elpenor himself, who is represented by his ψυχή (11.51), is nothing but the 'corpse' (σῶμα, 11.53), who tells Odysseus that it still has to be integrated in the realm of the dead by means of a proper burial (11.72), and the other being that the psyche is by itself (i.e., as a matter of poetic convention) a part of Hades. If this is a reasonable suggestion, then Otto may be right in positing that ψυχή denotes a *Totengeist*, namely in the specific epic sense that from the moment of physical death, it *represents* the person who is no longer living.

In those descriptions of the process of dying, on the other hand, where ψυχή is simply said to perish (*Il.*13.762; 22.325; 24.167),[21] or is classed together with concepts like θυμός, μένος and αἰών (cf. Warden, 1971, 99), it inevitably makes us think of the *life* of the dying. Here, in any case, it cannot refer to the *Totengeist*, which is precisely the representation that does not vanish. Hence, Warden states that

> The least that one could conclude from this is that as the semantic base of ψυχή shifts within the Homeric poems, it is dangerous and misleading to take it as a constant in an attempt to interpret 'Homeric' psychology or 'Homeric' religion. (Op.cit., 100)

Of course, we should be aware that the formulaic system produces a set of de-

20. See also Vernant, 1965, 334; and below p. 72ff.
21. See, in this respect Claus, 1981, 65.

scriptions, in which the meaning of the included concepts are directly linked to the specific meaning of the particular description. However, the fact that ψυχή may be capable of assuming different meanings in different linguistic contexts does not imply that the concept could be taken to mean anything whatsoever.[22] On the contrary, it may have important bearings on the understanding of Homeric eschatology that the psyche is so closely, although variably, associated with descriptions of death and never with any activity in life.

The concept of ψυχή does, however, also occur in the event of fainting, i.e., with the *temporary* loss of consciousness (*Il.*5.696; 22.467 ff.). Rohde is of the opinion that the psyche only leaves the person until consciousness returns, but nowhere is this stated directly in the epics.[23] Instead it is θυμός that returns to the φρένες (as in Andromache's case, *Il.*22.475). Various scholars have tried, on the grounds of etymological examination, to demonstrate that both ψυχή and θυμός carry a meaning close to *respiration* in the cases of swooning as well as dying.[24] The reason that we should perhaps prefer Bickel's notion of 'Vital-gefül' in this respect (1926, 49; 65 ff.; 74 f.), is that a person who has fainted does not, of course, stop breathing at all. However, the matter of translation, although important in itself, does not explain why ψυχή never reappears together with the return of consciousness (Böhme, 1929, 100). The only role that the psyche seems to play in association with a living person is that of leaving. From this moment

22. See, in this respect, Böhme who, after having admitted that the Homeric notions are strongly conditioned by conventions of style, states that '[d]as braucht uns nicht gegen diese Äußerungen mißtrauisch zu machen, als wären sie nicht Ausdruck realer Vorstellungen. Im Gegenteil, gerade da, wo wir bewußte dichterische Gestaltung spüren, können wir gewiß sein, die lebendige Vorstellung zu faßen', 1929, 93. Whoever may, or may not, have had these *Vorstellungen*, they are present as potentials of meaning in the text. Let it be repeated, however, that for the current investigation we shall in each case stick to specific *textual* potentials, while trying not to impose on them imaginative references external to the relevant frame of discourse.
23. See Otto, 1927, 24; Böhme, 1929, 101; also Bremmer, who nevertheless adds that 'we assume that the *psyche* returned', 1983, 15.
24. See especially Böhme, 1929, 19 ff.; 104 ff.; 113; but also Nilsson, 1955, 194, and Nagy, 1990a, 90 f. That ψυχή, as well as θυμός and μένος, may imply a concept of *breathing* makes it even more implausible that it should denote a free-soul in opposition to the body-souls. Thus, Hultkrantz tries to mediate, as it seems, between the views of Wundt and Arbman by writing that 'It appears probable that the life-soul, in its character a breath-soul, has emancipated itself from its immediate physical functions and in consequence of its airy consistency been assimilated with and finally absorbed the conception of the free-soul [ψυχή]', 1953, 205. See Bremmer, 1983, 23, for a contemporary formulation of basically the same idea.

onwards, ψυχή only reappears as being part of the world beyond.[25] Surely, this does not suggest that a man's psyche is gone forever in the event of swooning. The description of the swoon may either be borrowed from the description of the moment of death (which, perhaps problematically, implies that the word is used metaphorically), or it may be due to a manner of description, in which the meaning of ψυχή is not 'vitality' as such, but rather something like 'the image of vitality'.[26] If this is the case, it is obvious why the concept is never mentioned in any description of regaining consciousness. At the moment of death, on the other hand, we might intuitively prefer to say that *vitality* is precisely what leaves the body in order to become an *image of vitality*. But if we remember that Hades, in these descriptions, possibly alludes to *a realm of invisibility* (as suggested above, p. 32, n. 21), it should actually be more accurate to say that an *image of life* becomes invisible in order to reappear within the sphere of divine presence. If we take 'image of vitality' to be the basic meaning of the concept of ψυχή, it implies, however, that the suggested predications of 'life' and 'ghost' do not express any real dualism intrinsic to the concept (which would be odd to say the least), but are merely contextual variations of the same semantic potential. The difference between the living and the dead, which Otto, quite rightly I think, found to be decisive, may rather correspond to the difference between human existence, on the one hand, and divine existence, on the other, i.e., between the plane of mortality and that of immortality. It is this level of existence then, which makes the appearance of the psyche and the dream compatible.

Still, it remains to be explained in what precise sense the *mind* of the living is represented by the psyche of the dead. It is remarkable indeed that the inhabitants of Hades do not only regain the power of speech by the drinking of blood but even seem to be capable of *remembering* (cf., e.g., *Od*.11.489-91; 602; 617 ff.). Furthermore, the *psuchai* in *Od*.24 are apparently also in possession of these faculties even without the presence of any sacrificial blood. Yet if the libation of blood is primarily to be understood as an action which, as a matter of ritual

25. The notion of *life*, *breathing* or *consciousness*, which the concept of ψυχή may imply, according to Nagy, even in the state of death (1990a, 91 ff.), is, as I see it, basically due to these phenomena being irrevocably part of an invisible presence. Nagy's suggestion that the eschatological principle of vitality is due to the extraordinary keeping of φρένες and νόος, as exemplified by Teiresias, ibid., is, in my opinion, conflating different aspects of eschatology. This is a matter to which we shall, of course, be returning later.
26. We should remember that the concept of ψυχή does not only demonstrate an affinity with concepts of body-souls, such as μένος and θυμός, but with the concept of εἴδωλον ('image' or 'shadow') as well, cf., for example, *Od*.24.14, where the ψυχαί of Hades are described as 'weary images' (εἴδωλα καμόντων).

obligation, makes possible the communication between the living and the dead, it is immediately comprehensible that blood has no role to play, when the dead are solely speaking to each other. Contrary to the scene of *Nekuia* (*Od.*11), the scene of the so-called *Deutero-nekuia* (*Od.*24) has no obvious bearings on the cult of the dead. The introductory sequence of *Od.*24 is entirely of epic significance. But if the drinking of blood is not, from an epic perspective, a necessary precondition for the mobilization of consciousness in the state of death, there should be reason to believe that the psyche is, after all, an independent prolongation of the consciousness of the living and therefore essentially nothing less than the immortal soul of a human being.

Kessels may have an important point which argues against such a suggestion. He states that Homeric death is nothing but 'a memory of how life was' (1978, 56). Surely, the epics have the power to make the underworld shadows act just as people would act in real life, except that the stage on which they conduct their performance is not the stage of this life, but that of the afterlife. There is no continuation of earthlike existence in Hades, only a repetition of the lives that once were. The mental life of the dead is not a real mental life, but merely a reflection of it. Therefore the *psuchai*, which were sent to Hades by the wrath of Achilles, are not represented as the heroes 'themselves' (αὐτούς). From the moment a body becomes a corpse, the vitality and fate of its previous existence can only be repeated at a new level of representation.[27] The activity of the body-souls has vanished and their last moment of being has been transformed into one composite 'shade' (εἴδωλον), namely the psyche.[28] Ψυχή, the image of vitality, descends into a darkness, whence only the act of remembering can bring it back. It is invisible in the same sense in which Hades carries the meaning of

27. Much later this even became an object for philosophical reflection, when Socrates says that 'we must believe that the corporeal is burdensome and heavy and earthly and visible. And a soul is weighed down by this and is dragged back into the visible world through fear *of the invisible* (τοῦ ἀιδοῦς) and *of the other world* (Ἅιδου), and so, as they say, it flits about the monuments and the tombs, where shadowy shapes of souls have been seen, figures of those souls which were not set free in purity but retain something of the visible; and this is why they are seen', Pl.*Phd.*81c. This concerns, of course, the theme of *metempsuchōsis* (transmigration of souls), which shall be our object of study in *Chapter VIIIb*.

28. I am not sure that ψυχῆς ὄλεθρος should be translated as 'life that is destroyed', as rendered by Claus, 1981, 65, but rather as 'a life-image that is lost' from the point of view of the person, whose representation it has become by being a ghost. This is not the same as to define the concept of psyche as an abstract or metaphorical notion, as Claus seems to imply, cf. his criticism of Otto and Warden, op.cit. 61, n.4. It may only be from our point of view that 'image' is considered equal to 'metaphor', cf. Lloyd, 1987, 172 ff.

'Invisibility', namely by being a phenomenon of the other world, that is, the imagined sphere beyond the human world of immediate perception.[29] Actually, the theory of the *free-soul* as introduced by Arbman hits upon a definition, which at first glance seems to be quite similar. In Hultkrantz we read that

> From the psychological viewpoint the conception of the free-soul is of course identical with the memory-image of the dead person projected onto the supernatural reality; and the airy, ethereal shape of the deceased is like a condensation of human breath. (1953, 205f.).

Apart from the imaginative style of argument, which may remind us of the theories of Rohde, Spencer and Tylor, this description indisputably accounts for various facets of the Homeric ψυχή. Still, it does not follow from the understanding of ψυχή as a memory-image that it is a supernatural projection of the free-soul. Rather than being a *free* soul, ψυχή is the object of 'supernatural reality' that is *bound* to the act of remembering.[30]

Conclusively, we should be able to claim that the concept of psyche is to be comprehended from the meaning potential of three main aspects, each of them being characterized by their own quality of invisibility. Although we shall take 'image of vitality' to be the overall translation, ψυχή may in some contexts be closely associated with a notion of *breath*, which is, however, also an invisible phenomenon. In other contexts ψυχή may primarily allude to the *life*, which is no longer visibly experienced as the activity of the *living*, and lastly, ψυχή is, in a few important contexts, close to the meaning of *ghost* as being visible solely to someone whose eyes have been opened to the realm of Hades. The way in which

29. Vermeule describes Hades, the god, as 'a King of remembered images', 1979, 29; 39. The case that Rohde makes of *Il.*11.262; 23.244; 14.456, where it is not ψυχή but the actual names of the persons (i.e., their identity as Rohde would have it) that are said to depart for Hades, represents no real objection, since the relationship between the psyche and the name is likely to be one of mutual representation. In the typical Greek epigram '[t]here is a name and a beautiful image', as Burkert puts it, 1985, 197. This, and nothing more, is what ψυχή seems to stand for at the level of Homeric eschatology.
30. Arbman's original, and almost look-alike, formulation of the matter is even more problematic insofar as it speaks of psyche as 'Die Bildseele [...] das für die Vorstellung objektive Realität bekommen hat' and 'nicht anderes [ist] als die Persönlichkeit selbst', 1926, 100, compare, for example, Ehnmark who is of the opinion that 'psyche and personality do not coincide', 1948, 8. What Arbman seems to overlook in the case of Homer is that the context of reality, to which he is referring, is not objective in a sense that allows him to suggest the idea of a free soul, but eschatological in a sense that it even seems to deny this thesis. Boas could be right, on the other hand, in recognizing 'the objectivation of life and of the memory-image as the principal sources from which the manifold forms of soul concepts spring', 1940, 600, as Pindar, for example, gives us some prompting to suggest (cf. p. 96). It is still important, however, to emphasize that this is not the case in the semantic universe of the Homeric epics.

this last aspect interconnects the experiences of Achilles and Odysseus is significant in that both heroes separate themselves from the ordinary world of immediate perception. That Achilles does so by going to sleep (*Il*.23.59-60), and Odysseus by going into the House of Hades (*Od*.10.512; 11.22), presumably exemplifies alternative ways of approaching the sacred world of the dead. In this world, the 'shadows' (εἴδωλα) seem to be real beings on the level of immortal existence, but only experienced as such from within the exceptional state that the living participant is temporarily occupying.[31] The reason for establishing this exceptional encounter between the living and the dead has to do with *time*. In the epics, time is the *plot*, and the Homeric *psuchai* are playing the role of activating, or promulgating, the course of events.[32] Thus, the dead are not only aware of the past, but of the future as well. To put it differently, they do not seem to exist within the limits of time. The question of identity, or continuity, between the living and the dead, then dissolves into thin air. The House of Hades is not of this world. It does not only lie beyond the reach of immediate perception, but beyond the reach of human time as well. This is ἔσχατος, and the only way to get there is through the ritual, or epic, suspension of normal life and the human measure of time.

If both of these suspensions can be said to be ritual, or ritualistic, by way of making demarcations of separation, liminality and reintegration, it means that the epics effect an act of transformation on two levels. On the one hand, we are told about the corpse which is rendered invisible by the ritual fire, i.e., transferred to Hades (cf. *Chapter II*); on the other hand, we are told that 'the psyche went down into Hades' (ψυχή δ' Ἀϊδόσδε κατῆλθεν) by way of formula. Homer emphasizes the funeral obligations by distinguishing the unburied body, as being the self of the hero, from the psyche. Only the proper burial conveys ψυχή with the status of representing the whole person (cf. *Il*.23.244; 15.251; 14.456), whereby the corpse and the image of vitality are finally integrated in an invisible object of sacred memorization. Both levels of description, however, are poetic, and the very act of reciting the epics is, in itself, an act of sacred memorization. Moreover, ψυχή is, in all instances, and regardless of the matter of identity, the important object of representation. Hence, the Homeric discourse does, in the end, challenge the non-verbal cultic actions. The representation of a funeral practice

31. Thus, upon waking up, Achilles exclaims that 'even *in the house of Hades* (εἰν Ἀΐδαο δόμοισι) is the *spirit* (ψυχή) and *phantom* (εἴδωλον) somewhat, albeit the *living mind* (φρένες) be not anywise therein; for the whole night long hath the spirit of hapless Patroclus stood over me [...] wondrously *like* (ἔϊκτο) his very *self* (αὐτῷ)', *Il*.23.103-7[M]. Compare *Od*.11.632-35.
32. For this thesis, see Warden, 1971, 96.

notwithstanding, 'ψυχή δ' Ἀϊδόσδε κατῆλθεν' inevitably becomes a sovereign expression of the migration from this world of living beings to the other world of dead beings. Detached and abstracted from the level of ritual, the crucial transition is seen through the blind eyes of Homer.

IV. The State of Being a Hero

Soc. 'Don't you know that the heroes are demi-gods?
Her. 'What about it?'
Soc. 'They were all born because a god fell in love with a mortal woman, or a mortal man with a goddess'[M]

Pl.*Cra.*398c-d

The Homeric discourse seems to have been successful in creating a dominant image of the Greek hero. Even the hero-adoration at temples or tombs, which is almost neglected in the poems, reflects a profound epic influence from Geometric times onwards.[1] This is not to say, however, that the context of meaning was the same within these two otherwise divergent settings of religious communication. Rather, there are many indications of an overall, and eschatologically significant, discrepancy between the two.

As for the cult of heroes, Porphyrius passed on a testimony by Draco from around 620 BC telling us that paternal law obliged the Athenians to honour the gods and the local heroes with praise and sacrificial cakes of the first fruit according to their ability (cf. τοις 'Ατθίδα νεμομένοις, θεοὺς τιμᾶν καὶ ἥρωας ἐπιχωρίους ἐν κοινῷ ἐπομένοις νόμοις πατρίοις ἰδίᾳ κατὰ δύναμιν, σὺν εὐφημίᾳ καὶ ἀπαρχαῖς καρπῶν καὶ πελανοῖς ἐπετείοις, ap. Porph. *Abst.* 4.22, corr. Meursius). This is consistent to some extent with the picture Rohde wants to draw of local hero-cult, in which the cult of chthonic gods and the cult of ancestors were intermingled (1925, I, 108 ff.; 204 ff.).[2] Although the meaning of

1. See especially Farnell, 1921, 280 ff.; 340 ff. The matter has, of course, raised the difficult question of origin. Coldstream claims that the hero-cult, as we know it from archaeological findings from Geometric times, was generated by the epics, 1976, 17, whereas Snodgrass is inclined to see it 'as private, family cults, not as early examples of the state-regulated hero-cults', 1979, 31; see also op.cit. 38 f.; 1971, 190 ff. Others are of the opinion that hero-cult and epic song interacted to the effect of mutual advantage in the Panhellenic formation of both traditions, cf. Price, 1979, 221 ff.; Calligas, 1986, 232; Schmitt-Pantel, 1982, 185; Seaford, 1994, 159 ff. In this context I shall merely opt for the view that hero-cult and epic song co-existed from early Classical times.
2. Compare Farnell, 1921, 19 ff. The legends of the chthonic gods were often euhemeristic, whereas the ancestors often acquired a divine, or semi-divine, status in similar legends, Rohde, op.cit. 119 ff.; 146 ff. Rohde's view is heavily influenced by the famous, but generally discredited thesis of 'La cité Antique', 1864, in which Fustel de Coulanges claims that Classical Greek religion is developed from the local hero-cults.

the word 'ἥρως' may have carried different allusions from one time and context to another,[3] it may generally have been used as a category of extraordinary human existence. With regard to different conditions of afterlife, Hesiod thus characterizes the heroes as 'semi-divine' (ἡμίθεοι),[4] being the fourth of five human races (*Op*.159-160), in which the golden race becomes 'earthly demons' (ἐπιχθόνιοι δαίμονες, *Op*.122), and the silver race is honoured (cf. ἔμπης τιμή, *Op*.142) as 'the blessed of the underworld' (ὑποχθόνιοι μάκαρες, *Op*.141).[5] While these references are not, of course, to be seen as any unbiased testimony of the cult of the dead, it should nevertheless be safe to assume that they lent a voice to it. The fact that the complex of chthonic cult practice comprised heroes as well as gods was, in any case, understandable in terms of the ἥρως and the δαίμων, insofar as these concepts blurred the categorical distinction between mortality and immortality, i.e., between normal human beings (cf. θνητοί) and the gods (cf. ἀθάνατοι). Apart from this fact, we should perhaps keep Dietrich's point in mind, namely that the hero in the context of sacrificial adoration was basically referring to 'the spirit of a particular dead person, and not an underworld deity' (Dietrich, 1967, 46).[6]

The hero of the epics differs considerably. First of all, he plays the role of a

3. Inscriptions including the very word, ἥρως, have been found in Mycenaean tombs, in the dative form, cf. τρισήρωι ('triple hero'), and in the genitive, probably also denoting dedication, on a much younger fifth-century black-glazed sherd, cf. Jeffrey, 1961, 174; Coldstream, 1976, 14; Price, 1979, 220; Nilsson, 1927, 610; Chantraine, 1968, ad loc. ἥρως.
4. Similarly the epics have a 'race of half-divine men' (ἡμιθέων γένος ἀνδρῶν, *Il*.12.23; regarded as a late interpolation, cf. Ukert, 1850, 176, n.35), but only this once and without the eschatological context by way of which the notion of ἡμίθεος seems to take on a general significance in Hesiod.
5. Rohde, 1925, I, 107 ff., and Farnell, 1921, 14 f., agree in seeing the *post mortem* state of the silver race as well as the δαίμονες of the golden race as being comparable instances of hero- and ancestor-cult; similarly Nagy, who claims that 'together they form a complete picture of the hero in cult', 1979, 154. Although the deceased were often compared with, or even called, demons in the context of chthonic religion, the reliable version of Hesiod, *Op*.140, does indeed distinguish between the golden and the silver race. Plato, on the other hand, seems to conflate the conceptual demarcation of this distinction by calling the golden race 'holy demons of the underworld' (δαίμονες ἁγνοὶ ὑποχθόνιοι, *Cra*.397e-398a). This reading (or mis-reading) may thus opt for the suggestion that there was no clear-cut separation between demons and heroes in Classical times; on this matter, see especially Dietrich, 1967, 51 ff.
6. Similarly Nilsson, 1927, 584 f.; Dietrich directs this suggestion against what he believes to be the opposite view, in Rohde, 1925, I, 119 f., cf. Dietrich, 1967, 51. Dietrich is partly guilty of a misreading of Rohde, though; cf., e.g., Rohde, op.cit. 152-54, for a suggestion that is not basically different from that of Dietrich.

living being, strong and glorious by way of being an outstanding warrior, and he earns his ritual honour, τιμή, in life, not in death.[7] Gregory Nagy, who appreciates the importance of this, states, quite rightly I think, that

> [f]rom the standpoint of cult, however, this timé would be possible only after he dies, so that the epic perspective has the logical sequence reversed: by placing epic above cult, Homeric poetry allows the hero to have the kind of timé that befits a cult hero even before he dies. What he still has to earn by dying is kleos itself. (1983, 203)

On the other hand, it may be crucial to note that from the moment of his death, the epic hero is worshipped *solely* through the 'imperishable renown' (κλέος ἄφθιτον, *Il.*9.413) of poetic song.[8] No continuous, honorific sacrifices, appertaining to a general cult of the dead, are ever mentioned in the epics.[9] The deceased warrior is provided 'with a mound and a stele, for this is the due of the dead' (τύμβῳ τε στήλῃ τε· τὸ γὰρ γέρας ἐστὶ θανόντων, *Il.*16.456 ≈ 675), but there is no indication that the presence of a tomb entails any specific obligations in the future. The sacrifices that Odysseus learns to undertake in the *Nekuia* are mantic and not of the τιμή-type. Thus, when Sarpedon tries to stimulate Glaucus' readi-

7. There are two exceptions to this rule; in *Od.*5.335, where we are told that Ino, once a mortal being, 'now in the deeps of the sea has won a share of honour from the gods' (νῦν δ'ἁλὸς ἐν πελάγεσσι θεῶν ἒξ ἔμμορε τιμῆς), and in *Od.*11.304, where we hear of Castor and Polydeuces, the sons of Zeus, that 'they have won honour like unto that of the gods' (τιμὴν δὲ λελόγχασιν ἶσα θεοῖσι), and further that 'the earth, the giver of life, covers these two, albeit they are alive and receive the honour from Zeus even in the world below ' (τοὺς ἄμφω ζωοὺς κατέχει φυσίζοος αἶα· οἳ καὶ νέρθεν γῆς τιμὴν πρὸς Ζηνὸς ἔχοντες, 11.301-2[M]). These cases, however, refer rather to the topic of exceptional translocation, than to a general level of hero-cult, see further below, p. 86 ff.
8. Compare Nagy, 1983, 202; further Rubino, who writes that '[t]he hero's unfading glory lives in epic poetry: heroes and heroines live, suffer, and die to take on significance after death as the subjects of heroic song, the great significance of epic verse', 1979, 16; Vernant, 1981, 286; Humphreys, 1983, 145; M. Lynn-George, 1988, 153 ff.
9. In Homeric discourse it is only the *Hymn to Demeter* that explicitly connects τιμή with hero-cult, namely as a compensation for death, as Nagy points out, 1983, 200 f., cf. h.Hom.2.260-64. He further suggests that the epic formula, 'honoured of the folk even as a god' (θεὸς δ'ὥς τίετο δήμῳ, *Il.*5.78; 10.33; 11.58; 13.218; 16.605) etymologically carries a similar, although latent, meaning (as it parallels the other formula, 'give him burial there' (ἔνθα ἑ ταρχύσουσι, *Il.*16.456; 674), cf. Nagy, op.cit. 199), but, importantly, the epics make it refer merely to the state of life, op.cit. 197. In Hesiod, however, the sacrificial character of τιμή is emphasized in relation to the race of silver, who did not give 'honour' (τιμή, 138) to the Olympians (i.e., to serve them and sacrifice on the holy altars, cf. 136), but they nevertheless received 'honour' (τιμή) themselves, when they became blessed spirits of the underworld (142; compare D.S. 4.39.1). It should be safe then to agree with Nagy that the concept of τιμή was generally associated with ritual honours, for example, in the cult of the dead, op.cit. 213, n.36; 200 f.

ness to fight by assuring him that death in battle is the only secure way of winning glory,[10] he does not mean glory in the form of τιμή but in the form of κλέος.

If we allow ourselves to assume that the Homeric singers knew about actual sacrifices in the cults of heroes (perhaps even including honours bestowed on heroes of epic origin), we may be intrigued by their silence. Could it be that they were inclined to play down the importance of local worship to the benefit of a Panhellenic memory?[11] At any rate, they established a discursive representation of hero-adoration that may have had the effect of keeping various possible associations with existing ancestor-cults at bay. As ancestors, the heroes of *epic* 'were not the private property of those families which claimed descent from a particular hero', as Hack put it, 'but they belonged to the whole Greek People' (1929, 59). The hero of *cult*, on the other hand, was part of a local tradition, if only because his underworld existence was bound to a particular spot. Although we may not want to go as far as Snodgrass in suggesting that hero-cult 'originated in local attempts to consolidate the ownership of land' (1979, 39; 1982, 107 ff.), it is highly plausible that there was a connection between social status, household property and cult practice on the level of ancestor-worship. Insofar as the obligations of hero-cult, as referred to by Draco, for instance, have bearings on the cult of ancestors, which is, after all, a reasonable suggestion,[12] the Greeks must have felt a considerable tension between the *sacrificial* and the *epic* acts of heroic commemoration. In some respects, however, they must also have been mutually translatable, and thus it should be fair to say that the local perspective of hero-cult and the Panhellenic perspective of epic poetry both supported and challenged each other.

Furthermore, the rites and offerings, which were directed towards the gainful as well as baleful activity of the underworld dead (as richly testified in late sources),[13] are remarkably absent in the Homeric discourse. This discourse is not in any way concerned with the local power of the dead, but only renders the presence of the σῆμα ('memorial'). Apart from being statically represented by this visible sign-post, the commemorative and apotropaic cult is non-existent in the epics, and as an actual underworld being, the hero is exclusively presented as ψυχή, the invisible object of remembering. Even the ψυχαί of *Nekuia*, summoned by the blood of the black ram, are part of this discursively-controlled process (cf. *Chapter V*).

10. Cf. κυδιάνειρα, *Il.*12.325; εὖχος, 328.
11. Cf. Nagy, 1983, 189.
12. We might even imagine with Farnell 'that ancestor-cult is the original and prior phenomenon, from which hero-cult subsequently arose', 1921, 343.
13. See references in Deneken, *Roscher* I.2, 2477 ff.; Rohde, 1925, I, 173; 177; Focke, 1941, 37; Dietrich, 1967, 45; Kirk, 1974, 226.

It is tempting to assume that these dissociations between hero-cult and heroic song may have been generated by the Homeric desire to appropriate the memory of the hero - the psyche - by the act of Panhellenic recollection. Even if the heroic body, the σῶμα, might still constitute an important centre of religious identification in the local community, it would not thereby be independent of poetic representations. The corpse is described in the epics as being the dead person himself, yet also as being co-existent with the psyche by its final integration in Hades. More importantly, however, the *post mortem* existence of the hero is blatantly ignored in favour of the power and glory of his or her life. In this respect, Homeric discourse seems to minimize the danger of polemic confrontation with actual cult traditions by telling the story of *foreign* events. Neither the Patroclus of the *Iliad* nor the Elpenor of the *Odyssey* is being buried in their homelands.[14] The Achaeans, i.e., the Hellenes, who are unfortunate enough to die on their Panhellenic mission are privileged to live on forever, renowned in the minds of generations to come. The importance and significance of the cult of the dead thus seem to be ideologically challenged by the importance and significance of epic tradition.

It goes without saying that the eschatological discrepancy of this relationship also involved concepts of fate and destiny. Whereas there are several indications in relation to the cult of the dead of the fact that the deceased was continuously represented by an agent of fate, e.g., κήρ,[15] ἐρινύς[16] or δαίμων,[17] as equal to the

14. In contrast to the Lycian prince Sarpedon, whose corpse is ordered by Zeus to be carried to his native country by the divine twins, *Hypnos* and *Death*. See below, p. 92.
15. On the last day of the Anthesteria festival, *Chytroi* ('pots'), all the dead were anonymously summoned through meals (consisting of grains boiled in a pot with honey) and libations of water. When finally the festival was brought to a close, the participants ritually ordered the κῆρες to leave, cf. 'Exit keres, it is no longer Anthesteria!' (θύραζε κῆρες, οὐκέτ' Ἀνθεστήρια, Zen.4.33). That the κῆρες referred to the presence of the dead seems to follow from Photius: ὡς κατὰ τὴν πόλιν τοῖς Ἀνθεστηρίοις ψυχῶν περιερχομένων; see also, Rohde, 1925, i, 239; Deubner, 1909, 112 f. Bremmer opts for the variant reading, Κᾶρες ('the Carians'), 1983, 113 ff., following Burkert and Meuli, cf. op.cit. 116. I am not convinced that they are right. First of all, there was a general association, at least from Classical times, between winged εἴδωλα and winged κῆρες, to which iconographic material testifies (cf. *plate 2* and *3a*); both the process of dying in battle and in bed (*plate 3a and 3b*) as well as different states of being dead (*plate 7a and 7b*) seem to be represented by the figures of *kēres* thus embodying a continuity of the presence of the dead. At a festival, in which this presence was a feature, the ritual *legomena* 'θύραζε κῆρες, οὐκέτ' Ἀνθεστήρια' is therefore likely to have addressed the κῆρες rather than the Κᾶρες.
16. In the writings of tragedy, in which references to the complex of chthonic cult are particularly prominent, we find a close association between the vengeful 'mind' (φρήν,

ghost, εἴδωλον or ψυχή, there are no clues for such an identification in the epics. At best, a hero is described as acting 'like a daimon' (δαίμονι ἶσος, *Il.*5.438; 459; 884; 16.705; 786; 20.447; 493; 21.18; 227), but, in death, nothing suggests any similarity even of this kind. In singular as well as in plural, the κήρ is described as a female agent of death that is evidently different from the dying or dead person himself,[18] and as a concept it seems more or less synonymous with other concepts of fate associated with female divinities, especially μοῖρα and the μοῖραι,[19] although perhaps the *kēr* has a more specific reference to the fate of *death*[20] than any other agent. The ἐρινύς, who is invoked in curses and by oath-

A.*Ch.*323 f.) of the dead and the avenging erinyes, e.g., A.*Ch.*107; 157. In the Orphic poem of the so-called Derveni-commentary of the 4th Century BC, the chastising erinyes are further equated with ψυχαί (in the Classical meaning of souls, perhaps even immortal souls, cf. *Orph.Fr.* 226; 228).

17. Cf. E.*Alc.* 1003; A. *Pers.*619 f.; 641; as for later sources, see Tamburnino, 1909, 89; Reverdin, 1945, 133; Boyancé, 1935, 192; Sfameni Gasparro, 1996, 77; 94, n.70. One of the earliest testimonies of a close affiliation between δαίμων and the fate and *post mortal* existence of man, is Theognis, 348-50; see the detailed discussion in Nagy, 1985, 73 f. With regard to the Orphic and Pythagorean relation between ψυχή and δαίμων, see Hild, 1881, 22; Van der Horst, 1942, 62 ff.; Detienne, 1963, 63; 65; Van der Waerden, 1979, 121 f.; 156 f.
18. Rohde's (1925, I, 10, n.1) and Crusius' (*Roscher* II.1, 1160) view that the Homeric κὴρ θανάτοιο originally refers to the souls of the dead is not confirmable, according to Malten (*PR*, Suppl.4, 883) who specifies the general meaning of κῆρες as powers of death and decay (op.cit. 884), i.e., as 'Schadegeister', etymologically related to the process of 'Verderbnis', cf. κηραίνειν, op.cit. 886 f.; more specifically 'Verderbnis des Todes' according to Nilsson, 1955, 224; Harrison tries to mediate between this view and the view of Rohde by saying that 'Keres (ἀνθρώπιναι κῆρες) is not equivalent to the Destiny of man, it means rather sources of corruption inherent in man', 1903, 166. This becomes awkward, however, in the reading of the Homeric text at several passages, e.g., *Il.*2.302; 834; 18.535 ff.; *Od.*14.207 (compare Paus.5.19.6), which rather justifies Malten. See also, Chantraine, 1968, ad loc. κήρ. Apart from phonetic similarity, there is no decisive reason, neither in context nor in etymology, to believe, as Crusius does (op.cit.), that κήρ and κῆρ are semantically associated.
19. Compare for example *Il.*5.613 f.; 13.602, as for μοῖρα, with *Il.*2.834 ≈ 11.332, as for κῆρες.
20. See especially Dietrich, 1967, 247 f. The majority of cases, in which *kēr* seems to be synonmous with death, even leads Dietrich to conclude (with Harrison, op.cit.), that there is no specific relationship between *kēr* and *Destiny*, although he admits that a certain, but infrequent 'type of Keres frequently recalls the image of the agent Moira on which it was modelled', ibid. Since all the concepts of fate in the epics, not least the *moirai*, are somehow related to the fate of *death*, as Dietrich himself seems to be aware, for instance, op.cit. 64 or 250, I cannot see the precise point of this reservation. Surely, a female *kēr*, described in the act of grasping (cf. ἔχειν) living warriors as well as dragging (cf. ἕλκειν) the dead ones away, cf. *Il.*18.535-37, must evoke the figure of an *agent*.

taking, also play the role of a divine agent of fate, in Homer as well as in other genres. The difference, however, between Homer and, say, the writings of tragedy, is, in this respect, that in the latter the ἐρινύες represent the wrath of a deceased person, whereas in the former they relate to the wrath of gods or living beings. We encounter, once again, the contrast between the activity of the buried hero and that of the living one, or - in more general terms - between the sphere of chthonic undertaking, on the one hand, and the sphere of Uranic (or Olympic) undertaking, on the other. Although chthonic divinities are not entirely absent from the Homeric universe, the Olympic gods, with Zeus as their unrivalled leader, do, obviously, play a much greater role.[21] Hence, there is, undoubtedly, an indicative link between the dominance of Olympic religion and of the remote and past but living heroes, which is concomitant with the perspective of Panhellenism.[22] Apparently, the representation of chthonic religion was generally suppressed due to an incentive to subdue local contexts of identification.

Yet, even Zeus does not entirely control the chthonic powers of fate.[23] When μοῖρα assails a man, nothing can be done, even if he be a hero, or a protegé of the gods. It seems, in turn, that Zeus does not always want to decide the precise outcome of fate, as when he puts the κήρ of Achilles and the κήρ of Hector on his golden scales. In this case, it is explicitly stated that Zeus is only the administrant who brings the fate of death to work on its own.[24] Certainly, the decisions of the supreme god himself (as well as of the other gods) have the most direct consequences in the world of human affairs, but nevertheless seem to work on another level than that of chthonic powers. In the *Iliad*, Achilles accuses the gods of being immune to sorrow, while mortals are condemned to live in pain. 'For two urns', he says, 'are set upon the floor of Zeus of gifts that he giveth, the one of ills, the other of blessings' (*Il.*24.527-33). In the *Odyssey*, however, Zeus refuses to take the blame and returns it to the mortals inasmuch as they bring sorrows on themselves 'beyond that which is ordained' (ὑπὲρ μόρον, *Od.*1.34). Still, Agamemnon refuses to take responsibility for the outcome of events. Bringing us back once again to the *Iliad*, he says

21. The chthonic divinities such as *moirai, erinyes* and *kēres* are mostly anonymously present, while the Olympic gods and the heroes are often mentioned by their personal names. This clearly creates an important (and rational) bond between these two groups of protagonists as it makes their actions and decisions compatible and decisive in the overall scheme of events.
22. I largely subscribe to Nagy's view in this respect, cf. Nagy, 1990b, 52 ff.; 66 ff.
23. Cf. *Il.*16.433 ff.; *Od.*3.236 f., compare Pindar, *Pae.* 6.92-94; cf. also the case of Hypnos and Nyx, cf. Il.14.256-61.
24. Cf. '[T]hen he grasped the balance by the midst and raised it', ἕλκε δὲ μέσσα λαβών, *Il.*22.212.

Howbeit it is not I that am at fault, but Zeus and Fate (μοῖρα) and Erinys, that walketh in darkness, seeing that in the midst of the place of gathering they cast upon my soul (φρήν) fierce blindness (ἄτη) on that day, when of mine own arrogance I took from Achilles his prize. (*Il.*19.86-89)

To some degree this contradiction can probably be resolved by treating it as a contrast between the *Iliad* and the *Odyssey*, insofar as the theme of divine justice (*theodicé*) is only a salient expression in the latter. Though this suggestion has often been made,[25] it is not necessarily the end of the story. Both traditions can also, as a matter of fact, be seen as to reflect a general tension between the will of the gods and the will of the heroes as against the unavoidable conditions of mortality.

That a god stands behind every human act does not prevent Zeus from blaming the mortals; and Agamemnon, who seems to blame all the powers of fate he can think of, admits, at the same time, that it was *his* (cf. αὐτός) act that was the fatal one. In the *Iliad* as well as in the *Odyssey*, destiny - the course of events - has no single 'cause' (αἴτιον). Neither the gods, nor the mortals, are exclusively responsible, for the blame is on both. The level of determination, however, is expressed rather by the scheme of narration than by the workings of chthonic divinities which are predominantly associated with the fate of death as a *general* condition. Whereas personal gods play around with personal heroes within the frame of a story, the impersonal powers of, e.g., δαίμων, κήρ, μοῖρα and αἶσα, in a sense define the rules of the frame itself. In this sense, even the power and will of Zeus is limited, but in fact he surrenders nothing to the realm of chthonic religion. Rather, he delimits the scope of its influence to the level of elementary preconditions. Nevertheless, I shall not hesitate to admit that if it can be safely assumed that Zeus took a growing interest in the matter of justice, from the *Iliad* to the *Odyssey*, he had good reasons to transfer these basic kinds of determination to the range of his own government.[26]

As a dominant framework of interpretation and orientation, Homer may thus have succeeded - on the level of narration as well as of thematic choice - in influencing and fragmenting - if not transforming - notions of fate, and of being a hero, in contexts of chthonic discourse (such as local, earth-oriented cults and

25. See, most prominently, Dodds, 1951, 28 ff., who, among other things, refers to the apparent shift of perspective from the *Iliad*, where Zeus seems to be relatively unconcerned about the fate of heroes, cf. *Il.*8.70; 22.210, to the *Odyssey*, where he explicitly shows signs of concern, cf. *Od.*7.164 f.; 9.270; 14.283 f.; see also Dietrich, 1967, 335 f. Against this view, C.J. Rowe, who at least does not find the *Odyssey* to be 'a poem of justice', 1983, 268.
26. See Cornford, 1912, 12 ff.; 26 ff.

myths of death and fertility). The workings of fate, closely associated with this discourse, were inevitably to shift meanings of reference by being redirected to the level of narration. The epics only showed one side of the picture, namely *the powers of life in the image of death*, and not, as in cults of fertility, *the powers of death in the image of life*, or relatedly, as in the hero cults, *death as a kind of living and powerful existence*.

Despite these contrasts, however, the *hero* was generally an object of ambiguity, even in the epics. Being a child of an immortal and a mortal, as was, for instance, Achilles, or simply by being favourites of the gods, the fate of heroes inevitably tended to challenge the all-too-general distinction between mortality and immortality. In fact, a few epic characters were chosen to live an everlasting life in the beyond (cf. *Chapter V*), but, of course, these could be, and probably were, exceptions that confirmed the rule, namely that heroes became mere shadows of themselves in the hereafter. Yet, the tension between different modes of afterlife may have exerted its influence; and as selected objects of sacred recollection the epic heroes were already exceptional beings, closer to the gods than ordinary men. The existence of these heroes, however, was confined to the past, or more precisely, to the verbal re-creation of the past as it took place in the ritual act of recitation. Nagy even writes that 'the gap that separates the heroes of the past and the men of the present could not and would not be bridged' (1990b, 192).[27] This would be too affirmative, though. It may be, that the Homeric discourse formed a rather closed circle of interpretation, but it did also deliver a language of everlasting existence that could be, and indeed was, transferred to other frames of interpretation than that of narration.

City-founders, for instance, or soldiers who had given their lives for the sake of the people, were, although exceptionally, allowed an intramural burial, in some cases even in the centre of the city *agora*.[28] The bodies of the dead, which were normally treated as a source of pollution, and therefore banished from the dwellings of the living, were in this way being reintegrated by being reinterpreted as 'pure' objects of collective memory. The encounter between the cult of the dead and the cult of the epics, which was a consequence of this process, further established the option of transferring the verbal immortality of the epic hero to his actual presence in the earth. Despite the dominance of

27. Compare Bakhtin, who states that epic 'events and heroes receive their value and grandeur precisely through their association with the past, the source of all authentic reality and value', 1981, 18, and further that the discourse of epic 'is as closed as a circle; inside it everything is finished, already over. There is no place in the epic world for any openendedness, indecision, indeterminacy', op.cit. 16.
28. See Rohde, 1925, II, 349; Parker, 1983, 42; Seaford, 1994, 125.

Homeric, Panhellenic and Olympic ideology, the discrepancies between god and man, and between life and death, that were in several ways intrinsic to the state of being a hero, still had an uncontrollable source of reference in the depth of the soil. Some poets managed to take advantage of this situation in creating a model of afterlife as being the *real life*. Hence, they introduced a radical opposition to the authority of Homer, and, accordingly, they spoke in the name of Orpheus, whom they claimed to be his forefather. They became known as the Orphics, and with them the matter of eschatology came to the fore.

V. The Underworld

Perhaps they have carried me to the threshold of my story
Samuel Beckett, *The Unnameable*

a. Nekuia

As should be clear from the preceding chapters, the presence of Archaic eschatology in Homer is multiform as well as indirect. The epics do have an eschatology in the sense that they deal with representations of death and with a customary, ritual response to it; nevertheless, they do so primarily in terms of negation (i.e., by stating what existence in Hades *is not*, rather than what *it is*). If we wish to understand Archaic religion, and not merely the Homeric version of it, we might therefore want to know more about the rules of exclusion than is possible from the sources available to us. There are, however, in the Homeric text itself contradictions and irruptions of silence which might permit us a glimpse of the world beyond it. In a sense, the underworld of Homeric discourse is not only the invisible realm of the dead, but also the tacit (or silenced) world of other interacting discourses in the crucible of its representation. A closer understanding of different layers of meaning, connected with the theme of eschatology, therefore awaits the interpretation of the underworld as depicted in the narrative.

This brings us to the 11th and the 24th book of the *Odyssey*, the *Nekuia* and the *Deutero-nekuia* respectively. Starting with the *Nekuia*, or *Nekuomanteia* as it was also called,[1] we are led into an underworld which is absent in the *Iliad*. Whereas in the *Iliad*, the House of Hades stretches out with no exact boundaries below the surface of the earth, it is placed beyond Oceanus at the Groves of Persephone in the *Odyssey* (*Od.*10.509-11).[2] It is one of the places, to which Odysseus must go

1. The titles, νεκυία or νεκυομαντεία, refer to a sacrificial practice by which the dead were summoned for oracular purposes.
2. In Hesiod the realm of the dead is placed at the borders of Oceanus as well as in the depths of the earth (*Th.* 767-80). This underworld is not called by the name of Hades, though, but by the name of Tartarus (841; 851; 868). Tartarus is only mentioned twice in Homer (*Il.*8.13; 481), the first instance so closely reflecting the instances in Hesiod than one cannot help thinking of the possibility of interpolation in the Homeric case. The Hesiodic Hades is, on the other hand, mentioned exclusively as the God of the Dead (*Th.*311; 455; 768; 850), whereas the Homeric Hades is the name of the divine realm as well as of its divine king. However, differences and similarities such as these could very well belong to an underlying framework of a general Archaic topography,

in order to finally return home, and thus, the journey that Circe, the sorceress, demands him to undertake is a typical heroic ordeal, namely the so-called κατάβασις, *a descent into the underworld*.[3] There is disagreement as to the dating of other comparable accounts of this sort of adventure, such as, e.g., Heracles' and Orpheus' journeys to Hades,[4] but we have reasons to believe that the theme of katabasis was, in fact, already known as a popular element of heroic myth in the period when the epics were being composed.[5]

Certain obligations, however, follow the specific task of the Odyssean journey. Circe orders the hero to dig a pit at a certain place and to pour a libation to all the dead, first of milk and honey and then of sweet wine together with white barley meal (*Od*.10.517-20 ≈ 11.25-28). After this, he must make a separate sacrifice to Teiresias, which he conducts by slaughtering a black ram and pouring dark blood over the pit (10.524 ≈ 11.32). Then the 'soothsayer' (μάντις), thus summoned, should be willing to tell him about his jouney home (10.539-40). However, although Teiresias does deliver a prophecy of the events to come, it is actually Circe who gives Odysseus the specific nautical instructions, when he returns momentarily to her island (12.25-27). The visit to Hades (or Erebus, as it is called in the *Nekuia*, meaning a world of darkness) seems not to have had any immediate bearings on his returning home, but stands as a strange excursion

which means that there is no obligation to suggest a break of topographical tradition from the *Iliad* to the *Odyssey* in this respect.

3. See Albinus, 1998, for the tradition of katabasis.
4. Heubeck is convinced that the story of Heracles, who drags Cerberus up from the gates of Hades, is older than the epics (1989, 114), while Wilamowitz (1922, 341 ff.) cannot accept a date earlier than the 6th Century BC. The theme was later dealt with in, e.g., Bacchylides, 33.5.56 ff., and Euripides, *HF* 23-25, cf. Bond, 1988, ad loc.; and later in Paus.3.25.5. Merkelbach takes *Od*.11.605-8 to refer to the katabasis of Heracles, 1951, 191, which seems to find support in B. 5.73 and Apollod. 2.5.12. If this is acceptable, the conclusion we draw from it, however, depends on whether or not we consider the sequence of *Od*.11.602 ff. to be an interpolation, cf. below, p. 79.
5. The *Odyssey* suggests a familiarity with such matters as the katabasis of Theseus and Perithous (11.631), to which also a fragment by Hesiod can be seen to testify (*Fr*. 280) in a way that brings the *Minyad* to mind (Paus. 10.28.2); this poem is probably Orphic and explicitly treats the adventures of Theseus and Peirithous in Hades, see Wilamowitz, 1884, 222; Weizsäcker, *Roscher* III.2, 1781 ff. (see further below, p. 132). Also the Sumerian hero-epos, *Gilgamesh* (probably composed in the first centuries of the second millenium BC, cf. Ravn, 1953, 15) should be mentioned in this respect as Gilgamesh makes a journey to the underworld in order to meet his deceased friend Enkidu.

whose most important purpose is perhaps to bring the theme of katabasis into the frame of Homeric discourse.[6]

Eventually, Odysseus does not merely confirm his own status of being a hero in passing the ordeal of katabasis; he also learns what happened, long ago and far away, to other heroes, and gains some idea of the general fate of the dead. This knowledge, the acquisition of which seems to be the true purpose of the sacrificial ritual, comes from the dead themselves who by drinking the blood of a black sheep, sacrificed after the ram, were given the ability to speak the truth. There is little doubt that the 11th song[7] thus delineates ritual duties which reflected a real cult of the dead.[8] It is a matter of conjecture, however, to what extent such a practice influenced the epics, or *vise versa*, just as it is impossible to be sure of the chronology of such influences. These problems should not bother us too much, though, since it should suffice for the moment to assert that the Homeric *Nekuia* was or became an important representation of local cult practices which were thereby vouchsafed an overall epic voice.

Normally, the act of νεκυομαντεία took place at a particular grave,[9] i.e., in a local context, but in the epics the entrance is given a location which is purely mythical and therefore equally accessible (or rather inaccessible) to all peoples of Hellas. It may be significant in the light of this representation that Odysseus was not only instructed to make offerings of (non-animal) agricultural produce as well as libations of blood to the flocks of Erebus, but that he was also told to say a prayer to Hades and Persephone, the divine rulers of an underworld which is thus, on several levels,

6. Cf. Merkelbach, 1951, 221-24, and Kirk, 1962, 236 ff., regarding the connection between *nekuomanteia* and katabasis.
7. Cf. Circe's instructions in 10.517-25; 532-37, closely matched by Odysseus' administering execution in 11.25-33; 45-50.
8. See especially Blinkenberg, 1919, 26. It is noticeable that Circe instructs Odysseus to turn the victim's head toward Erebus, *Od.*10.528, since from other sources we have the general impression that Olympic gods receive their sacrifices (by day) of victims which are slaughtered with their heads held up against the sky, while chthonic gods, heroes and ancestors receive their due (by night) of victims which are being killed with their heads forced towards the ground, cf. Rohde, 1925, I, 149, n.1-3; the distinction 'Olympian' and 'chthonic', parallel to the distinction between gods and heroes, is noticed by Burkert, 1985, 205, albeit recently criticised for not being as clear-cut as one would like it to be, cf. Bremmer, 1994, 29; see further, Schmitt-Pantel & Zaidmann, 1989, 35; 37.
9. The πλουτώνια ('entrances into the underworld') were often located at, or in, 'pits' or 'caves' (χάσματα) which included, in this context, the graves of heroes, to whom oracular questions were addressed at that location, that is, at a specific νεκυομαντεῖον, cf. Rohde, 1925, I, 212 f.

emphasized as being Panhellenic. The *Odyssey* does incorporate chthonic religion in some respects (cf. Schnaufer, 1970, 88), but in such a way that, at the same time, it undermines the local basis of recognition. This actually seems to be the case on several interrelated levels, of which a few examples shall be given below.

Since Teiresias is meant to be the first to receive sacrificial honours, Odysseus begins his act of communication by chasing the other ghosts away as they are drawn near by the blood. The ghost of Elpenor, however, steps forward and starts to talk, apparently without having to drink blood in order to do so. He complains about not having been buried, or rather his psyche does so on behalf of the soma (σῶμα). The fact that this psyche is presently separated from the corpse may explain that it is not revitalized by blood. Yet, surprisingly, even the consciousness of those of the dead who *are* probably buried does not seem to be ultimately dependent on the consumption of blood. *Od.*11.390 has thus been transmitted differently. In some manuscripts we hear Odysseus say about Agamemnon that 'he knew me straightway, when he had drunk the dark blood' (ἔγνω δ'αἶψ'ἔμ'ἐκεῖνος, ἐπεὶ πίεν αἷμα κελαινόν), while in others the conditional clause is 'when he saw me with his eyes' (ἐπεὶ ἴδεν ὀφθαλμοῖσι).[10] Further, in 471, it is not stated explicitly that Achilles drinks the blood before speaking to Odysseus in recognition. Much weight therefore has to be laid on 84-89, where Odysseus, however hesitantly, refuses to let his mother approach the blood before Teiresias, and, in relation to that, on 153, where Anticleia immediately recognizes her son after having consumed the blood.[11] Let us assume that, in contrast to Elpenor, she has been properly buried. But so also have Agamemnon and Achilles and yet the possibility remains that their mental abilities are not conditional on the blood drinking. If it is true, however, that the general state of being a hero is somewhat ambiguous (see *Chapter IV*), we should perhaps not even think of the Homeric hero as fitting too nicely into a strict division between mortals and immortals. Possibly, for Anticleia, who is not explicitly a heroine, it is obligatory to partake of the blood-drinking, while for the deceased of a more strictly heroic status it is not.[12] From the continuity point of view (i.e., the expec-

10. Cf. Petzl, 1969, 39. The same formula is used of Heracles' recognition, *Od.*11.615, which is interesting insofar as he has been immortalized, yet one must bear in mind that this is an exceptional case and is within a context which is slightly different, see p. 79, below.
11. As it is stated through the mouth of Odysseus: '[...] my mother came up and drank the dark blood. At once then she knew me [...]', ([...] ἐπὶ μήτηρ ἤλυθε καὶ πίεν αἷμα κελαινεφές· αὐτίκα δ'ἔγνω [με] [...], *Od.*11.153).
12. Wilamowitz already noticed 'dass die Heroen in der Nekyia Bewußtsein haben und mit Odysseus reden, ohne Blut zu trinken', and added that '[d]amals lebte freilich der Heroenglaube', 1959, I, 305.

tation of correspondence between different discourses), the evidence of blood libation in the hero-cult would then be question-begging, but from the suspicion fostered by this current investigation, namely that the tradition of Homer and the tradition of hero-cult are at odds with one another, it is only to be expected that the traits of hero-cult which are represented in the epics are at the same time inverted. In Homer it is ψυχή - the 'shadow' or 'memory image' - which is able to exhibit mental abilities without the sustenance of blood, and only in the assumed co-existence with psyche does soma - the 'corpse' and the 'self' - seem to share the same faculty. In this respect the psyche obtains a greater amount of autonomy than the soma, not in the sense that it replaces soma as being the self of the person, but in the sense that it occupies the same place of activity in the epics as that which soma presumably occupies in the cult of the dead. It must be admitted, though, that while the Homeric discourse is available through a written and immediately representative body of statements, the sources of the hero cult are fragmented, mostly non-literary and, when literary, then not immediately representative. This makes it fairly difficult to conclude anything with certainty concerning the hero-cult. If, however, we are justified in supposing an interdiscursive polemic to be embedded in the discrepancy between the complex of local traditions and the Panhellenic setting of the epics (an interdiscursive activity that may even be intrinsic to the epics themselves), then it is also reasonable to suggest that certain inversions of the Homeric perspective on death will somehow bring about the orientation of *the other*, or at least some traces of an eschatological perspective that reflects a concrete cult activity. We may thus assume that if the object of blood libation - in the epics as well as in the hero-cult - was an entity of soma and psyche, the emphasis was on psyche as being the true recipient in the epics, whereas the emphasis was on soma as being the true recipient in the cult. If, furthermore, the hero of the cult becomes semi-divine by imbibing the blood, the deceased hero of the epics may be semi-divine precisely by being exempted from this engagement (understood as a normal precondition for communication). Hence, the epic hero inverts the cult hero through emphasis on psyche associated with there being no need for blood in the description of the former, as opposed to an emphasis on soma associated with obligatory consumption of blood in the description of the latter.

Yet the libation also has a role of its own to play in the *Nekuia*. Although the spirit of Teiresias, who appears with a golden staff in his hand (91),[13] speaks

13. The 'staff ' (σκῆπτρον) that Teiresias is holding is a typical priestly attribute, authorizing him perhaps to carry out all of his functions, but also, and more specifically, providing anyone, to whom it is handed over, with the right to speak; compare the sceptre of Minos, the underworld judge, *Od.*11.569; the heraldic sceptre in

before he drinks, he nevertheless begs Odysseus to give way and lower his sword so that he may partake of the blood and tell him 'the truth' (νημερτέα, 96).[14] If it seems to be the sceptre that *allows* him to utter his demand, then it is apparently the blood which *enables* him, as well as any of the dead (cf. ὅν τινα μέν κεν ἐᾷς νεκύων κατατεϑνηώτων, 147), to speak as an oracle. Hence, the blood of victims may not be unqualifiedly associated with the power of life, as Otto believes (1927, 34), but rather with the chthonic complex of heroic divination.[15] Prior to the mantic ability of the cult-hero, however, comes the ability as well as the obligation of the epic hero to recognize his epic counterpart, and this recognition tends to precede, or even to exempt its actors from the ritual actions. There is, moreover, certain restrictions to the scope of truth that the summoned person is able to deliver. Either he/she provides information relating to the narrative course which the applicant is to follow (as in the speech of Teiresias, 100-37), or he/she refers to his/her own share of the past which further serves to clarify the position of the applicant (the latter case being predominant in the subsequent speeches, 155-627).[16] The object of the oracular truth is the frame of the epic, the lives of heroes and heroines, of which the dark appearances from Hades are merely visual as well as verbal reflections. That the tale of Theban Teiresias stands apart in this respect, demarcated already by his priestly staff, is presumably due to his being in possession of both νόος and φρένες (10.493-94). But if the hero-cult seems to gain a foot-hold in this representation of the seer, who is, first of all, granted the use of his mental powers as a matter of exception

the assembly, *Il.*23.568, as well as the sceptre of Hesiod, which is given him by the Muses and associated with inspiration from a divine voice, cf. ἐνέπνευσαν δέ μοι αὐδὴν ϑέσπιν, *Th.*30-32.

14. Compare the testimony of Lycophron, which renders the oracle of the 'dead' hero as νημερτής, *Alexandra*, 1051.
15. A certain relationship between the power of life (or temporary revitalization as regards the cult of the dead) and the power of knowledge may, however, prove affirmative in the context of chthonic divination; see, for example, J.P. Schjødt, 1983, 91; 97, who accounts for the interrelation between the elixir of life and the elixir of knowledge in ancient Norse religion. If, on the other hand, such a relation is implicitly present in ancient Greek religion, it should be all the more important to assess the way that it is, or rather is not, regarded in the epics.
16. The words of Elpenor, 59-78, stand out as a demand for the fulfilment of the funeral obligations. In this way, albeit in this case only, the cult of the dead is linked with the mantic purpose of *Nekuia* on a personal level. Elpenor is not, however, one of the dead that drinks blood and, accordingly, not one that speaks the oracular truth. The singular (local) dimension of the heroic oracle is suggested without being explicitly represented. This may be due to a Homeric strategy of selected representation.

(cf. 10.495), the basis for this identification is at the same time dissociated from important local points of reference. Being an inhabitant of the realm of the dead, it is remarkable that Teiresias is dislocated from his homeland, as he does not appear from a Theban tomb but from the House of Hades at the edge of the world. Furthermore, he does not address a matter of local Theban importance, but one pertaining to the Panhellenic *nostos*, namely the fate of Ithacan Odysseus.

While it is true that Odysseus also learns about the fate of other heroes and heroines due to a general heritage of epic themes which frames Odysseus' own role and character on the epic level, it is also true that the words of the dead provide him with a general eschatological knowledge (which may, as a matter of principle, exceed the confines of the epic universe). One example is, of course, Elpenor, who warns against the wrath of the gods, should he, Elpenor, be left unmourned and unburied (11.72-73). Another example is Anticleia, the mother of Odysseus, who is allowed to approach the blood after Teiresias. She tells her son that is was πόθος ('longing' [for him]) that killed her (202) - the memory image, we might add, that drained her of life - and when Odysseus tries, thrice even, to embrace her psyche, she escapes him 'like a shadow or a dream' (σκιῇ εἴκελον ἢ καὶ ὀνείρῳ, 207), proving to have now become a figure of memory herself. In this way a strange affiliation is suggested between two instances of absence. Even though Odysseus has been alive all the time, while Anticleia is now actually dead, the two situations of loss are somewhat symmetrical, the one image of memory being generated by the other. Odysseus seems to acknowledge this and bitterly asks whether Persephone has merely sent him an 'image' (εἴδωλον) that he may lament and groan the more (213-14). Whether this question is posed rhetorically or not, and whoever is the real addressee, I take the answer of Anticleia to be pertinent to the eschatological perspective of the epics as thus providing the ritual applicant with knowledge. Persephone, the voice of the dead mother says, has not deceived him, 'for this is the appointed way with mortals when one dies ' (ἀλλ'αὕτη δίκη ἐστὶ βροτῶν, ὅτε τίς κε θάνησιν, 218). In death we are nothing but images of memory, Homer seems to tell us.[17]

Following the appearance of Anticleia, other women approach in turn, each telling the story of their own fate. In this catalogue of heroines, however,[18] the

17. Why Zielinski, who seems to follow this suggestion, finds *Il*.23.102 and *Od*.11.216-224 to be testimonies of religious innovation on this account (1934, 1021 ff.) escapes my comprehension. Even if we accept the eschatological perspective of the epics to be very different from that of the concrete cult of the dead, why does there have to be a chronological distance between differing discursive orientations?
18. About the genre of 'heroine-catalogue', possibly Boeotian (or even Hesiodic) in origin, see Kirk, 1962, 237; M.L. West, 1985, 112; Heubeck, 1989, 75, and not least Wilamowitz,

most salient reflection of hero-cult may be the mentioning of two male figures, the sons of Zeus and Tyndareus respectively, namely the dioscuri, Castor and Polydeuces, who 'even in the world below have honours from Zeus' (νέρθεν γῆς τιμὴν πρὸς Ζηνὸς ἔχοντες, 302[19]). In the *Iliad* as well as in the *Odyssey* it is expressed by part of a formula that 'the life-giving earth covers them' (τοὺς δ'ἤδη κάτεχεν φυσίζοος αἶα, *Il.*3.243), to which, however, the *Odyssey* adds that they are 'both living' (ἄμφω ζωοὺς, 11.301). The *Iliad*, which is silent about the extraordinary status of the dioscuri in the underworld, locates them 'in their dear native land' (φίλῃ ἐν πατρίδι γαίῃ, *Il.*3.244), whereas this reference is absent in the *Odyssey*, due as it may be to the Panhellenic dimension of the *Nekuia*. In the light of what we have already learned about the way the Homeric discourse seems to work, we should be tempted to regard the epic representation of these Lacedaemonian heroes as yet another instance of strategic selection characteristic of the Homeric references to issues of local importance.

After the catalogue of heroines, albeit with a break where Alcinous must urge Odysseus to continue, there follows the catalogue of heroes introduced by the spirit of Agamemnon. As in the case of Anticleia (172-73), Odysseus suggests a short register of predictable causes of death which might have sent his fellow king to the House of Hades (399-403), and once again he receives a tragic and unexpected answer. Agamemnon tells him that he and his comrades, the shades of whom appear around him, fell victim to the deadly betrayal of his wife, Clytemnestra, and her lover, deceitful Aegisthus (409-415). Apart from blaming Clytemnestra for being shameful in several respects,[20] he uses her to draw a parallel to Penelope, whom Odysseus is advised, therefore, to keep under control. It goes without saying that Agamemnon himself has failed to exercise such control. Even when this fact is discounted, the advice sits oddly when followed by his statement that Odysseus will not, in fact, find his wife to be unfaithful on his return home, wise and prudent as she is (by way of predication, 444-45). The shift from advice to judgement could perhaps be understood in the light of the assumption that the psyche of Agamemnon talks from a realm of timeless truth,

1884, 148, who analyses the possible relation between the aristocratic and genealogical interests of the Homeric and Hesiodic catalogue and the hero-cult.

19. Cf.: 'One day they live in turn, and one day they are dead; and they have won honour like unto that of the gods' (ἄλλοτε μὲν ζώουσ'ἑτερήμεροι, ἄλλοτε δ'αὖτε τεθνᾶσιν· τιμὴν δὲ λελόγχασιν ἶσα θεοῖσι, 303-4).
20. Thus, apart from calling Clytemnestra 'accursed' (οὐλομένη, *Od.*11.410) and 'guileful' (δολόμητις, 422) because of her deceit and her aid in the act of killing, Agamemnon reproaches her for abandoning, as a part of the death ritual, the conventional duties of closing his mouth and eyelids (426).

but we may still be left wondering, all the same, why he concludes by asking Odysseus about the fate of his own son Orestes. Odysseus is indeed taken aback by the question, and, being unaware of the answer, he ventures no response (462-64). What is the Homeric point in this? It may be that the ignorance of Agamemnon is just a matter of dramatic style, though this is hardly a satisfactory answer if we continue to restrict ourselves to locating 'meaning' in the context of epic diction. Without escaping this principle, we might, in turn, expect the 'mantic answer' to fit the 'mantic question'; hence, Agamemnon puts the *nostos* of Odysseus into perspective by referring to his own fateful *nostos*. He delivers an oracle of truth that fulfills the immediate epic goal, we could say, and, consequently, he has no similar access to the fate of Orestes, simply because this theme is beyond the immediate frame of relevance. On the other hand, we are undeniably left with a picture of two men in a conversation which does not explicitly credit Agamemnon for having any timeless knowledge whatsoever. It is rather as if he, or his psyche, is activated for the moment, provided only with the knowledge he had in life.[21] If this suggestion is preferable, which I think it is, we will have to conclude that the source of truth, which in all circumstances transcends the knowledge of the oracular applicant, does not exactly stem from the dead themselves, but from the frame of the epic story, of which they are merely the individual components. Not Agamemnon in person, but his 'oracle', reflects an epic voice which speaks from beyond, conveying advice as well as judgement - which, as a matter of principle, is relevant to the situation of Odysseus.

After Agamemnon has withdrawn, Achilles appears together with Patroclus.[22] He asks Odysseus why and how he has come to 'the unheeding dead, the phantoms of men outworn' (νεκροὶ ἀφραδέες ναίουσι, βροτῶν εἴδωλα καμόντων, 475-76). Odysseus explains his need to consult Teiresias and then surprisingly compliments Achilles on his circumstances while deprecating his own (482-86). He even addresses Achilles as the 'most blessed' (μακάρτατος, 483)[23] of all time,

21. The same is true of the following conversation between Odysseus and Achilles, cf. 11.492.
22. The motif is, of course, linked to the tragic perspective of the encounter between Achilles and Patroclus in the *Iliad*, where it is foretold by the shade of Patroclus that they will soon be together in the House of Hades (*Il.*23.82, cf. above, p. 38), but it further reflects the situation of an encounter between a living and a dead person, thus suggesting a parallel between Achilles' sleep (or incubation) and Odysseus' journey (or katabasis) as being corresponding preconditions for extra-sensual, or divine, contact.
23. Notice that 'blessed' (μάκαρ) is the word, Hesiod uses of the deceased ὑποχθόνιοι (the silver race, *Op.*141), who enjoyed continuous 'honour' (τιμή), as well as of the heroes (the fourth race), who have been translocated to islands far off in the depths of Oceanus (*Op.*171), where they will live free from sorrow and labour (172 -73); compare the pro-

since he rules mightily among the dead (cf. μέγα κρατέεις νεκύεσσιν, 485). The psyche of Achilles, however, reproaches Odysseus for seeking to play down the misery of death (488). He would prefer, as expressed in his famous answer, 'to serve as the hireling of another, of some portionless man whose livelihood was but small, rather than to be lord over *all the dead that have perished'* (πᾶσιν νεκύεσσι καταφθιμένοισιν, 491). What he implies is that the 'honour' (τιμή), which he enjoyed in life (cf. ἐτίομεν, 484), will not benefit him in death. All that the epic hero can hope for is the immortality of 'fame' (κλέος), but in Hades this fate is of no comfort.[24] This, of course, sheds a tragic light on Sarpedon's exhortation that one should strive to die in battle (*Il.*12.322 ff.; see above, p.60).

By his encounter with Anticlea, Agamemnon and Achilles, Odysseus is informed from various angles of the interrelated natures of 'death' and 'psyche'. Hence, the knowledge he receives is one of eschatological truth, represented as it is by the epic form of νεκυομαντεία. In the following sequence, however, the presentation of the catalogue of heroes (568-626) seems to challenge this fate of the psyche as hitherto represented. For this and other reasons, the sequence has been assessed as being an interpolation.[25] That this is actually not very likely, we shall see below. Odysseus introduces the catalogue by ἔνθα (568), a deictic marker that suggests that from 568 to 629 he is experiencing a vision of what is going on *within* the realm of Erebus, and this may in fact change the implications of his encounter with the dead altogether.[26]

mised translocation of Menelaus to the Elysian fields, *Od.*4.563; see further below,p. 86.

24. The epic κλέος is a compensation for death that is evidently of quite another nature than the τιμή, obtained by Demophoon in the *Homeric hymn to Demeter* (h.Hom.2. 260 f.). Although Demeter's attempt to render him immortal failed, meaning that he has to suffer death as well as any other mortal being, he is promised everlasting honours from his people (referring, no doubt, to ritual obligations of a hero-cult, cf. Nagy, 1983, 201). Apparently, the matter of hero-cult was less controversial in the genre of the hymns than in the epic tradition, see further below, p. 157; 169.
25. As Aristarchus had already done, cf. Schol.Hom.*Od.* ad loc.; Wilamowitz originally agreed in viewing the sequence of *Od.*11.566-631 as an Orphic interpolation supplied by Onomacritus, 1884, 199 f.; 220 ff., and he pointed out that the verse 632 comes naturally after 565, op.cit. 142. Later, however, he questioned the whole concept of Orphism, 1959, II, 198, n.1. Heubeck, who gives a general survey of the interpolation-theory (1989, 111) disagrees himself owing to what he takes to be a structural correlation between the first catalogue (of heroines) and the second (ad loc. *Od.*11.235; 568). Kirk, who believes the whole sequence to be an interpolation, refers to the fact that it dispenses with the imbibing of blood, 1962, 236. As we have seen above, however, the blood-sustenance is not always a prerequisite for the functioning of the deceased's mental faculties.
26. Heubeck thus finds the abandoning of drinking blood (due to the sequence in question) to be a logical consequence of the fact that the whole action now takes place in Erebus. The suggestion behind this must be that Odysseus simply has a vision of the dead as

Among other things, we hear of a scene of judgment which seems absent from the perspective of the *Iliad*. Divine punishment is known to the *Iliad*,[27] but it does not have a specific relation to the underworld, as is the case in the *Nekuia* of the *Odyssey*. Here, we are introduced to King Minos who, at the gates of Hades, has his throne of judgment (*Od*.11.569-71). However, keeping the words of Achilles in mind we might be inclined to compare the expression 'ϑεμιστεύοντα νέκυσσιν' (569: 'giving judgment to the dead') with 'μέγα κρατέεις νεκύεσσιν' (485: 'thou rulest mightily among the dead') as being merely instances of *seeming*.[28] However, it obviously makes a difference in the case of Minos that it is the dead themselves who 'ask him to judge' (cf. δίκας εἴροντο, 570), while they sit or stand about him (571).[29] Undoubtedly, this is to be understood as an autonomous activity within the realm of the beyond. If it is plausible, moreover, that δίκη has a root in the complex of chthonic powers, as Harrison among others has suggested (1912, 520),[30] and if it is, more specifically, related to a notion of fate, as Dietrich suggests (1967, 98; 204),[31] then we should perhaps regard King Minos as being a divine (rather than heroic) arbiter of the fates of human lives. Even if these fates might be preordained, they may nevertheless 'need' a mythical, 'earthlike' representation of their distribution and implementation in the world below. Minos seems to fulfill such a purpose.

they speak and act in a realm of their own. It could be a relevant point, of course, but as being quite independent of precise, textual information, it puts us at the risk of imposing a 'belief' in afterlife that has no real foot-hold in the epics themselves.

27. Cf. boastful Thamyris, *Il*.2.595 ff., and Lycurgus, who dared to chase Dionysos, *Il*.6.130 ff., were both blinded. Further, the erinyes punish the breaking of oaths and are given the task of fulfilling curses, *Il*.9.454 f.; 571 f. This punishment takes place *post mortem*, but is not explicitly related to any underworld mythology in the *Iliad*.
28. The mythologem of Minos, as represented in the *Nekuia*, draws on his legendary status as a Cretan Monarch, cf. *Od*.19.179; Hdt. 1.171; Th.1.4.1 Thus, Minos is first of all related to a Cretan mythology, and is represented only this once in the epics, while he appears several times in the Orphic poems and a few times in Plato's *Gorgias* (523e; 526d). It is not unthinkable, as we shall see later on, that a special eschatology evolved in Crete and became very popular through an Orphic adaption. Therefore the singularity of the Homeric representation could make us suspicious that it reflected a representation, as well as a marginalization, of this local discourse.
29. A scholion mentions this description of someone sitting before the judge to be *alogon* - i.e. irreconcilable with normal practice, compare, for instance, *Il*.18.505 ff., cf. Petzl, 1969, 14. Still, it is hard to understand the description in the *Nekuia* as referring to anything other than a situation of judgment, yet taking place, of course, on an eschatological level, compare Pl.*R*.614c.
30. Cf. also S.*Ant*. 450-51.
31. Cf. also *Od*.11.218, as mentioned above, p. 73.

Odysseus further experiences genuine activity on the part of the dead, namely Orion, Tityos, Tantalus and Sisyphus, the last three of whom act according to the punishments meted out to them. We may wonder, in this respect, why the actual crime is only specifically referred to in the case of Tityos. Supposedly, the stories of Tantalus and Sisyphus were generally known, which was probably the reason for not repeating them in this context. Be that as it may, the resulting silence may still reveal the fact that a notion of *moral reasons*, such as we may be inclined to think of it, was far from the perspective. The punishments simply revealed that the wrath of the gods had been aroused regardless of the specific reason.[32] Possibly, the grounds for bringing these issues of punishment together - within the frame of the *Nekuia* - were to enumerate instances of Olympian victories over chthonic agents (such as Orion, Ixion, Tityos and Tantalus) as well as mortal agents (such as Sisyphus), demonstrating, of course, the suzerainty of Olympian Zeus.

Another aspect of the punishments, which might be worth mentioning, is that they are perpetual. In death there is no change and therefore no release. Whereas the gods live on forever, free from sorrow and labour since there is no death for them, the mortals, when they die, are consigned to an existence in an everlasting, and incidentally painful, world of death. But these two kinds of 'eternity' also share a crucial property, namely that they only reach forward in time. The death of mortals and the birth of immortals are strangely, yet significantly, parallel in that they are the mythical, or narrative, beginnings of transcendent existence. Further, the state of death parallels the state of immortality in much the same way as chthonic powers parallel Olympian powers (as is the theme of the *Homeric Hymn to Demeter*, cf. p.170f.). This division actually goes through one and the same person, namely Heracles, the hero who was destined to become immortal the moment he died.

32. See especially Schnaufer, 1970, 107, and Rohde, 1925, I, 63, n.1. Sisyphus is called 'the craftiest of men' (ὃ κέρδιστος γένετ' ἀνδρῶν) in *Il*.6.153 as a sign of approval (and referring presumably to the myth, which is known to us through later sources, cf. Apollod.1.9.3; Paus.2.5.1). As is well known, he is sentenced to push a huge stone up to the top of a steep mountain (cf. *plate 4*). His efforts are unrewarding, since the stone immediately rolls down again after having reached the peak. He just has to start all over again and so the enterprise repeats itself infinitely, *Od*.11.593-600. The reason behind his punishment is that he has thwarted one of Zeus' erotic affairs. Hence, the sentence is obviously not due to moral sanctions but to a personal conflict, a matter of challenge, between a person (a hero) and a god. The hero that shows an effective and cunning intelligence is in the end overpowered by the supreme god; see especially Gordon (1977) for studies in this theme as typical in Archaic Greek mythology. Compare the cases of Tityos, *Od*.11.580-81, Ixion, Pi.*P*.2.21-48, Tantalus, cf. *Roscher* ad loc. 80 ff., and Prometheus, Hes.*Th*.537 ff.

While his ghost, or literally his 'image' (εἴδωλον), belongs to Hades, Heracles 'himself' (αὐτός) dwells among the immortals (*Od.*11.601-4).[33] Due to other instances of this semantic opposition (cf. p.44 above), we may expect αὐτός to refer to σῶμα ('corpse')[34], while εἴδωλον may implicitly encompass the notion of ψυχή. What, in any case, makes the distinction astonishing is that it is atypically conferred on the *afterlife*, so that the corpse, and therefore the self, are believed to survive in the world beyond *separated* from the realm of remembered images.[35] This is probably one of the things that made the scholiast believe that Onomacritus, who was actively involved in the distribution of Orphic poems, was responsible for the apparent interpolation (see p.102, n.6 below). There are indications contrary to this suggestion as well,[36] but even if the sequence may have been believed - by listeners to the Homeric poems - to somehow reflect Orphic eschatology or some other discourse, we must not forget that Heracles, more than anyone, is a figure of exception. If, for instance, the Orphic tradition was being represented by the verses in question then it was also, at the same time, being reduced to a marginal position by the *Nekuia* as a whole. As long as Homeric and Orphic discourses are viewed as living traditions, even in their transmission as written poems, different instances of mutual imitation are only to be

33. The verses 602-4 have been regarded as an interpolation by Onomacritus, cf. Schol.11.385, who apart from having contributed to an 'edition' (διόρθωσις) of the epics, has been associated with a recension of Orphic poems as well, see below (p.102, n.6).
34. Cf. Schol. A ad *Il.*1.4; B ad *Il.*1.4 ap. Petzl, 1969, 31, n.11; compare D.S. 4.38.5.
35. In *Od.*11.627, however, we are once more taken by surprise. After having spoken to Odysseus, Heracles is said to return to 'the House of Hades' (δόμος Ἄϊδος), which, if our analysis is even partly right, should be rather closely associated with the gathering of remembered images in the nether world. Still, the voice of Heracles, as well as Heracles 'himself', may be duly represented by his ghost, as may each and every one of the dead irrespective of their specific status. It is, after all, the world of darkness (Erebus) and invisibility (Hades) that reveals itself to the ritual gaze of Odysseus.
36. It is worth mentioning that the eschatology of Orpheus concerns the release of the psyche from the 'body' (σῶμα), which is regarded as the earthly and mortal element of human beings, cf. below p. 137 f. Yet the αὐτός of the specific sequence was interpreted by Lucian and Eusthatius as referring not to the soma but to the 'soul' (ψυχή), cf. Luc. *DMort.*; Eust. 19.21 ff. Another argument for viewing the sequence as an interpolation is that it is the only place in Homer that mentions Hebe to be the wife of Heracles. This does not specifically address an Orphic context, though, since the relation occupies several times in Hesiod, cf. *Th.*952 and *The Catalogue of Women*, *Fr.*229.9; 25.26-33, which also mentions the apotheosis of Heracles. Thus, if it was an interpolation, *Od.*11.602-4 rather drew on the tradition of Hesiodic discourse (cf. West, 1985, 112), from which *Works and Days* might even give us some reason to suggest that the apotheosis of the golden race included a resurrection of *corpses*, cf. *Op.*121-22.

expected, and do not make each discourse less Homeric or less Orphic. The discourse that represents another is exactly the discourse in charge, the one that, within certain limits of genre and context, decides what to select, and how to do it. This is what we might call an instance of 'selected representation', being an internalization of the voice of the other.[37]

It would be reasonable to suggest that the same applies to the Homeric representation of hero-cults and chthonic religion as such. The mythologem of Heracles, in which the Olympian resurrection of the corpse (or at least of the αὐτός) indicates as well as undermines the activity associated with *the heroic grave*, seems to be an example of this, not unrelated, however, to the orientation of Orphic discourse, as we shall see in some detail later (cf. *Chapter VIII*). The duality of Heracles' presence further seems to suggest (or confirm) that whereas the Uranian, or epichthonic,[38] existence is a state of immortality, the chthonic existence is a state of seeming. However, the measure of reality intrinsic to such concepts as 'existence' and 'seeming' might be alien to the epics in any ontological sense, with which it takes on meaning in later discourses. 'Reality' is therefore a notion we impose on the text as an *observer's category*.[39] Still, it is hard to escape the impression that *something* in the sense of ordinary, sensual accessibility, adheres to the state of *life upon earth* as being the model of the life that is lived on Mount Olympus. Were it fair to say that the world of transcendent powers is a world of its own reality, then it should be added that in the relation to the world of mortality, to which each and every one of its properties actually refer, the qualities of eternal being in the light of day on earth have a higher priority than qualities of eternal being in the earthly dark. The joy of life is a prevalent feature of Homeric discourse, and whereas the world of the Olympians is seen as positive because it assimilates the world of life, the chthonic world is rejected because of its dissimilarity. In this way Olympian Zeus of the epics subordinates the powers of the underworld to a world that is considered inferior as well.

If, in addition, the strategy of the supreme god reflects a strategy of Homeric discourse, we might say that it is not only the chthonic orientation of local cults which is seriously challenged by way of this devaluation, but also the perspective of Orphic discourse, in which the relationship between Uranian and chthonic powers, involving the fate of the psyche, was, in some respects, exactly the opposite of the way it obtains in the epics. Hence, instead of wasting too much

37. Cf. Bakhtin, 1973, 200 ff.

38. By *epichthonic* I refer to the distinction, in Hesiod, between the golden race, raised from their graves as epichthonic daemons, *Op.*122, and the silver race, confined to the depth of the earth as the blessed of the underworld, 141. See p.58, n.5 above.

39. Cf. Lloyd, 1990, 8.

effort discussing problems of genetic causality (e.g., whether some tradition influenced the other or *vice versa*), which may, in any case, prove unrewarding, we should perhaps enumerate the instances of correspondence, as well as of inversion, between different discourses as manifestations of interaction on a synchronic level. Viewed in this way, deducible elements of intertextuality may pave the way for analysing the ability of each discourse to continuously reproduce itself, concomitant, as it seems, with some restrained options of renewal. Perhaps through this approach we will be able to appreciate crucial aspects of traditional story-telling, whether it be the lips of Orpheus or those of Homer which gave it utterance.

More remains to be said about the mythologem of Heracles as represented by *Od*.11.601 4. Whether reflecting the editorial work of Onomacritus or not, these verses do probably, in any case, show a compromise between different versions of the popular hero's life and death. Diodorus from Sicily, for instance, claimed that Heracles was mostly honoured as a hero and that the Athenians were the first who made sacrifices to him as a god (4.39.1).[40]

Another point to be made is that the apotheosis of Heracles can in fact be interpreted as an eschatological reward for duties carried out in life,[41] a meaning potential that may, once again, turn our eyes towards the discursive context of the Orphics.[42] But even so, the destiny of Heracles was foretold by the oracle and brought about by the thunderbolt of Zeus (Apollod. 2.7.7; D.S. 4.38.4-5).[43] Nothing in the *Nekuia* implies on a general level that a person who might act in a certain way was entitled to look forward to a better fate in the afterlife, let alone that the enterprises of Heracles represented a model for imitation. Quite the contrary: the Homeric mythologem of Heracles represented an exceptional fate as regards the afterlife, an exception which proves the rule, since even as an

40. Cf. ὡς ϑεὸν ἐτίμησαν ϑυσίαις τὸν Ἡρακλέα; see also Hdt. 2.44.5; See above, p.69, n.8, as for the difference between offerings addressed to heroes and offerings addressed to gods. Heracles did also play the role of a god in the Orphic theogonies, but as a primordial being in the coming into existence of the cosmos (cf. *Orph.Fr*.54; *Orph.Fr*.58) and thus in an entirely different context, cf. West, 1983, 192-94.
41. The *Nekuia* only seems to mention the 'hard labours' (χαλεποὶ ἄεϑλοί, 622) as evidence of the fact that in life Heracles had 'woe beyond measure' (ὀϊζὺς ἀπειρεσίη), but the question is whether the 'immortality' (ἀϑανασία), which Diodorus relates directly to his carrying out of the twelve 'labours' (ἔργα, 4.8.1-20), is presupposed in the epic mythologem as well. We do not know. What we do know, however, is that the Homeric text, as we read it, does not represent *merit* as a salient theme.
42. As will be dealt with in *Chapter VIII*, Orphic discourse depicted mortals as being responsible for their own fate in the cycle of births.
43. The destiny of Heracles as declared by the Delphic Oracle, cf. D.S. 4.26.4; Apollod. 2.4.12, and according to 'the will of Zeus' (Διὸς Βουλή), D.S. 4.9.5.

exception it was represented in a way that only underlined the Olympian and Panhellenic dimension of the epics.

Odysseus would have wished to behold even more of the underworld, but the hosts of the dead uttered an 'ineffable cry'[M] (ἠχῇ θεσπεσίῃ, 633) that scared him off. Thus ended his encounter with the dead.

Conclusively, we must ask ourselves how it related to actual rituals of νεκυομαντεία[44] or even to rituals of shamanism, of which Karl Meuli took it to be a reflection (similar to the Argonautica, 1921, 25; 114 ff.; 1935, 164-71).[45] First of all, the Homeric *Nekuia* is no simple or immediate representation of either such rituals. Even if it were reasonable to speak of Greek shamanism, a point on which I would disagree (cf. Albinus, 1993), it should not pass unnoticed that Odysseus meets the ghosts of the dead with the same kind of naivety exhibited by Achilles in the *Iliad* (cf. above, p.38 f.). Explicitly surprised by the fact that the dead are merely reflections of the lives they once lived, Odysseus does not have the typical vision of a shaman. If, moreover, the *Nekuia* falls short of the notion of 'free soul', to which the notion of 'shamanic journey' is intimately related,[46] then not much remains to link the *Nekuia* with shamanism.

As for the ritual of νεκυομαντεία, the 11th song of the *Odyssey* represents an obvious connection, but in a manner that replaces the background of the cult with the background of the epic narrative. Odysseus is certainly initiated, though not into the cult of the dead, but into the timeless realm of epic memory. The sacrifice of blood that Circe orders him to undertake (thus representing a kind of aetiological myth for the cult) does not supply the dead with a voice from the underworld as much as it suppresses it. In the Homeric *Nekuia* the cult of heroes speaks with a voice that is no longer its own.

b. Deutero-nekuia

Deutero-nekuia, which introduces the 24th song of the *Odyssey* (1-204), speaks of the suitors' departure to Hades and of the subsequent conversations in the realm of the dead. The bodies of the suitors, brought into the courtyard at Odysseus' command, are obviously not going to be buried (*Od*.22.446 ff.). Yet Hermes seems to dispense with the ritual obligations insofar as he himself leads along the

44. The obvious connection, due to the content as well as to the title of the song, is discussed by Merkelbach, 1969, 221-24; Kirk, 1962, 263 f.; Page, 1955, 21-51.
45. See further Schwartz, 1924, 185 ff., and Thornton, 1970, 32 f. It is argued that Odysseus goes through a shamanistic initiation in which he meets the spirits of the beyond, cf. Eliade, 1951, 92.
46. See, for instance, Hultkranz, 1984, 28-34.

'ghosts' (ψυχαί) with his golden wand.[47] They are 'fluttering about with a sibilant noise'[M] (τρίζουσαι ποτέονται, 7)[48] like bats, thus reminding us of the winged creatures surrounding the wand-carrying Hermes on the sepulchral *lekythos* from Attica (cf. Harrison, 1903, 43 ff.; 1912, 205, cf. *plate* 2). The Homeric simile, as well as the thematically related, albeit Classical, iconographic representation, is not necessarily suggestive of any concrete and common imagination. The ghosts are parallelled and visualised by means of something imaginable, but that, however, is quite a different matter. Various Classical renderings of εἴδωλον (iconographic as well as literary) may, on the other hand, implicitly refer to the Homeric εἴδωλον without the opposite being equally true. The epic ghosts of the two *Nekuia*-poems share a profound difference from the type of winged person we find, for example, in the bosom of Persephone of Kamarina (*see plate* 7). This is, however, not very surprising, since the latter is intimately connected with the context of Orphic initiation (see later, p.146).

Deutero-nekuia may be a late-comer in the tradition of the *Odyssey*.[49] Nevertheless, it is well integrated in the overall discourse of Homer. By giving a retrospective account of the return home of the heroes it creates a narrative link between the *Iliad* and the *Odyssey* (even including references to *Nostoi* of the *Epic Cycle*).[50] One of the most remarkable contrasts to the first *Nekuia* is that blood-

47. In Pindar the function of ψυχοπομπός, similar to that of Hermes (*Od*.24.1-2; compare A.*Ch*.1 f.), is attributed to Hades (*O*.9.33). In both cases we hear of a wand, a ῥάβδος, which, as the σκῆπτρον (cf. p.71, n.13), signifies the power to perform certain acts. In this case, Hermes further 'lulls to sleep the eyes of whom he will, while others again he wakens even out of slumber', *Od*.24.3-4. As hinted at in *Od*.24.11, and as we shall account for specifically in the next chapter, a significant Homeric relation between sleep and death may be implicitly important in this respect. Compare also *Od*.10.238 where Circe uses a ῥάβδος in order to turn Odysseus' crew into pigs; see especially de Waele, 1927, 132 ff., Harrison, 1903, 44 ff., for a commentary on this chthonic function of the wand.
48. See especially Heubeck in Russo, 1992, ad loc. *Od*.24.5; 9-10. The same verb, τρίζω, is used of the sound uttered by the departing ghost of Patroclus, *Il*.23.101. Further, *Od*.11.605 and 633 (quoted immediately above) have similar descriptions of the dead, compare also the similes in *Od*.22.384-88 and 468-71 as for the teriomorphic representation, which probably points to the fact that the ghosts of the dead are no longer part of a human community, but rather part of the surrounding *nature* (as opposed to *culture*, if we follow Levi-Strauss' scheme of binary oppositions), or simply, as suggested by the θεσπεσίη (literally: *god-sent*) ἠχή (sound) in *Od*.11.633, the world of the divine.
49. Cf. Aristarchus' omission of *Od*.24.1-204; see Heubeck in Russo, 1992, 356 f., and Petzl, 1969, 44 ff.
50. See especially Schnaufer, 1968, 123 f. To mention a few things: *Od*.24.43-94 concludes the announcement, commenced in the *Iliad*, of Achilles' funeral: *Il*.23.83 f.; Agamemnon's view of Penelope in the *Nekuia* (11.441) is followed up by a final appraisal

drinking is entirely absent. Apart from the obvious reason that the context is not one of ritual contact, the fact that the dead speak freely with one another independent of living interlocutors may nonetheless seem to challenge the characterization of the inhabitants in Hades as being merely *memory images* or 'phantoms of men outworn' (βροτῶν εἴδωλα καμόντων, *Od.*11.476).[51] This invites us to address the matter of *metaphor*,[52] if only for the purpose of excluding it once again from the present context. Since the ψυχαί of the *Iliad*, for instance, are described as εἴδωλα καμόντων, we may wonder that they are, at the same time, 'substantial' enough to prevent Patroclus crossing the River Styx (cf. *Il.*23.72-73). Yet if some of these depictions are to be judged metaphorical, which of them would it be?[53] It is more helpful to our investigation, I think, if we permit ourselves to impose a notion of *otherness* in order to keep the references on a common wavelength. Abandoning categories of 'reality' and 'substantiality' - as referential implications in the notion of *literal meaning* tied to the Aristotelian concept of μεταφορά - and drawing instead upon a notion of similarity and dissimilarity, we will be able to say that the Homeric psyche, like any divine being in the epics, constitutes an invisible agent in the realm of the beyond. Admittedly, the epic gods frequently appear in disguise (in order to be immediately accessible to ordinary sense experience), but when they do not, their epiphany is accompanied by the same extraordinary state of experience as that in which ψυχή takes on the specific meaning of 'memory image'. The point is that this is not as incompatible with ascriptions of autonomous activity as one might believe at first glance. The conversations in *Deutero-nekuia* employ all those elements that would have made up a similar enterprise in life, save that they *do not* take place in life, nor even in any encounter with it. Rather Homer takes *us*, i.e., his listeners and readers, into

in the *Deutero-nekuia* (24.193 ff.), and as Clytemnestra is set in opposition to her as the guilty party in the *Nekuia* so are the suitors in the *Deutero-nekuia*. Moreover, the underworld topography of *Od.*24.11-14 is compatible with *Od.*10.511, 11.539, 573. See also Reinhardt, 1961, 469 ff.; Lord, 1960, 84.

51. Aristarchus' claim is that it is only the unburied who keep possession of their consciousness, but at least the presence of Achilles rather points to the fact, as noticed by Porphyrius, that *all* the dead are at least able to communicate *with each other* without the act of blood-drinking, cf. Petzl, 1969, 62.
52. Without necessarily appropriating the definition (and theoretical introduction) of the term by Aristotle, we may nevertheless take notice of the fact that he regarded it to be a major issue of poetry; see Lloyd, 1996, 205 ff.; cf. Arist.*Po.* 1457b6 ff.
53. Hence Foucault points out that '[t]he analysis of thought is always allegorical in relation to the discourse that it employs', 1969, 40 (cf. Sheridan Smith's translation from 1991, 27).

the underworld, the resonance of which happens to be that of the epic voice as well.[54]

From this point of view, the autonomous mental activity of the dead does not necessarily contradict the perspective of our interpretation as given hitherto, neither of the *Nekuia* nor of the concept of psyche in general. It rather seems that a certain *frame of diction and representation* in Homeric discourse allowed for variations and contributions that were, at the same time, *fenced-in* behind it. What matters in this respect is not so much the possible divisions in the exact textual chronology as the ordering of the result. It is the entire corpus of *Homerica* that defines the extension of Homeric discourse as delivered to *our* interpretation, not the single narratives or motifs that this tradition has managed to incorporate along the way. So as long as our interpretation consistently follows the text before us, not in search of its original layers but rather of its actual coherence, then we may reasonably hope to grasp at least some of the properties that made it a discursive formation of lasting dominance.

Yet the exposition of a consistent framework of eschatology is apt only for the synchronic, and intra-textual, dimension of our analysis. On the diachronic, and inter-textual level, we may expect various elements to have paved the way for, or been appropriated by, other contexts of interpretation. *Deutero-nekuia* is one such element. The very theme of dialogues between the dead can, it seems, be adjusted to suit a theme of immortality that is otherwise absent from the perspective of Homeric afterlife. This should not lead us to forget, however, that the knowledge of the speakers is also the one with which the poet addresses his audience. It is the voice from beyond. Still, independent of mortal perception, as it is insofar as it belongs either to the dead or to the blind, it is nevertheless *dependent* and *representative*, reflecting the narrative course of events, on the one hand, and the voice of the Muses, on the other. Reference to the latter may be conventional, but then again it is at the same time unavoidably tied to the potentials of serious meaning actually inscribed in the discourse. In the light of the negative eschatology that dominates this discourse, the *psuchai* of the *Deutero-nekuia* are

54. We will have to halt, if only for a brief comment, at the conversation between Agamemnon and Amphimedon, *Od.*24.106 ff. Unwittingly, Agamemnon addresses the issue of expected causes of death, much in the same way as did Odysseus in the *Nekuia*. It may be significant, in both cases, that the one part (Amphimedon) talks from 'the position of life' (from which the suitors have just departed), and the other (Agamemnon) from the position of death, save only that the author of *Deutero-nekuia* apparently dispels the significance of ritual allusions attached to this distinction in the *Nekuia*. This, however, may eventually leave the addressee of discourse with the impression that in the end the poetic access to knowledge is both able to encompass as well as to abandon all others.

not to be seen as immortal souls in their own right, but rather as extrapolated transpositions of mortal existence, i.e., transcendent reflections to which the Archaic poet had exclusive and inspired access. This in turn became a stepping-stone for claiming the divine nature of the mind, but that is another story for which we are not yet entirely prepared.

c. *Ēlusion*

In the fourth book of the *Odyssey*, Menelaus refers to the oracle of Proteus which has told him that when the time comes, he is not going to die but will be conveyed by the immortals to the 'Elysian plain at the edge of the world' (Ἠλύσιον πεδίον καὶ πείρατα γαίης, 563), where Rhadamanthys dwells and life is easy for men (i.e., without labour). While it is true that Menelaus is a son-in-law to mighty Zeus, many other heroes are likewise of semi-divine parentage without meriting such translocation. Translocation, which is in effect a kind of immortalization, is thus present, but, at the same time, marginalised in Homeric discourse. We find some parallels in the *Epic Cycle* such as Thetis' translocation of her son, Achilles, to the isle of Leuke, and the apotheosis of Telemachus and Penelope on the isle of Aeaea (cf. Procl.*Chr.*, *Homeri Opera* V (OCT), 106, 14-15; 109, 26).[55] Rohde goes further, citing the example of such heroes as Amphiaraus, Trophonius and Erechtheus whose living activity has been transferred to the underworld by divine intervention (1925, I, 113 ff.; 135 f.). Even though a thematic relation seems obvious, it is perhaps of some importance that Homer does not mention any cult in honour of Menelaus. A few dubious lines of Hesiod, on the other hand, confer 'honours' (τιμή) - that are most probably ritual[56] - on the heroes who are being translocated 'to the isles of the blessed' (ἐν μακάρων νήσοισι, 171). These isles and the Elysian fields arguably refer to one and the same mythologem, namely the location along the shore of Oceanus, at the edges of world, where Rhadamanthys rules.[57] That Hesiod and Pindar refer to distant islands in

55. The Cycle further tells us of Artemis' translocation of Iphigenia to the Tauri, where she is made immortal, Procl.*Chr.*, *Homeri Opera* V (OTC), 104, 18-19, and of the apotheosis of Memnon, 106, 6-7 (see below, p.92); see especially Rohde as for the theme of translocation (Entrückung), 1925, I, 70 ff.
56. Cf. τοῖς τιμὴ[ν ἔ]χει ὡς ἐ[πιεικές], *Op.*173c. On the conjecture of ἐπιεικές, see West, 1966, ad loc. and compare *Il.*23.50. As for the ritual implications in the notion of τιμή, see Nagy, 1983, 197 ff.
57. The scenery and topography of *Od.*4.564 and Hes.*Op.*171 are thus abridged by Pi.*O.*2.71; 74-75, which relates Rhadamanthys to the μακάρων νᾶσοι, cf. further A.R. 4.811; Plin. *HN* 4.58. As the theme of judgment is absent in the *Odyssey*, however, it might be a relatively late (probably Classical) element of the complex. See also Malten, 1913, 37.

a perspective that is emphasized as eschatological makes it highly plausible that Leuke and Aeaea also belong to the same range of ideas. In the *Iliad* such references are entirely absent, and although the *Odyssey* demonstrates awareness of the distant Elysian fields, the location of Erebus at the shore of Oceanus is certainly a more salient theme. Surely, we should not base any conclusion on a few, albeit noteworthy, passages in a text tradition as late as the summary of the Cycle (which has come down to us from Proclus), but at least it must be reasonable to maintain that the range of themes in this tradition is a fair reflection of the original one. We might therefore conclude that heroic immortality is a theme that is deliberately minimized in the Homeric discourse (in this respect, the *Iliad* and the *Odyssey*).[58] It does not immediately follow that the horizon of the Cycle is closer to that of hero-cults, but at least the Cycle does not seem to share the Homeric strategy of repression.

In contrast to his brother Minos, Rhadamanthys does not figure as a judge of the dead in Homer. He does, however, do so in the second *Olympian Ode* of Pindar (*O*.2.75), a fact that makes it highly plausible that a close relation between the two kings, due to their being Cretan brothers, is implicitly significant in the epics as well.[59] Further, we might relate this understated connection to a division between a 'dark' and a 'light' part of the beyond, that is, the difference between Hades, Erebus and Tartarus, on the one hand, and *Ēlusion*, the isles of the blessed and Mount Olympus on the other. First of all, Tartarus constitutes a negative reflection of *Ēlusion* in the 8th Book of the *Iliad*.[60] Homer makes Cronus the king in Tartarus (*Il*.8.479), to which Zeus has condemned him, whereas Hesiod and Pindar makes him the king of *Ēlusion* (Hes.*Op*.173a; Pi.*O*.2.70). The seeming confusion of the role of Cronus might reflect a similar division between Minos, as the judge in the underworld, and Rhadamanthys, as the judge in *Ēlusion*. The division is clearly present in Homer, but the important thing is that it is not explicitly accompanied by a moral distinction as it is in Pindar. Pindar presumably alludes to the 'place of the pious' (τόπος εὐσεβῶν)[61] and the 'place of the impious'

58. See Nagy, 1990b, 21 ff.
59. Bearing in mind the triad of Minos, Rhadamanthys and Aeacus which occurs in the *Gorgias* (Pl. *Grg*.524e; 526c-e), we should perhaps also add Aeacus to the original list of underworld judges.
60. Compare *Il*.8.478-81 to Pi.*O*.2.62 f.; 73 f.; Hes.*Op*.172 f., and *Od*.4.566-68, especially with respect to *Il*.8.481, where there is no joy 'in any breeze', and *Od*.4.567, where 'blasts of the shrill-blowing West Wind [...] give cooling to men'.
61. Undoubtedly reflected in the χῶρος εὐσεβῶν of the pseudo-Platonic *Axiochus*, 371c, which also mentions the presence of Minos and Rhadamanthys as judges (371b) in 'a dwelling beneath the earth where Pluto's palace is not inferior to Zeus' court'. I take it that this points to Orphic or Pythagorean influence in polemic opposition to the discourse of Homer.

(τόπος ἀσεβῶν) which Plato and Diodorus ascribed to the Orphics (Pl.*R*.363c-d; D.S. 1.96.4 ff.). This may be precisely the context that Homer avoided.

Malten finds the word Ἠλύσιον to belong etymologically to *Eleithyia/Eleutho*, the cult of whom is of Cretan origin (1913, 41).[62] The Cretan νθ-root in the name of Rhadamanthys, for instance, testifies to this.[63] Burkert, however, argues for a Mycenaean relation between Ἠλύσιον and ἐνηλύσιον (1960/61, 210 f.). According to the lexicographic authors, ἐνηλύσιον means a place struck by lightning (cf. Hsch.; Suid. ad loc.).[64] Apotheosis as well as translocation is often accompanied, or even brought about, by 'the thunderbolt of Zeus', Διὸς κεραυνός, and basically Burkert takes this to be decisive evidence of the fact that Ἠλύσιον - as a realm of the blessed - is derived from ἐνηλύσιον (op.cit.211 f.).[65] Two things, however, might be held against this claim. Firstly, nothing suggests that Menelaus will ever be translocated by the means of the Διὸς κεραυνός. Not Zeus alone, but 'the immortals' (ἀθάνατοι) as such, will transport him thither (*Od*.4.564). Secondly, Zeus does not use the thunderbolt solely to reward, but also to punish.[66] The Διὸς κεραυνός simply shows the power of the mighty god to remove someone from a certain situation, in some cases by way of translocation to *Ēlusion* or to subterranean caves, in others by way of deportation to Tartarus, the prison-like void of the cosmos.[67] Hence, if some association does exist in the end between Ἠλύσιον and ἐνηλύσιον, the order of influence is probably the reverse, namely the submission of Cretan mythology to the Panhellenic domain of Zeus (albeit primarily in his local manifestation as Kataibates).[68]

62. Likewise Gruppe, *Roscher*, ad loc. 89. Rohde takes the perfect root, ἐληλυθ-, of ἔρχομαι to be etymologically significant in Ἠλύσιον, which he thus translates to mean 'Land der Hintergegangen', 1925, I, 76. As for the change from θι to σι, see Burkert, 1960-61, 210. Likewise, Ἐλευσίς should bear the meaning of 'arrival' according the future tense, ἐλεύσομαι, of ἔρχομαι. If anything, we are dealing with ascriptions of meaning, which are probably not earlier than the etymological speculations of Classical times, cf. Malten, op.cit. Puhvel argues for a lost Ϝ in [Ϝ]ηλύσιον, which he thus takes to be a correlate to the Hittite *wellu*, a *valley* of the dead, 1969, 67 f.
63. See especially Nilsson, 1949, 623; against this suggestion, Burkert, 1960/61, 210.
64. The word for 'place' alternates between χωρίον and πεδίον, and it may worth noticing in this respect that the grave of Semele, who was struck by the lightning of Zeus, is called ἄβατον πέδον in E.*Ba*.10.
65. Thus Burkert takes ἐν in ἐνηλύσιον to be a preposition (i.e. ἐν Ἠλυσίῳ), 1960/61, 212; compare Chantraine, 1968, ad loc. Ἠλύσιον.
66. See, for instance, Rohde, 1925, I, 321.
67. Or the Διὸς κεραυνός may simply be used in order to separate two combatants from each other, as in the case of Apollo and Heracles, cf. Apollod.2.6.2.
68. Cf. A.*Pr*.361; compare *Od*.12.416; Hes. *Th*.854. Places as well as people who have been struck by the divine thunderbolt are generally consecrated to Zeus Kataibates, Cook,

Without losing its local implications, *Ēlusion* allegedly came to adopt the more general meaning of a place that was taboo for everyone[69] except those who were transferred to the ranks of divine beings by means of the Διὸς κεραυνός .

In the Sixth Book of the *Odyssey* (42-45), the Olympian home of the immortals is presented in terms that reminds us of *Ēlusion* in the Fourth (565-68), a parallel which is further strengthened by the mythologem of Heracles in the Eleventh (602-3, cf. *Od*.4.561). But whereas the Thessalian mountain is evoked as a centre of the world, exposed by the Panhellenic character of the pantheon and the supreme power of Zeus, *Ēlusion* is confined to the borders of the world similar to the House of Hades. Thus, the eschatological significance of *Ēlusion* is associated, on the one hand, with Hades through its topography as well as through the brotherhood of the Cretan kings, and, on the other hand, with Olympus through the conspicuous and parallel exceptions of Heracles and Menelaus. Yet the intervention of Zeus is at work in these cases of exception. Not the Cretan judges, let alone Cronus, but mighty Zeus is the final one in command, and while it appears that the distinction between the Olympian sphere and the chthonic sphere equals the distinction between *Ēlusion* and Tartarus, it is also clear that Olympus opposes, at the same time, the distant location of this duality, just as the underworld is underrated, as we have seen, in relation to the realm of the Uranians.

1965, II, 13 ff.; Nilsson, 1955, 72; Chantraine, 1968, ad loc. Ἠλυσίον.

69. Cf. Nilsson, 1955, 72; Nagy, 1983, 207; Compare E.*Ba*.10, see above n. 62.

VI. Sleep and Death

We are such stuff
As dreams are made on and our little life
Is rounded with a sleep
Shakespeare, The Tempest

As we saw in *Chapter III*, Rohde and Arbman drew on Pindar's association between psyche and sleep in order to ascribe a general, albeit not originally articulated, notion of 'soul' to the former. The obvious problem is, however, that whereas Pindar refers to the psyche (or εἴδωλον to be more precise) as the *subject of* the sleeper, ψυχή/εἴδωλον makes an *object for* the sleeper in Homer. If we are not satisfied with the way in which the theory of animism resolves this matter, we have no right to impose an implicit meaning of 'soul' on the epic notion of psyche. Yet, as we shall see in this chapter, it is, however, possible to point to some relations in the semantic framework of Homeric discourse that cleared the way for changing the concept of ψυχή into a new history of meaning. The potential lies in the lands of sleep and death.

In the *Odyssey*, Hermes' power to bring sleep and awakening to the living (24.4) is clearly associated with his power to lead the deceased to the underworld, that is, to 'the meadow of asphodel' (ἀσφοδελὸς λειμῶν, 13), which borders 'the land of dreams' (δῆμος ὀνείρων, 12).[1] Compared with the *Iliad*, in which 'the twins of sleep and death' (ὕπνος καὶ θανάτος διδυμάονε, 16.672)[2] are supposed to carry the corpse of Sarpedon to his homeland, we get the overall impression that the Homeric notions of sleep and death are significantly interrelated in the eschatological sphere.[3] Moreover, the similarity between the dream and the psyche (cf. above, p.48 f.) springs to mind in this respect. The question is in what sense the latter relationship corresponds to the former.

In Homer a person is never said to be *dreaming*, but only to be having a

1. A similar relation might be implicitly present in the εὐρυπυλὲς Ἄιδος δῶ of *Od.*11.571 as compared with the πύλαι ὀνείρων of *Od.*19.562.
2. We hear of this as information which Zeus imparts to Apollo, mirroring the earlier plea of Hera, 16.454; compare also, *Il.*14.231 f.
3. See also Vermeule, 1979, 148; 244, n.4, as for the iconographic representation of the twins of sleep and death which relates the motif to the winds of Boreas and Zephyrus, op.cit.150; 245, n.8, perhaps further implying the mythologem of *Ēlusion*, cf. *Od.*4.567. *See plate 5.*

dream by way of *seeing* one.[4] As a precondition for this act, however, the person must be sleeping, just as the psyche only appears to those who look into the realm of invisibility and darkness, either by sleeping (*Il*.23.62 ff.) or by performing a ritual to the same effect (*Od*.11.23 ff.). In the sleep of Achilles, the psyche of Patroclus even resembles a dream so much[5] that we may be tempted to interpret it as a dream, which I think, however, would be an unwarranted conclusion. Rather the psyche and the *dream* appear on the same level of encounter between different types of actors in the epic universe. The Homeric notion of 'dream' (ὄναρ, ὄνειρος) often refers to a message, or rather a messenger, sent by Zeus (in the *Iliad*) or Athene (in the *Odyssey*).[6] Typically it is disguised as a person who is known to the sleeper, e.g., by approaching Agamemnon in the likeness of Nestor (*Il*.2.20), or Penelope in the likeness of Iphthime (*Od*.4.797). It may relay orders to the sleeper (e.g., *Il*.2.6 f.; *Il*.23.65 ff.), or may just convey the coming events (e.g., *Od*.4.804 f.; 19.536 f.).[7] In other words, it has a narrative function in communicating a divine plan to mortals without revealing itself as such.

The Homeric characters are perfectly aware that a dream can appear in the mere likeness of a person (e.g., *Il*.2.57). Thus, Odysseus asks Anticleia whether her appearance is just an 'image' (εἴδωλον, *Od*.11.213) sent by Persephone 'in the like of a shadow or a dream[M]' (σκιῇ εἴκελον ἢ καὶ ὀνείρῳ, 207). This implies, of course, his sense of being deceived. Nevertheless, he is mistaken insofar as it is Anticleia herself who is present in the image; in fact she is nothing but an image. This makes the psyche a manifestation on the level of the sacred parallel to that of the dream, save only that the dream occasionally differs from psyche in taking on the look of *another*. The question is, however, whether there is more to the point in Odysseus' surprise, namely that the psyche and the dream may further correspond to each other in being manifestations that can only be comprehended

4. Cf. ὄναρ ἰδεῖν, *Il*.2.82; *Od*.19.567; the Homeric expression of ἐν ὀνείρῳ, *Il*.22.199; *Od*.19.541; 581; 21.79, merely points to the frame, or presence, of a dream; as for the objectivity of the Homeric phenomenon of the dream, see further Rose, 1925, 151 ff.; Böhme, 1935, 472; Kessels, 1969, 389 ff.; 1978, 157 ff.; on a general level of 'primitive' religion, see Lévy-Bruhl, 1918, 52-58. See also the Dodd's objection, 1951, 104, to the related scheme of development in the context of Greek religion suggested by Rose, 1925, 151 ff., compare Kessels, 1978, 30 ff., for a more balanced view of the history of attitudes towards the dream until the complicated system of interpretation, as we find, for example, in the writings of Artemidorus, also Meier, 1949, 110 f.
5. Thus the same phraseology is used of ὄνειρος and ψυχή, compare, e.g., *Il*.2.20 with *Il*.23.68 respectively.
6. In *Od*.6.20 it is, as by exception, Athene herself who visits the bed of the sleeper.
7. In this respect also, the dream parallels the psyche, see above, Warden, 1971, 96; and above, p.38.

by the human senses - or by the human imagination - in the shape of human likeness, that is, in their mortal form, while at the same time, a mortal manifestation is exactly what they are not. In this way, Odysseus is correct after all, in believing himself deceived. The *psuchai* and the dreams, and even the gods, are alike in that they appear as something else - being invisible by themselves. Accordingly, they appear either in disguise, or in situations, where normal visibility is excluded. These situations belong to the realm of darkness, in which the night and the soil, the bed and the grave, the land of dreams and the land of death, become intimately associated.

The motif of ὕπνος καὶ θανάτος διδυμάονε ('twins of sleep and death') is therefore suggestive of an indicative divine relationship, a path we might say, not immediately visible to the mortal eye, but a path in the dark which may lead from one position in the realm of *to eschaton* to the other, in effect from ψυχή to θεός, from mortal reflection to immortal being, anticipated in the very moment where the brothers are about to carry a corpse to its destination. Hence, if we follow Pestalozzi's reconstruction of *Memnonis*, we are able to relate directly the apotheosis of Memnon to the brothers of sleep and death who carry him away (probably back to the land of the Ethiopians).

Der Held ist tot, doch sein Tod ist ein Schlaf, die 'Zwillingsbrüder' - modern abstrakt ausgedrückt: die beiden Aspekte seiner jetzigen Zustandes - tragen ihm aus der irdischen Waltstatt in die Ferne - der Dichter wird sagen: ins Morgenland [i.e., to Eos, his Mother], *aus dem er gekommen ist.* (Pestalozzi, 1945, 14)

Apart from Pestalozzi's rhetorical way of putting it, I think he is justified in suggesting that each concept, sleep and death, potentially implies the other,[8] meaning that the inherent capacity of the sleeper to wake up also applies to the dead - in this case Memnon - denoting the kind of immortality that is allegedly associated with the cult of heroes.[9] Resting in his subterranean bed,[10] the hero

8. Cf., for example, the golden race of mankind, of whom Hesiod states that 'when they died, it was as though they were overcome with sleep' (θνῆσκον δ'ὥσθ'ὕπνῳ δεδμημένοι, Hes. *Op.*116).
9. Compare the motif of ὕπνος καὶ θανάτος διδυμάονε in *Il.*16.666 ff., where the divine brothers are supposed to carry Sarpedon to his homeland, and 'there shall his brethren and his kinsfolk give him burial with mound and pillar; for this is the due of the dead' (674-76; cf. 454-57). Skafte Jensen takes this as evidence against any inherent relation between ὕπνος καὶ θανάτος διδυμάονε and apotheosis, 1968, 37, but we have to bear in mind that it is only the Homeric representation of *post mortal* hero-adoration (cf. 674-76) that seems to preclude such a relation. If there is reason to suggest that *Memnonis* and the *Iliad* are closely related, as, e.g., Schadewaldt, 1959, 195 f., and Skafte Jensen, op.cit. 36, agree with Pestalozzi in believing, then it is noticeable that Polygnotus painted Memnon and Sarpedon side by side on his Delphic underworld painting,

was beyond mortality and immortality (or in a way ambiguously, and simultaneously, representing both). It is of no surprise then that the ancient Greek notion of ὄνειρος reveals its most profound connection with the sacred by way of incubation and subsequent divination, embedded, as this ritual process typically was, in the chthonic institutions of hero-cults.

Incubation (i.e., sleeping in a sacred precinct) was widely known in Hellenistic times as part of a healing process, but it is difficult to say exactly how old the tradition was, let alone in exactly what kind of ritual it originated.[11] In Homer the most probable clue to a ritual of incubation is the custom of the Selli of Dodona who were said to rest directly on the earth in order to receive dreams (*Il.*16.234 f.). The reference may suggest, however, that the Homeric singers considered such a custom strange and perhaps alien to the Greeks they knew of themselves.[12] On the other hand, we have already met several instances of sup-

according to Pausanias (10.31.5., see below, p.133 f.) who further speaks of a hero-cult which Memnon enjoyed at his grave in the homeland, 10.31.6. It may also be significant, in the light of this, that the corpse of Sarpedon is being dressed in 'immortalizing clothings' (ἄμβροτα εἵματα, *Il.*16.670, cf. Nagy, 1983, 208.

10. Regarding the actual cult of the dead, it is supposedly of no importance whether the deceased had been buried by inhumation or by cremation. The potent reference for the representation of the power - or even immortality - of the dead was probably not the visible likeness of the corpse, but the ritual manifestation of such a likeness in the *dark*. See n.18 below.
11. The ritual sleep, ἐγκοίμησις, which is mentioned as early as by Lycophron at the turn of the 3th Century BC and later by Diodorus, 1.53, and Strabo, 14.1.44, as well as the χρηματισμός, mentioned by Artemidorus (stressing the oracular aspect), are closely associated with divination by a priesthood in Hellenistic times, but it is doubtful that the ὀνειροπόλοι, of whom we learn in the epics, have a similar function, cf. Kessels, 1978, 26, who points out that the Homeric ὑποκρίνεσθαι does not mean 'to interpret a dream', but rather 'to discriminate between those of the dreams that are passing from the gate of truths and those that are passing from the gate of lies', op.cit. 30 ff., cf. *Od.*19.562-67; thus, in this respect the πολεῖν, implicit in ὀνειροπόλος, means 'to follow a dream back to its origin', ibid. Kessels may be right in suggesting this difference between the Archaic and Hellenistic attitude towards dreams, but it is difficult to see that it should preclude a ritual process in relation to the former, cf. Strabo, 6.3.9, who referred to the incubation-oracle of Calchas, mentioned as οἰωνοπόλος in *Il.*1.69, and cf. Aeschylus, who represents Prometheus as ὀνειροπόλος as well as a hero of healing, *Pr.*476 ff. See further Strabo, 14.1.44, and Meier's account of the Hellenistic institution of healing incubations, in which one of the duties of the priests was to discriminate between false and true dreams of the incubant according to the rule of σύμπτωμα ('correspondence') between the true dreams and their own dreams, 1949, 101.
12. The same can be said of the rather interesting information in Herodotus, namely that the Libyans used to sleep on their ancestors' graves, 4.172; Lycophron, however, refers to a similar practice at Colophon, *Alexandra* 1047 ff. Dodds further points to the fact

pressed cult practice in Homer, most importantly the complex of the hero-cult which was only represented selectively and carefully deprived of any grounds for local identification. That a straightforward representation of a common tradition of incubation is missing from the epics is therefore not in itself proof that there was none.[13]

Greek Tragedy, which apparently did not hesitate to refer to local traditions, not least to cults of the dead, often provides us with testimonies of traditions which are scarcely represented in the discourse of Homer. The tradition of incubation is no exception. We hear of it in the words of Euripides:

> Now when Apollo came and forced Themis, daughter of Earth (Γᾶς), from the holy seat of Pytho, nightly Earth (νύχια Χθὼν) brought forth from her womb shapes of dreams, which told many people of the first things, things to come thereafter, and things to come in the future, insofar as they slept on the dark earth-beds (ὕπνου κατὰ δνοφερὰς γᾶς εὐ|νας).
>
> (E.*IT* 1259-67)[14]

A similar practice is associated with the Classical cult of Amphiaraus, the hero and the seer, of whom Pausanias writes that at Phlius in the Peleponnesus he 'entered into ['the house of Divination' (οἶκος μαντικός)], *slept the night there* (τὴν νύκτα ἐγκατακοιμηθεὶς), and only then, say the Phliasians, began to *divine* (μαντεύεσθαι)' (2.13.7). Before this event Amphiaraus was just an 'ordinary person' (ἰδιώτης), but afterwards he became a *mantis* (ibid.). We hear of him in the *Odyssey* as the one who was loved 'in all manner of love' (παντοίην φιλότητα) by Zeus and Apollo (*Od*.15.246), an emphasis, we might believe, which indicates the possible exception of apotheosis. Nevertheless, Homer speaks simply of his death (252), whereas Pindar referred to a story of Amphia-

that since the Egyptians arguably conducted the tradition of incubation as far back as the 15th BC, the Minoans must inevitably have known of it (1951, 110), which is not to say, however, that they practised it themselves.

13. Compare, e.g., the ritual gesture of *Il*.9.569 f. (where the mother of Meleager beats three times upon the earth in order to summon Hades and Persephone) with Paus.8.15.3, which mentions a similar gesture related to the act of summoning the *hypochthonioi* (during rites of Demeter). The threefold repetition is also due of *Od*.9.65, where Odysseus calls upon the dead before leaving their bodies behind, and of *Od*.11.207, where Odysseus tries in vain thrice to take hold of his elusive dead mother. Compare further, *Il*.23.13-14; 24.14.
14. Although I am indebted to Vellacott's translation, cf. *Text ed.* (p.205), the one given above is prosaic and basically my own, based on the text edition and commentary in Platnauer, 1967, cf. *Text ed.* (p.205). I take the κατά of 1266 to express the condition under which dreamers receive oracles, namely in the institution of incubation as indicated by the δνοφερὰς γᾶς εὐνὰς. The meaning is not substantially changed even if we follow Linder, who suggests χαμεύνας instead of γᾶς εὐνάς, cf. Platnaur, ad loc.

raus being buried alive when 'Zeus clave asunder the broad breast of earth with his all-powerful thunder-bolt' (σχίσσεν κεραυνῷ παμβίᾳ Ζεὺς τὰν βαθύστερνον χθόνα, Pi.*N*.9.24-25). Further, Pindar compares the subsequent status of Amphiaraus to that of Diomedes who was made an immortal god by Athene (*N*.10.7-9).[15] Amphiaraus, who was later known for his skills in healing, also equalled Asclepius who became a god in Epidaurus, having previously been an ordinary mortal, albeit even in life a 'noble healer' (cf. ἀμύμων ἰατήρ, *Il*.4.194). Thus, when Aristophanes tells us of the custom 'to sleep the night inside Asclepius' temple' (νύκτωρ κατέκλινεν [...] εἰς 'Ασκληπιοῦ, *V*.123), he obviously refers to incubation as part of the cure. Likewise, Amphiaraus had a famous sanctuary at Oropus, where he resided as an 'immortal' hero - or perhaps rather a chthonic god[16] - addressing the practice of incubation and divination.

As for other connections to the Homeric discourse, Pausanias relates the Thesprotian νεκυομνατεῖον to the Homeric depiction of the regions of Hades (1.17.5),[17] and Plutarch refers to an 'oracle' (χρηστήριον) of Teiresias in Orchomenos (Plut.*Moralia* 434c). The ambiguity as regards the *post mortal* status of the departed also applies to Teiresias, and is even reflected in this case, as we have seen, in the epics. Thus, Strabo compares Teiresias, Amphiaraus, Trophonius,[18] Orpheus, Musaios and Zalmoxis[19] regarding their mantic abilities (16.2.39).

15. Compare Apollod.3.6.8: 'ἐκρύφθη καὶ Ζεὺς ἀθάνατον αὐτὸν ἐποίησεν' ('he disappeared, and Zeus made him immortal'[M]).
16. It is not clear whether Amphiaraus was regarded as a hero or a god, cf. Rohde, 1925, I, 125. Sophocles says of him that as 'a living soul he reigns' (πάμψυχος ἀνάσσει, *El*.841, cf. 833), and in Suidas we read that in Oropus he was honoured as the local Hades, s.v. πάμψυχος.
17. Cf. Rohde, 1925, I, 57, n.1.
18. Pausanias' famous description of the descent into the cave of Trophonius in Boeotia does not mention incubation as the oracular practice, 9.39.5 ff., which is, however, stated in Photius, ad loc. λύσιοι τελεταί; compare further Plutarch who says of the experience that is was 'of profound darkness' (σκότῳ πολλῷ), and that the ritual participant was not clearly aware 'whether he was awake or dreaming' (εἴτ' ἐγρήγορεν εἴτε ὀνειροπολεῖ, *Moralia* 590b). It is interesting that it seems to be the darkness which denotes the sphere of divine communication, connected with the option of *dreaming*, i.e., supposing an activity on the part of the human participant which is alien to the universe of Homeric discourse.
19. The nature of Zalmoxis is equally unequivocal, as he is both described as a god, Hdt. 4.94, and as a mortal, 4.95 (cf Hartog, 1988, 84-111) among the people of Northern Thrace; according to Herodotus, 4.94, they regarded themselves as οἱ ἀθανατίζοντες ('they who make themselves immortal'), probably connected in some way or another with Pythagoreanism, cf. Str. 7.3.5 f.; 16.2.39; see further, Voigt, Roscher, I.1, 1031 f.; Toepffer, 1889, 31 f.; Linforth, 1918, 23-33. Zalmoxis is often related to what is, problematically in my view, called 'Greek shamanism', cf. Meuli, 1935, 137 ff.; Dodds, 1951,

To conclude, it seems that the act of chthonic communication takes place in a chain of associations between the sleeper's bed, the dream, the dark, the earth, and the grave or residence of the hero. This field of meaning and interpretation may further imply an association between the ritual activity of the incubant and the ritual activity of the 'immortal' hero, creating the ground for a permanent, and extra-ritual, similarity between the mental abilities of mortal man and the hero as being one of the 'living dead'. This is precisely what is avoided, however, in the Homeric discourse, where the resemblance between the living and the dead is, at best, due to the latter resembling the former. The capability of the *mantis* is furthermore dissociated from the truth-telling of the dead in that Calchas, for instance, figures as a living *mantis* who receives his knowledge from Olympian Apollo (*Il.*1.69-72), whereas Strabo relates him to an incubation-oracle (6.3.9).

Hence, Homer significantly associates, but, at the same time, distinguishes between the act of divination (*Il.*1.62 ff.; 5.148 ff.), the act of carrying out a mantic ritual (νέκυια or νεκυομνατεία, *Od.*11) and the act of sleeping (as Achilles does within the general procedure of funeral rites, *albeit not as a specific rite*, (*Il.*23.59 ff.)[20] to the effect that the cult of incubation is suggested but at the same time marginalised. By means of selected representation, the epics appropriate and reject the same object of description in one and the same breath.

Nonetheless, we may finally suggest that the motif of ὕπνος καὶ θάνατος διδυμάονε, even in its Homeric representation, was pregnant with allusions such as between *sleep* as a place for the dream and *death* as a place for the psyche in such a way that the latter became involved with the chthonic complex of the all-nurturing power and mantic knowledge from below.[21] Thus, the notion of psyche undergoes a radical transformation of meaning which becomes explicit in Pindar's fragment 131b:

> [...] while the body of all men (σῶμα πάντων) is subject to over-mastering death, an image of life (αἰῶνος εἴδωλον) remaineth alive (ζωὸν), for it alone cometh from the gods. But it sleepeth, while the limbs are active; yet to them that sleep, in many a dream (ἐν πολλοῖς ὀνείροις) it giveth presage of a decision of things delightful or doleful.

The activity of psyche, as synonymous with εἴδωλον, is internalized in the state of sleep, namely as being the activity *of the dream itself*.[22] Pindar somehow relates

140; 160 f.; Burkert, 1972, 164 f.; but rejected in this respect by Eliade, 1983, 150 f.

20. Compare the dream of Agamemnon, *Il.*2.1 ff.
21. This line of association seems already present in Alcm. 3, *Fr.*1, PMG; and becomes generally evident in Classical and Hellenistic times, as in Theoc.21.66; Hdt.3.65.2; E.*IT* 44-45; Phld.1.22.39; Paus.5.18.1; *Orph.H.* 87.3; see further Lessing, 1769, 286 ff.
22. Similarly X.*Cyr*.8.7.21; Hp.*Vict.* 4.9; Pl.*R*.571d ff.; Arist. *Fr.*10 ap. Dodds, 1951, 157; Procl. *in R.* 122.22 ff.; Plut. *Fr.*178.

this state of knowledge, however, to the kind 'of happy fortune' (ὀλβίᾳ αἴσᾳ) and 'release from toil' (λυσίπονον) that is secured by 'initiation' (τελετάν) in the mysteries (Pi.*Fr.*131a). This leads us, eventually, to the discourse of the Orphics.

Part Two

Orphic Discourse

VII. The Orphic Tradition

I'll make it in my head, I'll draw it out of my memory
I'll gather it around me, I'll make myself a head,
I'll make myself a memory
Samuel Beckett, *The Unnamable*

a. Orphica

It is difficult to say how early a poetic tradition was established in the name of Orpheus. Probably, it reached far back into the 6th Century, if not even into the 7th,[1] but most of the surviving fragments and references stem from informants of Hellenistic or Roman times, and include parts of the tradition which were, at the earliest, born in a Classical context. It is, however, of interest to our present investigation that Homeric as well as Orphic traditions passed through the hands of an Athenian group of four poets, or rather editors, commissioned by Pisistratus in the 6th Century. It is beyond any reasonable doubt that the later division of the *Iliad* and the *Odyssey*, each into 24 books (or rhapsodies), as well as the compilation of 24 rhapsodies of the Orphic *Hieroi Logoi*,[2] somehow had their origin in this Athenian introduction of *Homerica* and *Orphica* as textual traditions.[3] As for the *Orphica*, they contained a *theogony* which seems to have

1. See especially Böhme who believes Orphic tradition to be even older than the Homeric tradition, 1986, 21 ff. When Plato speaks of the ἱεροὶ λόγοι of old (the general title for Orphic poems, cf. Hdt.2.81), concerned with punishment and salvation of the soul (*Ep*.7.335a = *Orph.Fr*.10), one may assume that they originated at least a few generations before his own; compare Pl.*Cra*.402b with Arist.*Metaph*.1.3.6 (=983b).
2. The Alexandrian grammarian, Aristarchus, published the *Iliad* and the *Odyssey* around 156 BC. It may be due to this model that Theognetus who, according to Suda, compiled the Orphic rhapsodies, made a similar numeric division, as he probably did, cf. West, 1983, 248. According to West, he lived and worked in Pergamum in the 1st Century BC, op.cit. 251, but drew on the material of earlier theogonies, op.cit. 246 ff. Not least the Derveni-find (comments on an Orphic poem, probably from the 5th BC) bears traces of resemblance to the Rhapsodic theogony, cf. West, op.cit. 75 ff.; Schibli, 1990, 35.
3. As for Homer, see especially, Merkelbach, 1951, 258 f.; Carpenter, 1956, 12; Skafte Jensen, 1968, 83 ff.; West, 1983, 249; against this view Allen, 1924, 225 ff. As for Orpheus, see especially Lobeck, 1829, 317; Malten, 1909, 427; Jaeger, 1947, 60; 217, n.21; *Orph.Test*.182-196; Böhme further discusses possible relations between the Pisistratean recension of Homer and of Orpheus, 1986; 22 f., cf. 90 ff.; 147.

formed the main stem of tradition, later referred to by the general title of *Hieroi Logoi*,[4] and whose style and content were primarily associated with the authorship of Pherecydes of Syros.[5] But other works as well, e.g., the (distorted) *Oracles* of Musaeus (Hdt.7.6 = *Orph.Test.* 182), *The Initiations*,[6] *The Mixing-Bowl*, *The Robe*, *The Net* and *The Peplos*, have possible links to the Pisistratean group of editors (*Orph.Test.* 223d; West, op.cit. 249 f.). Thus the same group of people contributed, it seems, to the textual fixation of Homeric and of Orphic tradition. This may show that, despite being different arrangements of discourse, they did not seem to entail any necessary correspondence with different or mutually exclusive groups on a social and institutional level. Rather they represented different contemporary, and therefore competing, systems of representing, and organizing, the stock of Archaic traditions.

Later, in the fourth and the third centuries, other texts came to light, namely the so-called *gold tablets*, related to Bacchic mystery cults and therefore probably Orphic (cf. Cole, 1980, 238; Graf, 1993, 250 f.). Explicitly eschatological as they were, dealing with the *post mortem* fate of the individual, they did not form a part of the Archaic theogony-tradition but were, as we shall see, obviously related to it. The same is true of the Orphic *Book of Hymns*, found together with the *Homeric Hymns*, but allegedly of an even earlier date.[7] Thus, the tradition of Orphic literature stretches over a vast period of time. Even so, we shall not put all our effort into discussing dates, *post quem* and *ante quem*, but rather characterize the overall framework of meaning that constituted a living tradition of producing

4. Cf., e.g., Pl.*Ep*.335a; *Orph.Test*.222 (= Clem.Al.*Strom*.II 81, 71); 223d; Kern, 1922, 140 f.; the ἱεροὶ λόγοι-title may also have denoted a more general range of poetry, as Herodotus, for instance, refers to an Orphic ἱρὸς λόγος which, in his opinion, explains the ritual taboo on burial in a garment of wool, 2.81 = *Orph.Test.* 216. See the commentary in Linforth, 1941, 39-49.
5. See especially Schibli, 1990, 35 f., with regard to the similarity between the Orphic *Theogony* and the *Theogony* of Pherecydes, and Suda, who even has Pherecydes responsible for 'bringing together' (cf. συναγαγεῖν) the poems of Orpheus, s.v. Φερέκυδες, ap. West, 1983, 20, with a critical commentary that casts doubts on the reliability of this information.
6. See further *Orph.Test.* 183-196 as for the Orphic authorship of Onomacritus; cf. Malten, 1909, 427; Jaeger, 1947, 60; 217, n.21; West, 1983, 249 f. (250, n.43).
7. Cf. Athanassakis, 1977, 7 ff.; Lesky, 1957/58, 738; Graf, 1992, 161, who argue for the period between the 2nd and the 3rd Century AD. Orphic hymns are also known to Plato, *Lg*.829d, and to Pausanias who refers to a collection of hymns that were used in sacred performances by the *Lycomidae* of Phlya, 9.30.12 (= *Orph.Fr.* 304), that is, in Classical times. There are no positive indications, however, that the surviving book of hymns owes much resemblance to the Classical hymns, of which they may nevertheless 'be a late, and probably faint, reproduction', according to Guthrie, 1935, 203.

texts in the name of Orpheus. This is exactly what ὀρφικά meant in Antiquity and what is meant by *Orphic discourse* in the present investigation.

In 1931, turning from his earlier view on the matter, Wilamowitz warned vehemently about speaking too confidently of Orphism as a specific theology (cf. 1959, II, 191 ff.). It is true that up till then, many unfounded speculations were fostered on this premise, while a growing skepticism, eventually formulated by Wilamowitz himself, resulted in making the very topic of Orphism problematic for many years. Confidence, however, is beginning to return, as new texts have been found (cf. Graf, 1993, 239 ff.; Burkert, 1998, 387 ff.). Still, the type of commitment that followers of Orpheus engaged in remains uncertain.[8] What we know is that Orpheus was believed, by the ancients themselves, to have introduced the 'rituals' (ὄργια) of 'initiation' (τελετή) in Greece and that the aim of this cult practice was esoteric and soteriological in respect of eschatological salvation, associated with the books that flourished in his and Musaeus' name.[9] We also know that this activity was closely related to the doctrines and rituals of the early Pythagoreans.[10] But while it is solidly testified that the Pythagoreans organised themselves into an exclusive community in Croton on Sicily, we have no evidence that the title of *Orphikoi* referred to a similar kind of organization.[11] 'Orphism', therefore, was rather a generalized practice of ritual participation, more or less open to anyone,[12] initiating a certain way of life,[13] arranged and conducted by some loosely organized parties of priests (*orpheotelestai*) in different parts of the Greek world.[14] 'If we must call something Orphism', Linforth writes,

8. Plato refers to 'those around Orpheus' (οἱ ἀμφὶ 'Ορφέα, *Cra*.400c) and Herodotus to the 'Orphics' ('Ορφικοί, 2.81). On the 5th Century bone-plates found at Olbia (at the Black Sea) we also find the inscription ΟΡΦΙΚΟΙ, cf. West, 1983, 18 f.; Graf, 1993, 240, n.5.
9. See, e.g., references to the 'bushel of books' (βίβλων ὅμαδος, Pl.*R*.364e); and the 'many writings' (πολλὰ γράμματα), E.*Hipp*.954, related to rites of purification and initiation. Likewise, the later testimonies of Pausanias, 1.22.7; 4.1.5; 9.27.2; 30.12.
10. Cf. Plut.*Moralia* 585e; Hdt.2.81 (discussed in Linforth, 1941, 39 ff.); Wilamowitz, 1931 (cf. 1959), 191 f.; Guthrie, 1935, 216 ff.; Zuntz, 1971, 321 f.; 227 ff.; Kingsley, 1995, 115; 144 ff.; 163 f.
11. See especially Burkert, 1982, 4 ff.; 12 ff.; 1993, 260.
12. Cf. Thphr.*Char*.16.11 = *Orph.Test*.207; however, only people of some social status are testified to have participated, Graf, 1993, 255 f.
13. Cf. the concept of an 'Orphic way of life' (ὀρφικὸς βίος, Pl.*Lg*.787c), by which Plato addresses the notion of purity related to the custom of vegetarianism, see Münzer, *PW*, 18, 1267, compare E.*Hipp*.952 f.; Porph.*Abst*.4.19.
14. Cf. Linforth, 1941, 49; Burkert, 1993, 260. Comparisons between the gold tablets from Thessaly, Crete and the Southern part of Italy show that they probably belong to the same tradition, cf. Graf, 1993, 250. Besides, the testimonies of, e.g., Diodorus (5.75.4; 77.3-4) and Strabo (10.3.11; 15-16), may be taken as further evidence that Orphic

> it must be the entire religion of teletae and mysteries with their magical ritual, the poems of Orpheus and others in which their sacred myths are told, and the ideas concerning god and man which were inherent in poems and ritual. The ancients did not call this religion Orphism, but they said what is in effect the same thing, in the Greek manner, when they said that Orpheus was the inventor and founder of it. (1941, 173)

This may be a sound definition as long as we pay respect to 'the Greek manner', that is to say, approach the object of investigation from the intrinsic perspective of the texts and ritual acts *actually ascribed to Orpheus and his associates*, and not according to some external idea of *mystery religion* and *soteriology* in general.[15] Some evidence, however, shall be drawn from the complex of Bacchic mysteries, since we know from various sources that the authority of Orpheus was intimately associated with it.[16] Thus, as a matter of exception, the gold tablets, evidently belonging to the context of Bacchic mysteries, shall be viewed as Orphic although they do not exhibit any reference to the name of Orpheus.[17]

b. The author as a mythical figure

Orpheus was a legendary poet like Homer but, contrary to Homer, it was the story of his life and death, more than the authority of Apolline inspiration, that defined the power of his song. Thus, as a potent figure of myth he assumed the character of a type of author that was quite different, eventually, from the blind singer of Chios. But who and what was he, this son of divine Calliope and mortal Oeagrus (*Orph.Test.* 22-26)?[18] Guthrie writes that

> Orpheus was not regarded as a god, but as a hero, in the sense of someone who could claim close kinship with the gods, in virtue of which he had certain superhuman power, but who had to live the ordinary span of life and die like any other mortal. (1935, 41)

initiation was spread all over Greece, where it not only addressed 'ordinary men' (ἰδιῶται), but 'city-states' (πόλεις) as well, cf. Pl.*R*.364e.

15. Cf. Kerényi, 1937, 40; Guthrie, 1935, 10; Wilamowitz, 1959, II, 192 f.; Linforth, 1941, 169-71, and West, who states that 'while ancient authors frequently refer to poems by Orpheus or attributed to Orpheus, they seldom refer to Orphics, except in the sense of authors of Orphic books, and never to 'Orphism', wherefore 'the name of Orpheus is the only unifying factor', 1983, 2 f. See further my discussion on the matter, 1997, 224 f. Unfortunately my critique of Burkert's argument did not take his own revisions of 1993 into account, for which I apologize.
16. See especially Burkert, 1993, 259; Graf, 1993, 240.
17. For one thing, the use of the hexameter in the main parts of the text on the tablets has also been held as evidence for the assumption that it belongs to the tradition of *Orphica*, Graf, op.cit. 243.
18. Some texts point to a tradition of regarding Apollo as the father of Orpheus, cf. Guthrie, 1935, 27; West, 1983, 4; Pi.*P*.4.176.

With these words, Guthrie may, at the same time, be touching upon an essential aspect of 'Orphism', namely that it was framed in a tension between the context of hero cult and the context of epic tradition. As anticipated above, we shall approach the topic of 'Orphism' as the tradition of poems, hymns and rituals that referred to the author - and authority - of Orpheus (and of his successors, Musaeus, Eumolpus and Linus), and we shall rather speak of this under the heading of *Orphic discourse*. The fact that this discourse, contrary to the Homeric one, specifically addressed the complex of ritual initiation, may further lead us to believe that the positions of *addresser* and *addressee* were somehow fused; the figure of Orpheus did not solely play the discursive role of the poet, as did Homer, but also played the exemplary role of the initiate. This was already reflected on the level of myth at which the two positions actually seemed closely related.

Begotten by a Muse, Orpheus was capable of enchanting everyone and everything by his playing on the lyre,[19] and when he went down into Hades in order to bring back his deceased wife to the realm of light and life, he even managed to put a spell on the guardians of the underworld.[20] That he actually failed in his attempt to resurrect Eurydice does not change the status of his mission as being a katabasis, i.e., a theme of heroic ordeal that also gave form to the ritual of initiation; and that he used music as a means of manipulation (or persuasion) may, in this respect, have symbolized the status of poetry as being somehow linked to the process of initiation, if not actually being a cryptical representation of it. We are told, moreover, that not only did Orpheus participate in several types of heroic ordeal during the expedition of *Argonautica*, but he also, and perhaps most prominently, delivered songs about the creation of the world

19. Cf. B.28b; A.*A*.1630; D.S.4.25.2-3; Ov. *Met*.11.1 f.; also Eisler, 1923, 93 ff.; Harrison, 1903, 457; Guthrie, 1935, 28. The musical skills of Orpheus may also have been related to a direct association with Apollo, in respect of which he further resembled other figures of Thracian legend, namely Abaris and Aristeas. Closely related to this type of character, Pythagoras represents another obvious parallel to Orpheus, being likewise referred to, occasionally, as a son of Apollo (Iamb. *VP*, 7.6; compare *n. 18* above). Compare further, Verg.*A*. 3.98, Guthrie, 1935, 47, and Burkert, 1972, 91 f.; 141, as for the thematic relationship between the two associated with 'the Hyperborean Apollo'.
20. The precise date of this motif eludes us. Oldest references are found in E.*Alc*.357-59 (= *Orph.Test*. 59) and Pl.*Smp*. 179d (= *Orph.Test*. 60); D.S. 4.15.4. Cf. also the marble relief (Guthrie, 1935, plate 3 = Richter, 1959, 133, plate 174), the style of which brings us back to the last quarter of the fifth Century, c. 420 BC. The reference given by Isocrates, ὁ μὲν ἐξ "Αιδου τοὺς τεθνεῶτας ἀνῆγεν ('he [Orpheus] led the dead [in plural] back from Hades'), *Bus*. (11) 8, seems to imply that Orpheus had a general ability to restore the dead to life. For the theological interpretation in Pl.*Smp*. 179d, see further Linforth, 1941, 11 ff.

(A.R.1.494 ff. = *Orph. Fr.*29).[21] Thus, it was a feature of his character to act both as a poet and as a hero, a dual aspect that also seems to be reflected, albeit in a different manner, in other poems ascribed to Orpheus and in which he departed for the underworld in order to receive oracular dreams.[22] Regarding this specific issue, however, it remains an open question whether 'receiving a dream' and 'descending into the underworld' were actually two expressions for one and the same event.[23] Somehow the poems must have been instructions for, or reflections of rituals of initiation, and while the exact correspondence between certain acts of myth and certain acts of cult remains enigmatic to us, it was probably obvious to many of the ancients themselves - and only *mysterious* in the sense that there was a taboo on mentioning the subject. In the discourse of Homer, the correspondence between ritual acts and their verbal representations in the narrative was of a different kind. First of all, the content of the epics had no direct bearing on the ritual of their performance and only incidentally alluded to the act of recitation. Secondly, the rituals that did play a salient role in the Homeric universe were explicitly referred to as some common acts of obligation which were basically independent of their epic representation, as, for instance, the ritual of bringing the dead to the House of Hades. At the same time, however, this precise act was also parallelled and even, in some sense, replaced by the epic depiction as such (cf. *Chapter II*). In the discourse of Orpheus, the relationship was rather the reverse in that it was the myth that was acted out and even, in some sense, replaced by ritual.

21. The two enterprises were nevertheless connected insofar as Orpheus was said to have saved the Argonauts by outsinging the Sirens, cf. West, 1983, 4.
22. Cf. the poem *Descent to Hades*, *Orph.Test.* 174; 176; 221-224; and *The Mixing-bowl* (Κρατήρ, *Orph.Fr.*296.21); see also Dieterich, 1913, 147 ff.; Eliade, 1951, 45 f.; 72; West, 1983, 12.
23. Plutarch suggested that while searching for his wife, Orpheus only went as far as to the 'bowl' (κρατήρ), from which dreams drew their mixture of truth and falsehood. Plutarch, who might have had either the *Descent to Hades* or *The Mixing-bowl* in mind, further states that Orpheus referred to his endeavour as a descent to the oracle at Delphi shared by Apollo and Night, Plut. *Moralia* 566b; compare *Orph. Fr.* 103, which speaks of the Oracle of Night. Thus, the 'descent' might itself be another word for 'receiving the oracle', cf. Gruppe, *Roscher*, 3, 1130, cf. also note 5. Let us not forget, however, that we are dealing with a world of myth, in which the katabasis of Orpheus precedes the ritual, as is also the case, for instance, in the katabasis of Odysseus. Given that the theme of katabasis may be viewed somehow as a narrative representation of the overall frame, or some part of the ritual, it does not follow, however, that the two events can be reduced to one another. No one, I gather, would regard Odysseus' journey to the underworld as being merely a metaphor for carrying out a *death-oracle*.

An example of this, which also points to the role of Orpheus as an initiate within the frame of his own discourse, may be the theme of 'tearing asunder' (σπαραγμός) as it appears in the myth, when Orpheus, mourning over his dead wife and wandering about in solitude, meets a band of raging Thracian women who tear him to pieces with their bare hands.[24] The context of this slaying is the Dionysian 'madness' (μανία) which, at the level of myth, always seems to entail dreadful consequences. In turn, the mythologem allegedly reflects a ritual context where the *sparagmos* of wild animals and the ὠμοφαγία ('eating the raw flesh') which followed it were, in some form, part of controlled cult activities. That the god, Dionysus, was thought to be present in the sacrificed victim (a topic to which we shall soon return), reinforces the relationship of the Dionysian context to the Orphic discourse, in which we also find the story of how Dionysus was torn to pieces by the Titans and subsequently served up as food (cf. below, p.112). That Dionysus as well as Orpheus was typically regarded (by the Greeks themselves) as coming from Thrace[25] further indicates that there was a close association between the two, Dionysus being even one of the most prominent gods in the Orphic discourse, and in some respects parallel to the mythical figure of Orpheus himself.[26] However, just as the complex of Dionysian cult and myth in Greece cannot, in point of fact, be reduced to a Thracian origin, which is probably equally true of Orphism, we should not regard Dionysian cults and Orphic discourse as fully interchangeable.[27] Yet the Dionysian theme of

24. Cf. *Orph.Test.* 39; 115; Ov. *Met.* 11.23 ff.; earliest iconographic sources on red-figure vases from early 5th Century, cf. Guthrie, 1935, 64, n.8. The death of Orpheus at the hands of Maenads was also the theme of the lost play *Bassarai*, cf. *Loeb, Aeschylus II*, 386 f. (= A.*Fr.*23-25 N); Harrison, 1903, 460 ff.; Linforth, 1941, 11 ff.
25. Cf. Str.10.3.16; for the Thracian 'origin' of Dionysus, see also *Roscher*, 1033 f.; and for the Thracian 'origin' of Orpheus, see *Orph.Test.* 30-37; Graf, 1974, 17, n.66. With regard to these testimonies it is important, however, not to conflate information of a mythical and of a historical kind.
26. Cf. Procl. *in R.*398. A theme that further connects the two is the attempt to bring a dead person back from Hades. Thus, like Orpheus, Dionysus departs for the underworld in order to make a woman (his mother Semele) immortal, cf. D.S. 4.25.4; Apollod.3.5.3; Paus.2.31.2; 37.5; Plut. *Moralia* 556a.
27. See especially Guthrie, 1935, 42; 46-48. Guthrie follows Gerhard's view that Orpheus was originally a figure in Apolline cult, op.cit. 45, and suggests that only later was he adopted as high priest in Dionysian Religion, op.cit. 48. Be that as it may, the fact that Apollo does certainly not play any salient role in the complex of Orphic mythology, leaves the suggestion rather unimportant with regard to the analysis of Orphic discourse as it presents itself on the surface of statements and ritual acts. On this level Orphism is Bacchic, or Dionysian, regardless of its earlier, genetic roots. See especially Linforth, 1941, 207 ff.; West, 1983, 26 ff.

sparagmos, which seems applicable to the fate of Orpheus, may still be a relevant point of comparison. In the Orphic story of Dionysus, it is the victim's heart that survives dismemberment, while in the story of Orpheus it is the head. The body of Orpheus is not restored as is the body of Dionysus, but his head continues to sing even when severed from his body.[28] Surely, the two themes must be related, and yet they are also significantly different in one respect, namely that Dionysus is a god, while Orpheus is a hero (cf. Guthrie, loc.cit.).

Orpheus was not just any hero, though, but a hero among singers and poets.[29] While being a son of a Muse, his authority, however, was not merely one of inspiration bestowed on him by the Muses, but an authority in its own right insofar as he was even regarded as a rival to Apollo, the master of the Muses.[30] Thus, the surviving head of Orpheus was depicted in the process of dictating an oracle.[31] Even after his death, he was in immediate possession of divine knowledge and continued to show a 'superhuman power' (cf. Guthrie, op.cit. 41). Hence, the issue of 'survival' did not stem from the song or oracle itself, or from the frame of myth as a world of its own, but rather from the singing and revelatory hero, that is, the part of him that resisted death and oblivion. Orpheus did not merely become a ghost in the Homeric sense but one of the living dead, a continuous being that encompassed the life of an epic hero as well as the 'power' (δύναμις) of a hero in the context of the cult of the dead.[32] An added consequence of this appears to have been the framing of a new role of ritual participation in the context of initiation, namely a *mimesis* - one way or another - of the fate of Orpheus, and of Orphic characters such as Dionysus and the Titans. A similar kind of imitation might have appeared irrelevant within the frame of Homeric recitation. The devotees of Homeric discourse belonged to an audience

28. Thus Conon reports that the head of Orpheus 'was still singing, and in no way harmed by the sea, nor had it suffered any of the other dreadful changes which the fates of man bring upon dead bodies. Even after so long a time it was fresh, and blooming with the blood of life', *FGrHist.* 26 Fab.45 (translation taken from Guthrie, 1935, 62).
29. Orpheus was even regarded as a weakling by a scholiast who suggested that he was only included among the Argonauts in Apollonius' story because his singing would allow them to pass the Sirens, *Orph.Test.* 5.
30. Cf. Harrison, 1903, 467; Guthrie, 1935, 35 f.; compare the red-figured *Kylix* of the 5th Century, op.cit. 38, fig.7; also Graf, 1974, 11, n.31 (The writer on the left has been interpreted as Musaeus, cf. ibid.).
31. See Guthrie, 1935, 36-39, fig.6-8. Conon is speaking of the oracles of the singing head (*FGrHist.* 26 Fab.45 = *Orph.Test.* 115).
32. Conon speaks of the locals at Libethra who found the head of Orpheus and '*buried* (θάπτουσι) it under a great *mound* (σῆμα), and fenced off a *precinct* (τέμενος) around it, which at first was a *hero-shrine* (ἡρῷον) but later grew to be a *temple* (ἱερόν)', Conon, Fab.45, ap. *FGrHist.* 26 Fab.45 = *Orph.Test.*115 (translation taken from Guthrie, 1935, 62).

of obedient listeners, whereas the participants in Orphic discourse belonged to a group of active partakers, much in the likeness of Orpheus himself.

As being first of all a figure of myth, Orpheus differs from the other figures of Archaic authorship, but does, nevertheless, belong to a similar frame of discursive authorization. The crucial point is not, in this respect, whether the poet is a construction of myth or not, but that he takes up the position of an author who is no longer present, no longer speaking his own words. As a figure of transcendent authority, Orpheus, as much as any other of the Archaic poets, was represented by a tradition that referred itself to a remote origin. Orpheus, however, was not only held to be an author from time immemorial, but was actually the 'father of song' (Pi.*P*.4.176) and an ancestor of Homer (*Orph.Test.* 7-9; Gorgias B 25 DK, Hippias B 6 DK).[33] Thus, Orpheus and Musaeus were probably the very poets who were said to precede Homer and Hesiod, according to the account of Herodotus (2.53), although, in his own opinion, they were actually of a later date.[34] Surely, Herodotus must have been thinking of historical individuals, and obviously several authors, who may have contributed to the complex of Orphic tradition, come to mind in this respect.[35] Yet, the mythical reference is informative as it stands, if not in respect of historical dating, then as a strategy that characterizes a certain kind of discourse. Referring to Orpheus as the eldest of poets is, at the same time, a way of endowing his name with the highest kind of authority.[36]

Homer was also a figure of myth, represented in the act of carrying out the ritual of recitation (*Hom.Hes.Gen.Ag.* 313; h.Hom.3.172 ff.; compare Paus. 10.7.3). If, however, we recognize behind both these references (i.e., to Homer and Orpheus) a common model which represents the original poet as an active *addresser* of his own discourse, we must remember that Orpheus was not depicted in his role as a bard, but rather in the role of performing initiations. Thus, Pausanias relates a story of Orpheus and Musaeus, in which they refuse to participate in a Delphic song competition preoccupied as they are with their initiations (10.7.2).[37] The representation of Orpheus was fundamentally a double

33. Hippias renders the chain of succession as Orpheus, Musaeus, Hesiod, Homer, *Orph.Test.* 252; that Musaeus was a son of Orpheus is also stated by Diodorus, D.S. 4.25.1. See also Graf, 1974, 17, n.62.
34. Compare *Orph.Test.* 11.
35. Apart from the Thracian Orpheus and Orpheus of Camarina, who both seem to be fictitious persons, Orphic poems were ascribed to Orpheus of Croton, who was a member of the Pisistratean four-man group, see West, 1983, 249 f.
36. See especially Nagy, 1990b, 55, and Bakhtin, 1994, 182.
37. That Classical and Hellenistic references often mention Orpheus together with his son and successor, Musaeus (and also with the Eumolpus, the son of Musaeus), may point

one. On the one hand, he was a figure of myth in the age of heroes, on the other hand he was associated with the frame of legends concerning 'divine men' (θεῖοι ἄνδρες) of a recent past, 'divining healers' (ἰατρομάντεις), such as Epimenides, Aristeas, and Pythagoras (cf. Burkert, 1972, 147 ff.; 1987, 31; Lloyd, 1987, 84).[38] Hence, the rather complex figure of Orpheus appears out of a paradox of myth and history, or rather through two kinds of reference, the border between which was apparently beginning to emerge in Classical times.[39] The strategy of assigning the greatest amount of authority to Orpheus obviously drew on different types of legitimacy, just as the discourse that was successfully established in his name developed in a combination of different discursive orientations. On the one hand, the most famous, and influential, part of the Orphic tradition was composed in the style of the theogony-genre and applying the hexameter; on the other hand, the poems were thought of as parallel to, if not the source of, philosophical theories of the immortality and salvation of the soul.[40] However, ambiguities such as these may only have made Orphic discourse all the more attractive, insofar as it reflected, and probably built upon, the problem of relating the past to the present which was an issue of general concern in Classical times.[41] Surely, the Greeks must have distinguished between Orpheus as a heroic bard, and Orpheus as an author of texts and rituals, just as they must have distinguished between the world of myth and the contemporary world of their own lives. Just as obviously, the two worlds were regarded as two sides of

to the importance of succession in the discursive system, following the rule of imitation of Orpheus, as it is said of Musaeus that he 'copied Orpheus in everything' (τῇ ἐις πάντα μιμήσει τοῦ 'Ορφέως, Paus.10.7.2). Just as the Homeridae claimed the right of representing Homer, the representatives of Orphic discourse probably claimed to be descendants of Orpheus (as did, e.g., the Eumolpidae of Eleusis).

38. Linforth thus holds that there might have been some confusion as to whether there were two persons by the name of Orpheus, 1941, 168; Kern considers Orpheus to have been an entirely mythically constructed character (1920, 16 ff.), whereas Nilsson suggests that the myth might to some extent originate in a historical person (1955, 681 f.). I tend to agree with Kerényi in that 'Orpheus ist und bleibt Mythos, und als Mythos bietet er sich als Idee dar' (1937, 12), insofar, namely, as his function as an author draws on his mythical qualities.
39. As exemplified by Herodotus, 2.53, or by Aristotle who doubts that the *Orphica* was written by a single poet called Orpheus, *Fr.*7; *De An.*410b; Paus.1.14.3.
40. See, for example, Pl.*Ep.*7.335a = *Orph.Fr.* 10. Pl.*Men.*81b.
41. A tradition, reported by Euripides, tells us that Orpheus carved out the Thracian Tablets, later found on Mount Haemus (*Orph.Test.* 82; compare Ps.Pl.*Ax.* 371a; likely to relate to Moses' receiving the Law on Mount Sinai). The mythologem may express a concern of the sort mentioned above, namely an awareness that some part, at least, of the discourse was born as a textual tradition, while, at the same time, it did not fall short of Homer in respect of age and sanctity.

the same coin. So, it may not be from each side of the gap, but rather in some implicit theological interrelation of past and present, myth and history, that we should estimate the importance of the figure of Orpheus. In comparison herewith it may only have been of little interest that Homer was likewise a person betwixt myth and history, since it was neither 'him' nor 'his' discourse that created a thematic link between the past and the present, but only the Muses insofar as they were themselves present, at any moment of invocation, to bear witness to what happened long ago.

Occupying different roles as authors, Homer and Orpheus also identified certain differences of authorization. The criterion for ascribing certain works of poetry to Homer (by defining them as *Homerica*), followed rules of composition as a minimum, whereas the criterion for ascribing certain works to Orpheus (by defining them as *Orphica*, including works ascribed to Musaeus, Eumolpus and Linus in the family line of succession) was due to their use in the context of purifications and initiations. Apart from the thematic discrepancy following from this incompatibility, the main difference in form between Homeric and Orphic discourse was thus the relation between words and acts. Homer recreated the heroic deeds of the past in a representation that was purely verbal, whereas Orpheus represented similar deeds as a person who was, at the same time, the creator of initiations. Hence, Orphic discourse invited its participants to *act* out the past according to a certain frame of myth, whereas the Homeric discourse invited its participants to *listen* to the past according to a certain frame of ritual.

VIII. Continuity of Being

Immortals are mortal, mortals are immortal: each lives the death of the other, and dies their life.
Heraclitus, B 20 DK

a. Death and resurrection

One of the most prominent themes of Orphic eschatology is the dismemberment and recreation of Dionysus. It is also the part of the theogony-tradition that most evidently combines the level of theology with the level of ritual practice. Hence, we have good reason to believe that it may take us to the heart of Orphic discourse.

Briefly, the story is as follows: Dionysus, the offspring of Zeus and Kore, is destined to become the new king of the gods. Hipta, his nurse, carries him in a basket to the cave of Mount Ida, where he is guarded by the dancing Kouretes. Yet the Titans, who whiten their faces with gypsum, lure the child away with toys. They tear him apart in seven pieces which they boil, roast and start to eat. Athena, however, discovers the deed in time to rescue the beating heart, which she takes to Zeus in a basket. In his anger, Zeus blasts the Titans away using his thunderbolt, and Apollo inters the remaining parts of the child in Delphi. Eventually, Zeus resurrects a new Dionysus from the surviving heart, and creates mankind from the residual soot of the lightning.[1]

It is generally held that the myth alludes to a ritual process of initiation. I am not sure, however, that it is helpful to regard this process in the light of shamanism, as West does.[2] Rather, it seems more promising to relate the theme

1. The summary rests on various Orphic fragments, of which the most important ones are quoted by Clement of Alexandria, and the Neoplatonists, Proclus and Olympiodorus, cf. the collection in West, 1983, 74.
2. The 'Titanic' toys are clearly ritual instruments, and the dismemberment may, on the symbolic level, quite safely be regarded as an ordeal in the process of initiation. The immediate context, however, is most likely to be the general one of transition from childhood to adulthood, cf. Jeanmaire, 1951, 390, as, e.g., in the Cabeiric cult, Guthrie, 1935, 123 ff., and the Cretan cult of *megistos kouros*, cf. the *Hymn of Palaikastro* (Harrison, 1912, 1 ff.), rather than some specific shamanistic initiation, as West suggets, 1983, 144 f.; 156 f. For the Orphic influence on, or perhaps even transformation of, the Cabeiric and Cretan initiation cults, see Str.10.3.7; *Orph.H.*38.14; D.S. 5.64.3-4; 5.77.3 (also West, 1983, 132; 166 f.). The correspondence, for example, between archaeological findings

of dismemberment to Dionysian violence, namely the *sparagmos* (as mentioned above, p.108).[3] In several myths, the theme of *sparagmos* appears as a punishment for neglecting the cult of Dionysus, as was the case when the daughters of Minyas and the daughters of Proitus happened to kill their own children in a state of madness,[4] but since the cult itself indulges in similar behaviour, such punishment cannot be the explanation for it. The victims of the ritual killing are not humans but wild animals, and yet, the victims in myth and the victims in ritual seem to unite, symbolically, in the figure of Dionysus as he appears both as a child and as a goat's kid. In order to justify this identification, however, we will have to get behind a veil of esoteric references.

A myth tells us that two nurses of Dionysus, Ino and Athamas, were driven mad by Hera, and as a consequence killed their own sons. Thus, Athamas hunted down Learchus as if he was a deer, and Ino threw Melicertes in a boiling cauldron. Dionysus, however, was saved by Zeus who turned him into a 'kid' (ἔριφος), and he was finally surrendered to the care of the nymphs (Apollod.

and the 'ritual toys' in *Orph.Fr.* 34; 214 makes it probable that the motif of initiation, as it appears in Orphic myth, refers directly to the esoteric context of Orphic soteriology.

3. See especially Kerényi, 1976, 197; lately also Seaford, 1994, 292. It was pointed out, back in antiquity, that Dionysus became a victim of his own violence, Firm. 6.2-5 (p.88 f., cf. *Text ed.* p.205); Photius s.v. νεβρίζειν. Thus the verbs used of the Titanic act in *Orph.Fr.* 34-36 and 210-11 are διασπᾶν and δαισπαράττειν, which are, of course, suggestive of σπαράγμος. The relevance of this has not survived undisputed, though. I shall only mention a few of the reasons why. The structural analysis, delivered by Detienne, 1977, 171 ff., suggests a polemic relationship between the Orphics and the cultural codes of the city-state and points out that the Titanic preparation of the meal rather stands as a counter-motif to the Dionysian *ōmophagia* than as a parallel. While this analysis is interesting for what it is worth, it may, however, not legitimately be used in order to discredit other thematic relations, which are plausible on other premises (see also the criticism in Seaford, 1994, 293 f.). M.L. West, on the other hand, rejects the relevance of *sparagmos* and *ōmophagia* by pointing out that a knife, which, according to some accounts, was used by the Titans to cut up their victim, is not compatible with 'the rite of omophagy', ibid. This is not entirely true, however, insofar as a relief actually shows a maenad about to kill a kid with a knife, cf. Bianchi, 1976, plate 80. It is more likely therefore that the myth of the Titanic deed simply represents *ōmophagia* in a ritualized form , due to the Bacchic cult practice; we shall deal with this further below.
4. Cf. Kerémyi, 1951, 253 f.; references op.cit. 865 f. Agave's killing of her own son, Pentheus, as it is known to us through the *Bacchai*, 38 ff.; 1445-69; 1646, is, of course, a related theme, although Euripides exposes it as a motif of tragic error, since Agave is quite precisely not neglecting her ritual obligations. Kerényi, however, has interpreted Pentheus (*the suffering*) as representing the god himself, that is, Dionysus in the role of suffering the fate of his own violence, 1976, 259. This interpretation suggests that Euripides also alluded to the ritual killing in the mystery cult, see immediately below.

3.4.3; Ael.*VH* 3.42). Most likely, this myth was a circumscription of the ritual sacrifice of goats that was undertaken in Delphi and 'handed over to the women' (cf. αἶξ παραδό : γυνα|<α>ιξί, LSCG, 18 Δ 36-40, cf. *Text ed.* p.205). That the sacrificial meat was consumed as a part of the same ritual further points to the motif of *ōmophagia*, i.e., a cultivated, or rather ritualized, form of it (cf. Henrichs, 1982, 144), as was also the mode in which it appeared in the myth of the Titans (cf. Kerényi, 1976, 197 ff.). Furthermore, according to Plutarch, the priests of Delphi, 'the holy ones' (ὅσιοι), carried out 'a secret sacrifice' (θυσίαν ἀπόρρητον) 'in the shrine (of Apollo) where 'the remains of Dionysus rest' (τὰ τοῦ Διονύσου λείψανα ἀποκεῖσθαι παρὰ τὸ χρηστήριον),[5] and 'the *Thuiades* [i.e., the female devotees of Dionysus] wake the God of the Basket' (ὅταν αἱ Θυιάδες ἐγείρωσι τὸν Λικνίτην, Plut.*Moralia* 365a^{M}).[6] Similar implications may be traced from the late *Orphic hymns* in which the Dionysus child is lulled to sleep in the damp cave of the nymphs who nurse him until he wakes up again (cf. *Orph.H.* 51; 52; 53). In the Orphic myth, the Titans thus play the destructive role of the 'nurses' (τιθῆναι),[7] while the nymphs play the recreational role of bringing him back to life, carrying him in the basket (reflecting also the motif of Athena, see above, p.112). It seems that in this case we actually have an opportunity to trace the esoteric correspondence between myth and ritual insofar as the divine child may obviously be identified with the sacrificial kid,[8] while the nurses and the nymphs may together define the role of the *Thuiades* who attend the ritual.[9] Probably taboo, in this respect, was any mention of the ritual participant's complex role of killing, eating and resurrecting the victim, who was none other than the divine child himself. This is a suggestion for which we actually have some evidence.

5. As for the Delphic grave of Dionysus, see also Philoch.*Fr.*7; cf. Kerényi, 1976, 187 f.
6. The basket (*liknon*) which was used to carry first fruit offerings, as well as various items of mystery ritual, e.g., a phallus, also served, on the level of myth, as a cradle for *Dionysus Liknetes* (cf. Kerényi, 1976, plate 71 = Bianchi, 1976, p.89), i.e., as a token of nursery; compare also, E.*Ion*.222 f. Thus, Hesychius speaks of 'the Basket in which children sleep', cf. Hsch. s.v. Λικνίτης.
7. It is, of course, tempting, however impossible to prove, to regard the phonetic resemblance between Τιτᾶνες and τιθῆναι as significant. Τιθῆναι is, at any rate, the word that is often used of the mythical attendants of Dionysus, cf. *Orph.H.*53.6; *Il.*6.132; S.*OC* 679-680. See further, Kerényi, 1951, 93 f.; 246 f., for the relations between Titans and the role of nurses in Orphic mythology.
8. Thus, 'kid' (ἔριφος) was actually an epithet of Dionysus, cf. Hsch., s.v. Ἔριφος ὁ Διόνυσος; see also Harrison, 1903, 594 f.
9. In Kerényi's interpretation it means that '[s]ie töteten das Unzerstörrbare, den Gott, nur scheinbar: sie bewahrten und erwechten ihn wieder, periodisch, in jeden zweiten Jahr. Das waren ihre grossen Mysterien', 1976, 209.

According to Porphyry's quotation from *The Cretans* (Porph.*Abst*.4.19 = E.*Fr*.472 N),[10] Euripides refers to a Bacchic ritual of initiation at the Idean cave. The ritual takes place in honour of Zagreus, the mystery name of Zeus as well as of Dionysus,[11] and is undoubtedly Orphic.[12] Referring to a ritual of *ōmophagia*, the 'initiate' (μύστης, 10) confesses to 'having accomplished the raw feasts' (cf. τοὺς ὠμοφάγους δαίτας τελέσας, 12) of the god and is then 'sanctified and named as *Bakchos*' (cf. βάκχος ἐκλήθην ὁσιωθείς, 15) by the *Kourētes* (i.e., the priests, see also above, p.112, as for the mythical reference). Finally, as a confirmation of the completed ritual, the new-born *Bakchos*, who is 'dressed in a white garment' (πάλλευκα δ'ἔχων εἵματα, 16), declares that he is able 'to escape mortal birth' (cf. φεύγω γένεσιν βροτῶν, 16-17), by avoiding 'the coffin' (νεκροθήκης, 17), and by abstaining from the habit of 'eating meat filled with life' (τὴν εμψύχων | βρῶσιν ἐδεστῶν, 18-19[M]).[13]

We can quite safely assume that the act of *ōmophagia* in this respect bears strong connotations to the Titanic murder,[14] and that the *mustai*, having engaged in this sinful deed, must purify themselves for each to become a *bakchos* who will never again eat animal food. Hence, the ritual is an initiation into Orphic life according to which no killing is allowed[15] and vegetarianism thus prevails.[16] This rule of abstinence, which is shared by the Pythagoreans, addresses the idea of metempsychosis and the final (i.e., eschatological) release from the cycle of births

10. The translations below of this fragment are mine, although indebted to Guthrie, 1935, 111 f.
11. See especially Harrison, 1903, 479 f., and Guthrie, 1935, 111 ff.; cf. later p.123.
12. Cf. D.S.5.75.4; Harrison, op.cit.; Guthrie, 1935, 111; compare Kerényi, 1976, 349, n.19; Henrichs, 1982, 144.
13. If this confession is, in fact, related to an actual ritual of initiation, and therefore expected to be kept secret (i.e., *aporrheton*), we may wonder why Euripides chose to reveal it. It may be worth mentioning, in this respect, that Diodorus actually states that 'in Crete it has been the custom from ancient times that these initiatory rites should be handed down to all openly, and what is handed down among other peoples as not to be divulged, this the Cretans conceal from no one who may wish to inform himself upon such matters', 5.77.3.
14. Diodorus, for example, states that 'Orpheus has handed down the tradition *in the initiatory rites* that he [the Cretan Dionysus] was torn into pieces by the Titans', 5.75.4 (italics mine).
15. Cf. Aristophanes, according to whom Orpheus introduced rites of initiation and the taboo on killing, *Ra*. 1032.
16. Cf. E.*Hipp*. 953 f.; Pl.*Lg*.782c = *Orph.Test*. 212; Porph.*Abst*. 2.20; 4.19; 3.25 f.; 4.22; *Orph.Test*.111; 112; Graf, 1974, 36, n.71-73; Guthrie, *HGP*, III, 239; that it is difficult to distinguish between the Orphic and the Pythagorean way of life in this respect, see Dieterich, 1913, 84 f.; Graf ,1974, 93 ff.; Kingsley, 1995, 285 ff., and further Iamb. *VP* 240; Arist. *Fr*. 194, with regard to the sacrificial customs.

(as hinted at in 17-18).[17] Yet before turning our attention to this topic, let us dwell, for a moment, on the status of becoming a *bakchos*. As is probably well known, Dionysus is also *bakchos*, so to bestow this title on the initiate simply means to identify him or her with the god himself.[18] The implication may be that the initiate is somehow believed to suffer a fate similar to that of the god, that is, to die in order to be reborn. Actually, 'ritual death' is a typical motif of initiation rituals in which it represents the transition from one state to another (cf. Eliade, 1958, 14; 75 f.). The state which is overcome, in this respect, is explicitly the state of mortal birth and of being 'locked up' in a coffin (cf. E.*Fr*.472, 18 N)[19] - i.e., the mortal and earthly condition of human kind - and it follows that the state attained is instead one of immortality. Perhaps this state can best be described as *the continuity of being (through the process of death and resurrection)*, that is, in Kerényi's words, Dionysus 'als der unzerstörrbaren Leben'. Thinking of the Orphic myth, this 'principle of life' may, moreover, be the part of the soot, from which human beings are born.[20] As the issue, however, of the Titanic transgression, these humans are polluted with a sin[21] that they must apparently repeat ritually, if only in order to reject it once and for all.[22] Heraclitus was

17. See also Porph. *Abst*. 3.25 f.; 4.22; Iamb. *VP* 21.98, and compare with Diogenes Laertius who was accustomed to think that Pythagoras 'forbade even the killing, let alone eating, of animals *which share with us the privilege of having a soul* (κοινὸν ἡμῖν ἔχοντα ψυχῆς)', D.L.8.13, immediately before stating that 'he was the first, they say, to declare that the soul, bound now in this creature, now in that, thus goes on a round ordained of necessity', 8.14.
18. As Cole puts it: 'The worshipper and the god are both described by the activity of the ritual. Bakchos therefore is not a name but an epithet. Because the worshipper is in some sense identified with the god, both god and follower can be called by the same term', 1980, 229.
19. Compare Pl.*Cra*.400c, cf. below, p.126; 137.
20. Cf. Olymp. *In Phd*. 61c, p.2.21; 3.9, Norv. = *Orph.Fr*.220; *Orph.Fr*.107 (p.172, Kern); Olymp. *In Phd*. 68c, p.48.20, Norv. = *Orph. Fr*. 235; Plut. *Moralia* 996c; the theme is clearly associated with Mesopotamian anthropogony, as Burkert has pointed out, 1982, 8. It is further interesting that in the Babylonian Atrahasis-myth, god and man are said to be mixed in *clay* and that a spirit may rise from the god's flesh, Atrahasis I 212-7 (Lambert and Millard), ap. Burkert, op.cit.
21. Cf. Pl.*Lg*.701b; Plut. *Moralia* 996c; Xenocrates, *Fr*. 19-20, Heinze; see further Harrison, 1903, 494 f.; Frankfort, 1946, 248; Kerényi, 1937, 38; 1976, 194 ff.; Guthrie, 1935, 156; however, Linforth, 1941, 359 f., and West, 1983, 164 f., rightly react against what they regard as applying too much theological speculation to this theme.
22. On the ritual 'mechanism' of purification by self-infliction, see especially Douglas, 1966, 170 f., compare *Orph.Derv. Col*.III; *Col*.VI.4-5, with which Emp. B 115 DK should further be compared. See the commentary by Tsantsanoglou, 1997, 112-114. Yet he fails to deal adequately with the seeming parallelism between the daimones, being 'responsible' (αἰτίην [ἔ]χουσι) and 'unjust' (ἄδικοι), cf. *Col*.III, and the human 'souls' (ψυχαί) being

probably reflecting on this when he remarked, somewhat sarcastically, that

> [T]hey purify themselves by staining themselves with other blood as if one were to step into mud in order to wash off mud. (Heraclit. B 5 DK, cf. *Text ed.* p.205)

It is almost certain that he was referring either to Orphics or Pythagoreans and that the blood, from which they sought to purify themselves, was the blood of ritual killing. Moreover, the reference to 'mud' (πηλός) was not incidental. It is likely that Heraclitus even used it consciously as a loaded metaphor for the earthly condition of man[23] in order to make the Orphic act of eschatological release seem all the more ridiculous.

Should Heraclitus, in fact, thus succeed in the eyes of a modern reader, it would be the appropriate time to turn more specifically to the topic of immortality and 'reincarnation' (μετεμψύχωσις) in trying to assess some of the theological, and indeed eschatological, implications behind the ritual process of Orphic initiation.

b. Metempsychosis and Immortality

Turning from the discourse of Homer to the discourse of Orpheus, we move (assuming we can trust the ancient philosophers) from the field of epic myth to the field of epic theology.[24] What they probably meant was that Orphic myth was not merely a 'story' (μῦθος), but also an 'account' (λόγος), of the gods, or more precisely, of the exact nature of the relationship between man and god, between mortality and immortality. Thus, at least, they were inclined to interpret it. Yet, although the proclamation of the immortality of the 'soul' (ψυχή),[25] transmigrating from body to body according to 'a wheel of births',[26] was indeed associated with Orphic discourse, it was, however, generally thought (by Neoplatonists and other Hellenistic writers) to originate with Pythagoras or Pherecydes.[27] True, both of these writers were associated with Orphic writings,

Eumenides (or Erinyes, cf. *Col.*II.4-5) on behalf of whom sacrifices are made (cf. *Col.*VI.7-10). That the daimones are said to be 'enemies to souls' (ψ[υχαῖς ἐχθ]ροί, *Col.*VI.4) - should we trust the reconstruction - is understandable in terms of self-defilement (as a kind of *kakodaimonia*) and subsequent salvation (as a kind of *eudaimonia*), cf. Albinus, 1997b, 2.6.4.; ***2.8.1.***

23. See especially below, p.138 and West, 1983, 183.
24. See especially Arist. *Metaph.* 1017b27; cf. 1091b4; *Fr.* 60; Iamb. *VP*, 145.
25. Cf. *Orph.Fr.*226; 228; Arist. *De An.* 410b28; D.L.8.30.
26. Cf. κύκλος γενέσεως, *Orph.Fr.* 229; γενέσεως τροχός, *Orph.Fr.* 230.
27. As for Pythagoras, cf. D.S. 1.98.2; 5.28.6; 10.6.1 f.; D.L.8.14; 30-36; Porph.*VP* 18-19; 30; as for Pherecydes, cf. Cic.*Tusc.*1.16.38; Suda s.v. Φερεκύδης, being regarded as the teacher of Pythagoras, D.L.1.119. See also Long, 1948, 14; Detienne, 1963, 62 f.; and

and perhaps correctly so,[28] but they were also regarded as theologians and philosophers in their own right. The point may be that the concepts of immortality and metempsychosis were primarily associated with a philosophical doctrine[29] and only deducible from Orphic poetry by way of allegorical interpretation.[30] On the other hand, Orphic discourse apparently exhibited a way of expressing such matters within the frame of traditional storytelling, either because a mythos was devised for the purpose or simply because it originated in a context that was suggestive of similar ideas. Some evidence, in fact, points to the latter, leading us back, once more, to the cult of heroes.

Contrary to the perspective of the Homeric discourse, the hero was, in the complex of chthonic tradition,[31] in some way regarded as one of the 'living dead',

Burkert, 1972, 120 ff. The earliest, and therefore historically the most reliable, testimony of the notion of metempsychosis in relation to Pythagoras is reported by Diogenes Laertius to come from Xenophanes who, mockingly, said that Pythagoras recognized a friend in the presence of a dog (B 7 DK), cf. Lesher, ad loc.; Long, 1948, 16 f.; Kerényi takes this as a confirmation of his suggestion that μετεμψύχωσις did not in the context of early Pythagoreanism constitute a doctrine of the wandering soul, but rather a belief in the survival of *life* itself, 1950, 20-31, thus drawing on the Archaic meaning of ψυχή, as elucidated by Otto, cf. above, p.49. I find it hard to see the precise difference, although the Archaic notion of ψυχή must, of course, be taken into consideration. As suggested in *Chapter III* this notion was, however, closely related to the *name* and the *image* of a person, that is, the 'identity' in some sense, and not merely the *life*. Strangely enough, Kerényi does not deny Pherecydes the honour of introducing metempsychosis as a soul-doctrine, op.cit. 20 f.. As for comparison with Pythagoreanism in the Classical age, see Arist. *De An*.407b 20; Philol. B 10 DK; B 13 DK.

28. See Suda s.v. Φερεκύδες; Burkert, 1972, 129-31; 1977, 7-8; Graf, 1974, 92 ff.; Kingsley, 1995, 115; 144.
29. Formulated by Olympiodorus, with reference to the *Phaedo* dialogue, as 'one psyche that clothes itself in different bodies' (μία ψυχὴ διάφορα σώματα μεταμπίσχεται, *In Phd*. p.54, 25); see also Kerényi, 1950, 24; 31, and Stettner, 1934, 3 ff., who relates it to the concept of 'regeneration' (παλιγγενεσία), ibid.; likewise Harrison, 1903, 526, who, in addition, sees a connection with the complex of hero-cult, 1912, 271.
30. Thus, against Harrison (1903, 526) and others, cf. Burkert, 1972, 126, n.32, for references. Burkert himself agrees that 'Metempsychosis is not attested directly for Orphism in any ancient source', ibid., and that metempsychosis 'does not offer a mythical narrative, a picturesque story which gives the interpretation of a ritual, but a general doctrine which claims to be immediately true', ibid. Further, it is argued by Long (1948, 89-92) and Jaeger (1947, 62) that this doctrine was not invented by the Orphics. Surely, this is a matter of whom we actually understand 'the Orphics' to be, but I agree that the *Orphica* - and this is what matters here - are not likely to have encompassed the notion of metempsychosis in the form of a doctrine.
31. In this respect I refer not only to the ritual complex of local hero cult, but also to the genres of poetry that addressed it, e.g., the *Elegies* by Theognis, cf. 340 f.; cf. Nagy, 1985, 72 f., and the *Oresteia* by Aeschylus, which, however, both refer to the wrath of the dead

who sent forth dreams and cures from below (as we have seen above, p.93 ff.). Persons, who visited a chthonic oracle thus slept in the *abaton* of the temple, or descended into a hallowed cave, in order to receive the message.[32] In both cases, which were, as we have seen, correlative and sometimes even combined, the contact between the participant and the hero (or the chthonic deity)[33] was established by a ritual of separation. Even so, that very contact may have prompted the suggestion of some kind of immediate affinity between *addresser* and *addressee*. Pindar, at any rate, held the 'soul' (ψυχή) to be the divine part of man that was active in sleep and was even capable of delivering oracles itself (cf. *Fr.*131b).[34] Thus, when Pythagoras, according to legend, claimed to have remembered himself from earlier lives, e.g., as being Aithalides, Euphorbus (known from *Il.*17.1 ff.) and Hermotimus,[35] he may have drawn upon a similar context of identification (cf. Max.Tyr.10.1c d).[36] But there is even more to the case. As the hero was, by his presence in the earth, also a person of the past, it seems to have been the property of continuation more than anything else that mattered in the example of Pythagoras. In the context of hero-commemoration, he became a hero himself, not in the sense of being *one* specific person of the past, but by assuming the very *continuity of being* that made him several different persons in life, while only one and the same beyond the changes of this condition. Exactly

being also able to invoke the spirits of revenge.

32. In Lebadeia, the visitor who wished to receive an oracle from Trophonius had to descent into the 'chasm' (χάσμα, Paus.9.39.9) of his cave. As a mantic preparation for this, he sacrificed a ram over a pit (like Odysseus), which is a chthonic gesture especially related to the complex of hero-cult. Cf. Paus.9.39.5-14. See further below, p.129. According to the reference in Plutarch, *Moralia* 590b, the visitor was 'not clearly aware whether he was awake or dreaming'.
33. As mentioned above, p.58; 95, it is difficult to distinguish between the two. The terminological problem may be one of modern concern only, yet not unrelated, of course, to the Homeric emphasis on heroic mortality.
34. See also Cic.*De div.* 130; Phot. *Bibl.* 439; and above, p.96.
35. Cf. D.L.8.4-5; D.S. 10.6.1; Max.Tyr.10.2b, and the comments in Rohde, 1925, II, 417 f.; Long, 1948, 17 f.; Kerényi, 1950, 18 ff.; Burkert, 1972, 137.
36. Cf., e.g., the famous passage in Diogenes Laertius, where it is stated in relation to the teachings of Pythagoras that 'the whole 'air' (ἀήρ) is full of 'souls' (ψυχαί) which are called 'daemons' (δαίμονες) or 'heroes' (ἥρωες); they are those who send 'men' (ἄνθρωποι) 'dreams' (ὀνείροι) and 'signs' (σημεῖα) of future disease and health, and not to 'men' alone, but to sheep also and cattle as well; and it is to them that purifications and lustrations, all divination, omens and the like, have reference', D.L.8.32[M]; compare Pythag. B 40 DK; Olymp. *Comm.In Arist.*382a6, and Porph. *VP* 30. The traditional complex of tradition that is referred to is notably the hero-cult, cf. also Hes.*Op.*121-26.

why and how this process of identification came about remains obscure, but it is almost certain that the Orphics had something to do with it. In the context of the gold tablets, the Orphic initiate was promised immortality (*Orph.*A4.4), i.e., permitted to rule beyond death with the other heroes (*Orph.*B1.11), belonging to the group of *mustai* and *bakchoi* (*Orph.*B10.16). We remember that the participants in the cult of Idean Zagreus likewise received a gift of immortality, namely by becoming *bakchoi* and escaping life's mortal condition. The identification with Dionysus, presumably being the most crucial matter of *aporrhēton* that lurks behind this process, further evokes the heroic figure of Orpheus who, after having suffered the Dionysian fate of dismemberment, continued beyond death to give oracular pronouncements. That he also, while still alive, received dreams himself by way of descending into Hades, adds to the suggestion that incubation, associated with katabasis, was not merely a matter of establishing a ritual contact with some hero (as in the hero-cult), but also of undergoing an ordeal in the process of *becoming* a hero (as in Orphic initiation). Yet the final identification was between the participant and the god.

According to Alexander Polyhistor (D.L.8.3), Pythagoras visited Crete and 'went down into the Idean cave' (κατῆλθεν εἰς τὸ Ἰδαῖον ἄντρον) together with Epimenides.[37] Legends also tell us that the visit included a long sleep (Max.Tyr.10.1; 38.3) and that both Pythagoras and Epimenides were nursed in the cave by nymphs (D.L.1.114-15; Porph.*Antr.*60.6; 61.8), as was the sleeping child Dionsysus (*Orph.H.*51; 52). Here, behind the frame of legend, we get a glimpse of the secret rites, allegedly Orphic,[38] in which the *mustai* went into a symbolic state of death by descending and sleeping, and from which they were subsequently resurrected by being woken and permitted to ascend from the grave, meaning that they were initiated into a new mode of existence.[39] Hence,

37. Epimenides was another legendary sage who identified himself with Aeacus. Aeacus was an underworld judge like Rhadamanthys and Minos and together they formed a mythologem which was probably of a Cretan origin, cf. D.L. 1.114; Pl.*Grg.*525d, see above *Chapter Vc*.
38. The suggestions and arguments in Taylor, 1824, vii ff., and Rohde, 1925, II, 107 f., are not as easily dismissed as it has conventionally been claimed, cf. immediately below.
39. Compare in this respect the sources of D.L.8.41; Procl.*in Ti.*291; Iamb. *VP* 145.20 ff.; and not least D.L.8.14, where it is reported that Pythagoras '*returned to the land of the living* (παραγεγενῆσθαι ἐς ἀνθρώπους) [...] after two hundred and seven years in Hades'; likewise, it is cryptically reported by Demetrius that Epimenides 'became old in as many days as he had slept years [in the cave]', cf. D.L.1.115, and similarly by Plinius, *HN* 7.52.175, who nevertheless held him to have reached the age of 157 years, likewise in D.L. 1.111 (with a slight variation, i.e., 154 years, ascribed to a statement by Xenophanes, cf. B 20 DK).

the affinity between sleep and death, with which we are already familiar from the Homeric representation (cf. above *Chapter VI*), apparently carried the meaning potential of *immortality* in the context of mystery initiation, which, in contrast to the epics, made it an immediate consequence of ritual imitation.[40] Obviously, this is what enabled Pythagoras' 'soul' (ψυχή) to move freely about on earth and in Hades (Pherec.Syr.B 8 DK), similar to its general capacities in sleep.[41] Furthermore, the same ability was associated with the notion of metempsychosis (transmigration of the soul), since both Pythagoras and Epimenides, still according to legend, claimed to have lived several previous lives.[42]

40. We are not, in this respect, dealing merely with a single and final ritual of initiation, but also with a repetitive ritual of establishing a mantic contact with chthonic divinities. Thus Pythagoras made this contact repeatedly through katabasis and incubation, Burkert, 1972, 185 f.; 112 f.; 154 ff ; Kingsley, 1995, 283 f. (compare Paus.9.39.5-14). Deubner even thought that 'the Pythagorean way of life coincides with incubation rituals', 1900, 30. The katabasis of Parmenides may be another testimony to a similar, repetitive context of initiation, which was likewise related to Orphic discourse cf. Cornford, 1912, 214 f.; Tarán ,1965, 27; Burkert, 1969, 11 f.; Kingsley, 1995, 251; Albinus, 1998, 88 ff.
41. Cf. above, p.96, n.22. Legends of Pythagoras further associate him with *bilocation*, which categorizes him together with the Thracian figures of Abaris and Aristeas, as well as with Hermotimus (cf. Plin.*HN* 7.52.174), who was said to be Pythagoras himself in one of his earlier lives (cf. D.L.8.4). Thus, he was seen at the same time in Croton (where he organised his society), and in Metapontum (cf. Ael. *VH* 4.17), where he later died. Meuli takes this legend to be an example of Greek shamanism (1935, 159; cf. also Dodds, 1951, 143), which, in my view, is a typology that is barely helpful. I agree with Vajda that 'Der Schamanismus ist keine einmalige willkürlige Erscheinung, sondern eine Dauereinrichtung; er verfolgt auch keine individuell-privaten Ziele, sondern dient der menschlichen Gemeinschaft', and that 'Keine komponente reicht allein aus, den ganzen Komplex zu determinieren', 1964, 291. If we accept these criteria, Pythagoras can only, but still not convincingly, be associated with shamanism because of the sectarian life of his society in Croton, not because of *bilocation* as such or other so-called shamanistic characteristics that legend happens to apply to just one man. The same, of course, must be said of the figure of Orpheus in relation to 'Orphism', which also, and mistakenly I believe, has been seen as a phenomenon of shamanism (cf. Eliade, 1951, 187; 352; Meuli, 1935, 124; ; Burkert, 1972, 162-65; West, 1983. 5 f.). The fact that there are traits in Pythagoreanism and Orphism that are obviously similar to the complex of shamanism as an institution in certain cultures (such as the Tunguse, from whose language the name has been taken) does not make Orphism and Pythagoreanism examples of this phenomenon, but merely examples of esoteric legitimation of extraordinary capacities related to the ritual process of initiation.
42. Cf. D.S. 10.6.1; Max. Tyr.10.2b; D.L.8.4-5; D.L. 1.114; Procl. *In R.* 614b (113, 24 f., Kroll). The association is explicitly made by Pherecydes of Syros, cf. B 8 DK, in relation to Pythagoras, who is said to have received his divine ability from Hermes, cf. further D.L. 8.42. In Diodorus' account there is even a hint that Hermes is related to the mystery

To reach a closer understanding of this specific motif, we shall once more turn to the context of initiation at the Idean cave. The hymn from Palaikastro (cf. Harrison, 1912, 7-8) addresses a ritual of initiation at the cave of Dikte (op.cit. 5), affiliated to, if not the same as, the cult at the Idean cave (cf. Rohde, 1925, I, 218). Attending the cult are the δαίμονες, who, as followers of Zeus, 'the great youth' (μέγιστος κοῦρος), are to be identified themselves as 'youths' (κουρῆτες, Harrison, op.cit. 12 f.; Burkert, 1985, 127; 398, n.15). Referring to Strabo's comparison of different mystery cults,[43] Harrison claims that these ritual participants went through an initiation from childhood to adulthood, in the process of which they identified themselves with the divine youth in the cave, thus each of them being called by the title of νέος Κοῦρος.[44] Furthermore, one of the cult societies referred to by Strabo is the Cabeiri, and it is therefore significant that, in the remains of their temple at Thebes, archaeologists have discovered a piece of a black-figured vase from around 400 BC that apparently testifies to a similar rite of initiation (cf. Harrison, 1903, 652, fig.175 = Bianchi, 1976, plate 53). A 'child' (ΠΑΙΣ) is shown, offering a libation at an *eschara*,[45] standing in front of an adult male, who is the *Kabiros* (ΚΑΒΙΡΟΣ). According to Harrison (1903, 652 f.) and Guthrie (1935, 124 f.), both figures must be identified as Dionysus, who is thus mysteriously present at two different ages simultaneously. In the Cretan context of Orphic discourse this god is known as Zagreus who represents the son, Dionysus, by way of the father, Idean Zeus, and the father by way of the son. The two are one and the same (cf. op.cit. 111 f.; 116 ff.). Perhaps it is the mystery of this *double* that is denoted by the verse of some unknown poet, quoted by Clement of Alexandria, saying that: 'The bull begets a snake, the snake a bull'

rites of Orpheus, and that Homer was following this relation when he wrote the verses, *Od*.24.1-2. Although Hermes is subsequently, and, of course, interestingly, mentioned as a mediator between the lands of sleep and death, cf. p.90, nothing in the Homeric discourse suggests any context of mystery initiation. Since we cannot use Diodorus as a trustworthy source on the chronology of influence, it is difficult on this account to decide whether the context of initiation is a topic that is being suppressed in Homer or a phenomenon that is simply of a later date. See, in addition, Rohde, 1925, II, 417 f.; Long, 1948, 17 f.; Burkert, 1972, 137, on the topic of metempsychosis.

43. Strabo thus defines the cultic function of *daimones* to be that of, e.g., *bakchoi* and *kourētes*, 10.3.7; 11; compare E.*Fr*.471.14. The discursive frame of identification is undoubtedly Orphic, compare *Orph.H*.38.5-6; 14; D.S.5.64.3-4; Iamb. *VP* 145.20 ff.; see West, 1983, 132; 166 f.
44. Cf. Str.10.3.11 and Harrison, 1912, 20; likewise Guthrie, 1935, 117; cf. also Eliade, who refers to the ancient Greek rites of initiation in the light of the general character of puberty rites, 1958, 109.
45. An *eschara* is the hollow hero-shrine that may have 'functioned' as a channel to the underworld.

(ταῦρος δράκοντος καὶ πατὴρ ταύρου δράκων, *Protr.*2.14). The context is, at any rate, Orphic and refers to the chthonic Zeus who in the form of a snake begets Persephone (*Orph.Fr.*58; 153; cf. West, 1983, 73; 94), with whom he later has 'a child, which has the form of a bull' (παῖδα ταυρόμορφον, *Protr.* 2.14). While this may explain in what sense the bull-god had a snake-god as father, it remains unclear in what sense the bull is also a father of the snake. Although here we are on the shaky ground of guess-work, I believe the answer lies in the context of initiation, in which the participants handled snakes, probably as fertility symbols,[46] after having participated in the ritual feasting on the bull.[47] So maybe the god - killed in the likeness of a bull - reappeared as a snake. This is compatible, at least, with the general class of dracomorph epiphanies that seem to mark the chthonic level of cyclic regeneration as seen in lots of iconographic representations.[48] In any case, the important point is that the snake and the bull might have been two representations of the same, albeit shape-shifting god who was father as well as son, and known by the alternating names of Zeus, Zagreus, Sabazius and Dionysus. Perhaps the Orphic theogony reflected a similar aspect of *doubling*, if we are right in suggesting an underlying identity between Phanes,

46. Cf. Clement of Alexandria who relates the *legomena*, mentioned above, to the Mysteries of Sabazios, and to a serpent, the true nature of which is revealed as 'the god through the bosom' (ὁ διὰ κόλπου θεός), when it is 'being pulled through the bosom of the initiates' (διελκόμενος τοῦ κόλπου τῶν τελουμένων, *Protr.*2.14), compare Plut.*Alex.* 2.6; Arnobius 5.21, and Marc *N.T.*16.18 as to the handling of snakes in a Christian context; see also *LIMC* V[2] 382.22; 384.38-45, as to the handling of the snake by Hygieia, and further *plate 8 + 9* (in this book); Bianchi, 1976, plate 51 + 52, in relation to the Eleusinian Mysteries. The bosom, *kolpos*, must here refer to the 'fold of the dress' that the initiates are wearing, but probably carries, at the same time, undertones of sexual significance. As the ritual snake unavoidably evokes phallic symbolism, perhaps even representing 'phallic impregnation' (as Burkert suggests, 1983, 152), it may also be suggestive of Dionysus as the *phallus* carried in a *liknon*, cf. Bianchi, 1976, plate 85; 88; 92; Kerényi, 1976, plate 135; thus, Guthrie refers to the snake that curls around the sacred *kistē* in mystery cult - correlating in myth with the basket (*liknon*) that is used to carry the child to the cave as well as the heart of Dionysus after the Titanic slaying, 1935, 112. For the snake as connotative of the relation between death and sexuality, see Eitrem, 1909, 31, and Burkert, op.cit. 269; compare further Clem.Al.*Protr.*2.30, cf. Kerényi, 1976, 209; p.246.
47. Cf. above p.115. Porph.*Abst.*4.19; the Delphian ritual of sacrificing [Dionysus as] a kid may actually have become identified with the Cretan ritual of sacrificing [Dionysus as] a bull, insofar as Plutarch is speaking of Dionysiac 'statues in the form of a bull' (ταυρόμορφα ἀγάλματα, *Moralia* 364f.); and this correspondence may be due to, or is at least 'to some extent analogous to the Orphic mythical complex', West, 1983, 154.
48. See especially Harrison, 1903, 18 f.; 325 ff.; 1912, 278 ff.; a general study can be found in Küster, 1913. Compare also the etiological reference to the Bacchic custom of crowning oneself with snakes, E.*Ba.*100-4.

or Protogonos (i.e., *the first born*), and Dionysus (cf. D.S.1.11.3 = *Orph.Fr.* 237)[49], and between this god and Dionysus as 'twice born' (δίγονος), i.e., Dionysus-Zagreus, as well as 'thrice born' (τρίγονος), i.e., the resurrected Dionysus. This is, at least, what Guthrie (1935, 82), and Wili assume (1944, 74 ff.). Hence, the latter locates in this motif the allegorical Orphic representation of a doctrine of metempsychosis. The god changes, yet remains the same (op.cit.79).

Actually, a related motif may be hidden, by way of esoteric abbreviation, in the inscription 'life - death - life' (βίος - θάνατος - βίος), which we find on the bone-plates from Olbia on the coast of the Black Sea (cf. West, 1982, 18 ff.; 1983, 15-20; Graf, 1993, 242 f.; Burkert, 1998, 395 f.), referring directly to the context of ὀρφικοί.[50] The tripartite structure which appears together with the dualities of 'peace - war' (εἰρήνη - πόλεμος) and 'truth - lie' (ἀλήθεια - ψεῦδος) seems to suggest a continuity of life through death that breaks with the cycle of opposites changing into each other. The inscription may thus indicate, and confirm, the initiatory release from the process of metempsychosis that took place in Orphic mystery cults (cf. West, 1982, 18). Again, we are reminded of the Orphic theogony tradition insofar as this presents a succession that is structured by a similar process. Here, the birth of Phanes, or Protogonus, is made possible through the unity of the egg. However, together with the rest of the world, the god is subsequently swallowed by mighty Zeus in whom everything becomes one[51] until restored to external existence once again by being 'brought up from his holy heart' (ἐξ ἱερῆς κραδίης ἀνενέγκατο, *Orph.Fr.*21a.9[52]; Oprh.*Fr.*168; cf. West ,1983, 88 ff.).[53]

49. See especially, Guthrie, 1935, 101 ff.; West, 1983, 206.
50. The rendering of ΟΡΦΙΚΟΙ has become consensual, although, as Burkert has recently pointed out, the last letter is actually 'undeutlich', 1998, 395, n.45, meaning that we are either dealing with ''Orphiker' (oder allenfalls 'Orphisches')', op.cit. 396.
51. *Orph.Fr.*167; compare the fragments of the Derveni papyrus, cf. *Orph.Derv.Col.*XIII (=IX, ZPE 47); *Orph. Derv.Col.*XVI (= XII, ZPE 47)). In West's reconstruction of the 'Derveni' theogony (1983, 114), the 4 crucial lines, 21-24 (from XII, ZPE 47), prefixed with 'a fifth by way of supplement' (op.cit. 88, cf. 114, line 14 = IX, ZPE 47) are translated as follows: '[So Zeus swallowed the body of the god,] | *of the Firstborn king, the reverend one* (Πρωτογόνου βασιλέως αἰδοίου). *And with him* (τωῖ δέ) all | the immortals became one, the blessed gods and goddesses | and rivers and lovely springs and everything else | that then existed: he became the only one' (ibid.). See Laks & Most for a slightly different suggestion, 1997, 16.
52. This specific formulation is from a Stoic version, cf. West, 1983, 89 f.
53. Earlier in the Stoic version we read that Zeus is the head and the middle, and that everything is accomplished from him (cf. 'Ζεὺς κεφαλή, Ζεὺς μέσσα· Διὸς δ'ἐκ πάντα τελεῖται', *Orph.Fr.*21a.2). The same line is found almost identically in Oprh.*Fr.*168.2 equal to *Orph.Derv.Col.*XVII (=XIII, ZPE 47): 'Zeus the head, Zeus the middle, and from

Now Musaeus is reported to have said that 'all things proceed from unity and are resolved again into unity' (ἐξ ἑνὸς τὰ πάντα γίνεσθαι καὶ εἰς ταὐτὸν ἀναλύεσθαι, D.L. 1.3). In the Orphic theogony tradition we hear of no resumed unity. Yet a passage in *The Laws* indicates how this might be implicated. Plato's character, the Athenian, refers to 'that god who, according to an *ancient tale* (παλαιὸς λόγος), *encompasses* (ἔχων) *the beginning* (ἀρχή), *the end* (τελευτή), and *the middle* (μέσα) of all things that exist[M]' (*Lg*.715e).[54] Who would that god be if not Zeus, the supreme god, remaining the unity of his own creation, and thus combining the beginning and the end? In the light of this, a probable interpretation of the sequence of βίος - θάνατος - βίος points to a related, if not identical, structure of development as a matter of Orphic eschatology.[55] From life, the ritual participant went through a state of death by way of which he or she was initiated into a new and final state of life.[56]

The original context of initiation at the Idean, or Dictean, cave in Crete may have been that of puberty rites (cf. above, p.122); yet, as a rite of passage, it seems to have been transformed by the Orphics into a cult of esoteric initiation,[57] which was the form in which Strabo, and others, recognized its occurrence in various places. Thus, e.g., in Crete, Delphi, Thebes and Olbia, local traditions of different origins were being identified as belonging to the same kind of mystery cult (and we might add that by keeping the true content secret, problems of diversities were effectively suppressed and, perhaps, even eliminated in the course of time). In Croton, however, a sect was organized under the exclusive authority of Pythagoras. However, he might still have originally gained this authority

Zeus all things are made' (Ζεὺς κεφα[λὴ Ζεὺς μέσσ]α, Διὸς δ'ἐκ [π]άντα τέτ[υκται]·), for comparison, see West, op.cit. 89; 114, line 27.

54. For comparison, the scholiast quotes: Ζεὺς ἀρχή, Ζεὺς μέσσα, Διὸς δ'ἐκ πάντα τέτυκται, which can be safely identified as Orphic, cf. *Orph.Fr*.168.2 = *Orph.Derv. Col*.XIII (ZPE 47); 21a.2, as commented on immediately above.
55. Compare Aristotle who has Alcmaeon saying that men 'die because they cannot connect the beginning with the end' (ἀπόλλυσθαι, ὅτι οὐ δύνανται τὴν ἀρχὴν τῷ τέλει προσάψαι, Arist. *Pr*.916a35 = Alkmaion B 2 DK, cf. later p.197). Hence the way in which Empedocles, most likely an Orphic initiate, describes the cosmic cycle: 'at one time it grew to be one only from many, at another it divided again to be many from one' (B 17.1-2 DK). And, as we shall see, Empedocles regarded himself in some sense as a god (B 112 DK), cf. below, p.131, n.4; 134.
56. Compare, for example, Plut. *Fr.* 178, *Loeb*, and Graf, 1993, 248, further below, p.141.
57. Thus, Epimenides, who like Pythagoras and Empedocles became a sage after his initiation, was, for example, called 'one of the *Kouretes*' (cf. D.L.1.115), cf above, p.120, n.39; n.40; and see Eliade, 1958, 77 ff.; cf. 68 ff., for other examples of phenomenological resemblance between puberty rites and initiation into secret societies that may be relevant for comparison in this case.

through Orphic initiation, as reported by Iamblichus (*VP* 146), and perhaps more specifically through the context of the Idean cult, by way of which he internalized the *continuity of being* that made him a 'divine man' (ϑεῖος ἀνήρ),[58] or a 'beneficial daemon' (ἀγαϑὸς δαίμων, Arist. *Fr.* 192),[59] as he was also called. The same context may have provided him with decisive inspiration, as well as legitimacy, for proclaiming a doctrine of metempsychosis, that is, the wandering of the soul beyond death and resurrection, if we trust this to be somehow reflected in his actual teachings (cf. n.27 above). The doctrine was eschatological in the sense that the Pythagoreans thought it possible to escape the condition of perpetual rebirth. The ascetic way of Pythagorean life was one method in this respect, and it was exactly the way by which Pythagoreans distinguished themselves from being merely 'Orphics'. It is in the discourse of Orpheus, on the other hand, that we may further pursue the initiatory role of Dionysus which concerned not only a matter of regeneration[60] but a matter of redemption as well. Thus, Dionysus Lysius (*Orph.Fr.*232) had the power to 'redeem' (λύειν) those he wished.[61] The immediate context was that of purification from ancestral sins, but if we are right to suggest that the Titanic deed was but a cryptical representation of exactly this sin (cf. Graf, 1993, 243 f.), the act of expelling it may further imply the real, and overall, goal of initiation (cf. Pl.*R.*364e). As the carnal state of man is actually in Orphic discourse predicated as a punishment,[62] it follows that the final result of purification is a release from this state as being the cycle of births (cf. *Orph.Fr.*229; 230).

Pindar, who was familiar with the religious milieus of Sicily and Italy, including Orphic and Pythagorean cult practice,[63] represents an important source of information in this respect. It is generally agreed that by the 'ancient grief' (παλαῖον πένϑος) of Persephone (being the Orphic mother of Dionysus), he addressed the esoteric myth of the Titanic murder (*Fr.*133, cf. Graf, op.cit. 244). Persephone, however, is inclined to accept the 'atonement' (ποινή) that mortals have suffered on behalf of this deed, and 'their souls she will send forth again into the upper sun in the ninth year' (ἐς τὸν ὕπερϑεν ἅλιον κείνων ἐνάτῳ ἔτει ἀνδιδοῖ ψυχὰς πάλιν).[64] In this act of redemption, Persephone seems to be

58. See especially Detienne, 1963, 87; 133; Vernant, 1965, 142 f.; 387; Burkert, 1972, 147 ff.
59. Compare [Ps.]Pl.*Ax.*371c, cf. below, p.131, n.4.
60. Hence, the Palaikastro hymn and the Orphic hymn address the regeneration of the 'year' (cf. ἐνιαυτὸν, Pal.6, Harrison; cf. ὥρα, *Orph.H.*53.7), which , due to the context of vegetation cult, parallels the condition of man within 'the cycle of births'.
61. Cf. West who relates this act to the doctrine of metempsychosis, 1983, 99.
62. Cf. Pl.*Cra.*400b-c; *Phd.*62b; Xenocrates, *Fr.*20; see further below, p.137.
63. See in this respect, E. Reiner, 1938, 89-91; Bowra, 1964, 89, n.1 Vallet, 1985, 285 ff.
64. Translation taken from Graf, 1993, 244, n.13.

substituted for Dionysus Lysius, which is exactly what is suggested on the *Gold Tablet* from Sicily (A1-3, cf. later, p.142).[65] It even becomes clear that Pindar actually referred to a deliverance from metempsychosis, when we think of a parallel passage in the second Olympian ode, in which it is said that 'whosoever [...] have thrice been courageous in keeping their *souls* (ψυχάν) pure from all *deeds of wrong* (ἀδίκων), pass by the highway of Zeus unto the tower of Cronus, where the ocean-breezes blow around the *Islands of the Blest* (μακάρων νᾶσος)' (*O*.2.68-71). What Pindar means by 'thrice', however, is not entirely obvious until we acknowledge the esoteric role that number 3 actually seems to play in an underlying numerology.

This role is recognizable, we should believe, in the *nine* years that must pass before Persephone delivers the human souls, and the *nine* years in which the gods are banished from Olympus when they swear false at the waters of the Styx (Hes.*Th*.793-804), since according to Orpheus these gods are punished in Tartarus and can therefore probably be identified, in Orphic discourse at least, as the Titans (*Orph.Fr*.295).[66] Moreover, Empedocles, who himself believed he had been born before,[67] puts himself in the position of the daemons who, by the sin of perjury, must pass through a state of mortal incarnations in '3 x 10.000 seasons' (τρίς μυρίας) before being able to return to the society of gods (B 115 DK).[68] Relatedly, Proclus refers to Orpheus as author of the idea that 300 years will pass before the soul is reborn in the realm of the divine (Procl. *in R*. 173 = *Orph.Fr*.231), while Plato makes Socrates say that the soul will be able to fly off to its divine home after 3 x 1000 years of choosing a philosophical life (Pl.*Phdr*.249a).[69] Generally, 3 seems to be the number of times the soul has to

65. That the roles of Persephone and Bacchus are similar, and to some extent, interchangeable, is further suggested by the Pelinna texts, as when the initiate is ordered to 'Tell Persephone that Bakkhios himself *has set you free* (ἔλυσε)', cf. Graf, 1993, 241, from which the translation is taken.
66. On this point, see further below, n.68; p.131, n.4; and p.138.
67. Compare D.L.8.77 with Hdt. 2.123 and Pl.*Phdr*.249a, on the explicit relation to the belief in metempsychosis, and accordingly, the immortality of the soul.
68. Empedocles further equates the crime of perjury (B 115 DK) with the crime of bloodshed (B 136 DK) as incidents of 'Strife' (Νεῖκος), cf. Vernant, 1965, 149, which is noticeable insofar as he seems to have defiled himself with the latter in a ritual similar to the Cretan initiation (cf. above p.115). It seems that the gods, who swear false at the river of Styx, are used as a model for the exiled souls, cf. Vernant, ibid.
69. A similar span of time is mentioned by Herodotus, 2.123. Long sees a profound incongruence between the Plato-Herodotus reference and the Pindar-Empedocles reference, claiming that the former addresses more explicitly the notion of metempsychosis and stems directly from Pythagoras, 1948, 22 f., while the latter are closer to Orphic writings, op.cit. 50. Comparison between Hdt.2.123; Pl.*Phdr*.249a, and D.L.8.77,

make the right choice in order to finally prove its righteousness (Pi.*O*.2.68; Emp. B 115.6 DK; cf. Dieterich,1913, 119).

Although themes and numbers differ in detail in the specific frames of discourse, 3 is still the basic figure throughout, and there should be no reason to doubt that this is due to a common numerology that dealt with the final release from metempsychosis. The precise doctrine may have found its formula in the discourse of the Pythagoreans; the general impact of mythical compatibility, however, may have been due to the Orphics.[70]

An important notion in this composite theology is, of course, the notion of immortality, which, apart from its appearance in philosophical discussion,[71] also seems to be related to the complex of mythical themes. Thus, among the interpreters of Pythagoras' hidden meanings, Numenius, the Neoplatonist, is reported by Porphyrius to have identified the underworld River Styx in Hesiod and in Orpheus as corresponding to the Ameles in Plato and to the 'outflow' (ἐκροή) in Pherecydes; according to Porphyrius, Numenius understood these waters to be a stream of semen that holds the 'soul' (ψυχή) (Porph. *Gaur*.2.2).[72] That the soul is incarnated through the agency of semen is a thought that actually occurs as far back as the *Timaeus* dialogue (Pl.*Ti*.73c; 86c; 91b), while in the *Phaedo*, Socrates speaks of the rivers that flow into and out of the 'chasm' (χάσμα) of Tartarus (*Phd*.112a). After one year in this chasm, the souls that are not deemed incurable of their sins are sent back by the 'outflow' (ἐκροή, 112d) into 'the generation of living beings' (εἰς τὰς τῶν ζῴων γενέσεις, 113a).[73]

Thus, it was not only in the minds of neo-Platonists and Christian writers that running water in the underworld was associated with the ejaculation of

points, I would say, to a common complex of belief in metempsychosis.

70. Cf. Dieterich, 1913, 123, and Schibli, 1990, 122, n.38, who thus predates it to the recension of Onomacritus. West further takes the Orphic fragments to be the oldest in form, 1983, 99 ff., and refers their content to the *Protogonos*- and *Derveni*-theogonies, op.cit.101.
71. As well known from several of the Platonic dialogues, *Phd*.85 c ff.; *Phdr*. 245 c ff.; *R*.608d ff.
72. See especially, Schibli, 1990, 113 f. According to Apponius, a Christian writer, Pherecydes of Syros proclaimed the idea of a double soul, which came from heaven and from the seeds of the earth, Pherecyd.Syr. F86b (Schibli). Apart from connotations of Christian theology, the mythologem is surely not unlike the one we actually find in Plato, *Ti*.69a-c; 90a. In any case, the divine part of the human soul was thought by the ancient philosophers in Pythagorean and Platonic tradition to originate from outside the flesh, and even from outside matter as such. The notion was ascribed to Orphic theology that souls were borne into the body by the wind, *Orph.Fr*.223.
73. The theme of banishment is also suggestive of the gods, who are punished for nine years in Tartarus, as mentioned above, cf. *Orph.Fr*.295.

semen and related to the immortality of souls due to the condition of metempsychosis.[74] Moreover, when the souls are in a state between death and (re)birth, reincarnation is, for Plato, a consequence of drinking from the underworld rivers of Ameles and *Lēthē* (*R*.621a). Although these rivers are not precisely recognizable as a metaphor for semen, it might be worth mentioning, in this respect, that the chthonic springs of *Lēthē* (*Forgetfulness*) and Mnemosyne (*Memory*) had a ritual function of demarcation between 'this' world and 'the other', or between the 'profane' and the 'sacred' (cf. Vernant, 1965, 151 f.). Accordingly, the ritual participant, who went down into the cave of Trophonius' oracle in Lebadeia, had to drink water from both springs in order to forget his mortal thoughts and 'to remember what he has seen after his descent' (μνημονεύει τὰ ὀφθέντα καταβάντι, Paus.9.39.8). Plutarch held that such a visit granted knowledge of metempsychosis (*Moralia* 590a-f; cf. 944d-e) and that the real purpose of the katabasis was for the souls to learn how to avoid the 'chasm' (χάσμα, 590f.).

Schibli suggests that Numenius got it wrong when he interpreted the river of Ameles as the flow of semen (1990, 116). I am not so sure. However, it may be *the running water of the underworld* that is the significant mythologem,[75] and a mythologem for which the flow of semen was but one of the metaphors used to illustrate how the soul was being transported from the world beyond to earthly life in the body. Another metaphor was the drinking of water from the Ameles, by which Plato drew on ritual imagery (cf. later p.143) in order to express the attitude of a soul that would inevitably slip back into the cycle of births. The divine part of the soul, Plato claimed, would be able to escape this cycle only by an 'exercise in death' (μελέτη θανάτου, *Phd*.81a, cf. 67c), that is, by way of philosophical 'recollection' (ἀνάμνησις) (cf. Vernant, 1965, 144). The soul had to *remember* its origin beyond the world of changes and, accordingly, to free itself from the desires of mortal life. Otherwise it would fall victim to the endless flux of time, represented by Ameles, 'whose waters no vessel can contain' (ἀγγεῖον οὐδὲν τὸ ὕδωρ στέγει, Pl.*R*.621a). Hence, by the 'lack of exercise' (in death),

74. Cf. Schibli, who claims that the association may exclusively apply to the concept of 'outflow' as it appears for the first time in Pherecydes, 1990, 114-17. It may be noted in this respect that running water was also, in the Archaic myth, associated with sexuality and birth, as when the sea swept away the genitals of Uranus, until Aphrodite was born from the 'white foam that spread around them' (ἀμφὶ δὲ λευκὸς ἀφρὸς ὤρνυτο, Hes.*Th*.190-91); compare the way in which the motif was, according to Proclus, represented in the Orphic *rhapsody*, namely as a matter of cyclic regeneration, cf. ad *Cra*.406c = *Orph.Fr*.127.

75. Pindar may be alluding to the same mythologem in the phrase, 'streams of darksome night' (νυκτὸς ποταμοι, *Fr*.130), cf. Schibli, 1990, 114, n.23.

which was obviously what Plato took ᾿Αμέλης to mean etymologically, the soul was destined to stay in life's earthly prison (cf. later p.137). Further, in the *Gorgias* dialogue, Socrates refers to some Pythagorean or Orphic, who compared the emotional souls of the uninitiated to leaky jars (*Grg*.493a-b; cf. *Phd*.107c-8c). He takes it to mean that this lower part of the soul is 'unable to *contain* (στέγειν) anything because of its *unbelief* (ἀπιστία) and *forgetfulness* (λήθη)' (*Grg*.493c^{M}). So by drinking immoderately from Ameles and *Lēthē* (Λήθη), as the souls of the dead do in the *Republic* dialogue, they are filled with the dimension of time and with ignorance of the reality beyond it (i.e., of the continuity of being), and Plato seems to imply that this is in effect the same as to be born (again) from the flow of semen. Thus, Proclus recognized Ameles as 'the terrible outflow' (τὴν δεινὴν ἐκροήν, Procl.*in R.122*, cf. Vernant, 1965, 145, n.36). However, while Plato referred to the underworld waters (using metaphorical expositions that were slightly changing from context to context) in order to expose the real philosophical project behind a veil of myth, he nevertheless drew on a potential of meaning that was rooted in actual myth and ritual.[76] It is in this complex of tradition, not in philosophy, that Orphic theology and initiation have their place, and it is within the limits of religious discourse that the underworld water figured as a *ritual* limit between the worlds of life and death. Beyond the water, the purified souls could rest, free from the labours of incarnation, in the land of 'heroes' (Pi.*Fr*.133; *Orph*. B1.11). However, they had to go through a ritual exercise in death in order to get there. It is time to take a closer look at this ritual.

76. Cf. my article on this matter, Albinus, 1998.

IX. The Lake and the Meadow

According to Diodorus of Sicily, Orpheus 'brought from Egypt most of his *secret initiations* (μυστικῶν τελετῶν),[1] *the orgiastic rites* (ὀργιοζόμενα) that accompanied his wanderings, and his *fabulous account* (μυθοποιίαν) of his experience in Hades[M]' (D.S. 1.96.4). Further, Orpheus introduced 'the punishments in Hades of the impious and the meadows of the pious' (τὰς τῶν ἀσεβῶν ἐν ᾅδου τιμωρίας καὶ τοὺς τῶν εὐσεβῶν λειμῶνας, 1.96.5[M]).[2] By addressing a situation in the afterlife, divided by a bad and a good fate, these 'introductions' actually seem to reflect the traditional opposition between Hades and *Ēlusion*, as we know it from Homer and Pindar, among others,[3] but since the notion of 'piety' (εὐσέβεια), related to judgment, suggests a religious attitude that is unknown, at least as a salient concern, in the Homeric epics, the overall framework of interpretation must be different. Yet in the main aspects it seems to fit the motif of 'the righteous councils of Rhadamanthys' (βουλαῖς ἐν ὀρθαῖσι ʽΡαδαμάνθυος) which is, in Pindar (*O.*2.71-75) and later in Plato (*Grg.*523e-524a), related to the *Islands of the Blest*. This is the place, beyond the water, where the souls become 'sainted heroes' (ἥρωες ἁγνοὶ) after a final judgment has been passed on them (Pi.*Fr.*133; cf. *O.*2.68 ff.).[4] Orphic discourse, however, did not seem to emphasize an aspect of *righteousness* in any moral sense, but rather addressed the aspect of *piety* as a

1. Thus, the complex of ritual and myth that relates to Osiris and Isis has obvious parallels to the complex of ritual and myth that relates to Dionysus and Demeter, as Diodorus remarks himself, 1.96.5; 1.22.6-7; see however West, who objects to the modern historical adoption of this view, 1983, 140 f., claiming that the Orphic myth of the dismemberment of Dionysus 'cannot be derived from the Osiris myth', ibid. Likewise Burkert, 1987, 82 f. Compare Kerényi's view on the matter, 1976, 226 ff.; 359, n.23.
2. Compare the λειμῶνας ῞Αιδου in Plut. *Moralia* 943c.
3. Cf. above, *Chapter Vc*, especially n.57. See also Malten, 1913, 46 ff. In Hellenistic times, and perhaps much earlier as well, the eschatological division between Hades and *Ēlusion* was associated with an astral symbolism, cf. Guthrie, 1935, 184 ff.; Schibli, 1990, 117, n.32. Plutarch, for example, identifies Hades with the dark side of the moon, and *Ēlusion* with its face, *Moralia* 944c. Compare Iamb. *VP* 82; Pl.*R.*614c; D.S. 1.96.7; *Od.*24.11-14; Pherecyd. F88, Schibli, 1990, 118, n.32. See later, p.175, n.12.
4. The souls also achieved the status of sages and kings, Pi.*Fr.* 133, which might indicate the potential of meaning that induced Epimenides to identify himself with Aeacus, the underworld judge (cf. above p.125, n.57, and immediately below). This status, however, should probably not be taken in a literal sense, but should rather be seen as a reference to the post-ritual state of initiation, as when Empedocles referred to himself as a god in relation to his fellow men in Acragas, B 112.4 DK; see also Guthrie, 1935, 175; 184.

ritual attitude, that is, as a matter of purification (cf. Pl.*R*.364e). Somehow this implied the mythical scene of the 'meadow' (λειμῶν), which Diodorus, a little later in his account, renders as *'the mythical dwelling of the dead* (τὴν μυθολογουμένην οἴκησιν τῶν μετηλλαχότων)[5] [...] a place near the *lake* (λίμνη) which is called Acherousia' (1.96.7).[6] Such a lake, Acheron or Acherousia, that the deceased had to pass in order to gain entrance in Hades, was also known in the *Odyssey* (10.513) and by the painter Polygnotus who in the 5th Century[7] painted a large picture of the underworld on the wall of the Cnidian meeting room (*Lesche*) in Delphi (Paus.10.25.1; 28.1, see *plate* 6). Pausanias, who is our prime witness to this lost source, found in it several representations of the Homeric *Nekuia* (30.1 ff.), but also of the *Minyad* poem, from which he was convinced that the motif of the ferryman Charon (10.28.2) had been taken, related as it was to the presence of Theseus and Perithoüs (29.9).[8] There are

5. This mythical place, often named as the χῶρος εὐσεβῶν, as in [Ps.]Pl.*Ax*.371c and in various epigrams from the Classical period, did not necessarily contradict the Homeric representation of Hades as the one and all-encompassing realm of the dead, cf. Rohde, 1925, II, 383, n.5; West, 1983, 99. Already in Diodorus' account we get the impression in 96.7 that the Orphics were speaking of only one domain of the dead despite 96.5 (which seems to distinguish between Hades and the meadows), corresponding to the Platonic story of Er, in which all the dead, the righteous as well as the unrighteous, were gathered in a meadow, 614e. Likewise, in the *Gorgias* dialogue where the souls were summoned to the meadow before the court of Aeacus, Minos and Rhadamanthys, who sent the righteous to the *Isles of the Blest* (μακάρων νῆσοι) and the unrighteous to Tartarus, 523e-524a. The difference in relation to the Homeric discourse consists in the motif of a final judgment that divides the future afterlife as a matter of eschatology. It is this eschatology that is absent in Homer.
6. Compare the Pseudo-Platonic dialogue *Axiochus*, 371a-c, in which it is stated by Socrates that 'the river Acheron, and then Cocytus [cf. *Od*.10.513-14], receive those who must be ferried across in order to be brought to Minos and Rhadamanthys [...] interrogating each of those who arrive, concerning what kind of life he has lived and amid what pursuits while he dwelled *in his body* (τῷ σώματι)[...] then, all whom a *good daemon* (ἀγαθὸς δαίμων) inspired in life go to reside in a *place of the pious* (χωρὸς εὐσεβῶν)', 371b-c. The account is said to originate from some bronze tablets from the Hyperboreans, undoubtedly Orphic, cf. Hershbell, n.61 (*Text ed.* p.205); and above, p.110, n.41. Both this reference to the Hyperboreans, and Diodorus' reference to Egypt is a matter of *interpretatio Graecae* that should not be taken too seriously as historical testimonies.
7. *Datum ante quem* 447 according to Wilamowitz, 1884, 223, n.19; about the year 458 according to Robert, 1892, 76.
8. And not from Hesiod's catalogue to which Pausanias also refers the katabasis of Perithoüs and Theseus, 9.31.5. The *nekuia*, on the other hand, only deals with the theme insofar as Odysseus expresses his regrets that he did not manage to encounter these heroes, *Od*.11.631-33 ap.Paus.10.30.10.

reasons to believe that this poem was Orphic.[9] Orphic characters and themes did, in any case, play a prominent role in the painting. Apparently, Polygnotus was not favouring one discursive framework over the other, but simply trying to encompass them in one and the same imagery. This may give us some prompting to believe that Homeric as well as Orphic motifs were actually part of a common cultural horizon as early as in the 5th Century. Thus, Orpheus was sitting with his 'lyre' (κιθάρα) on the right part of the painting,[10] while on the left Odysseus was kneeling at the mound of the sacrificial pit (cf. Robert, 1892, 74, cf. *plate* 6).

Pausanias further reports a depiction of women 'carrying water in broken pitchers' (10.31.9), referred to by an inscription which states that they are 'of the uninitiated' (τῶν οὐ μεμυημένων, 31.10),[11] that is, in Pausanias' eyes, 'those who held of no account the rites at Eleusis' (31.11).[12] It is uncertain whether or not these ΑΜΥΗΤΟΙ ('uninitiated') reflected an Orphic source (cf. Robert, 1892, 80), but our reference to the *Minyad*, namely Charon's crossing over the river of Acheron (Paus.10.28.2), makes it rather likely. Thus, Pausanias recognizes,

9. Pausanias takes Prodicus to be the author of the *Minyad* (4.33.7), and this same author was also associated with the *Descent into Hades* (Clem.Al.*Strom*.1.21 = *Orph.Test*.222), a poem which was traditionally ascribed to Orpheus (cf. *Orph.Fr*.293-96; Kern, 1922, 304-7). Otfried Müller's claim that this poem was even identical with the *Minyad* is further supported by Wilamowitz, 1884, 223. Regarding this matter, Robert suggests that *Od*.11.630-31 might be seen as an interpolation that was meant to account for the difference between the *Nekuia* and the *Minyad*, 1892, 64 f. I doubt, however, whether the ancients would see the point in such a separation. That Polygnotus apparently drew on both the Homeric and the Orphic tradition did not, of course, change anything in respect of the eloquent differences in the framework of their orientation.
10. Pausanias emphasizes the Greek appearance of Orpheus, 10.30.6, which may indicate that various Thracian and other 'foreign' aspects of the mythical figure were assimilated in the Greek representation at the time.
11. Thus Robert takes the inscription to have been ΑΜΥΗΤΟΙ, 1892, 68.
12. This identification is supported by Robert who claims that Polygnotus was himself among the initiated in Eleusis, 1892, 84. The uninitiated were, according to Pausanias, condemned to fill a jar ceaselessly with water from the broken vessels, 10.31.11, compare Pl.*Grg*.493a-b, which relates the motif to the topic of metempsychosis, cf. above p.130. See also the gloss given below p.137, n.29. Another possible context is indicated by Attic black-figure amphoras from the 6th Century which, according to Vermeule, 1979, 59, exhibit *choēphoroi* (libation-bearers) in the act of pouring libations in jars that lead to the underworld; likewise, Felten, 1975, 41. In the Polygnotus painting, however, the filling of the *pithos* takes place *in* the underworld, which definitely makes it a motif of punishment *post mortem*, cf. D.S. 1.96.5. Thus from the 3rd Century, the maidens were explicitly identified as the Danaids who were each condemned to fill a bottomless jar, since they murdered their spouses-to-be, cf. Gruppe, *Roscher*, 84; Harrison, 1903, 613 ff.; Rohde, 1925, I, 327.

among the passengers in Charon's boat, Cleoboea as a maiden 'holding on her knees a chest such as they are wont to make for Demeter' (ἔχει δὲ ἐν τοῖς γόνασι κιβωτὸν ὁποίας ποιεῖσθαι νομίζουσι Δήμητρι, 28.3).[13] It should be reasonably safe to say therefore that the Mysteries of Demeter, or some other cults of initiation, were being represented in the *Minyad* (thus enhancing the probability of its belonging to Orphic discourse). Pausanias does not directly mention any presence of the *initiated*, but such presence may nevertheless be inferred from the presence of listeners to Orpheus' singing,[14] and from other figures around him who apparently enjoy their stay in the underworld.[15] Since the 'place of the pious' (τόπος εὐσεβῶν) and the 'place of the impious' (τόπος ἀσεβῶν) belong to the same mythologem in Orphic eschatology,[16] we should also trust 'those around Orpheus' and the *amuētoi* to be part of the same reference, for which *Minyad* may have been the main, if not the only, source. Perhaps Polygnotus thus, side by side with the negative eschatology of Homer, addressed the Orphic issue of soteriology. Why else should he make a 'maiden' (παρθένος) arrive in Hades with the shrine to Demeter?

Let us now, in any case, take a closer look at what we actually know of this issue. First of all, in the *Republic* dialogue, Adeimantus refers to Orpheus and Musaeus, somewhat disapprovingly, for the ritual practice of '*remissions of sins* (λύσεις) and *purifications for deeds of injustice* (καθαρμοὶ ἀδικημάτων), *by means of sacrifice* (διὰ θυσιῶν) and pleasant sport for the living, while *for the dead*

13. Although Pausanias uses the word κιβωτός ('chest') he obviously associates it with what is often referred to as the sacred κιστή in the Eleusinian Mysteries, see below later p.180. Elsewhere, however, the *kibotos* was explicitly distinguished from the *kistē*, cf. *LS*.
14. Amongst them is Promedon, of whom Pausanias had heard that he was especially fond of listening to the music of Orpheus; another is Pelias, who also figures in the *Minyad* (cf. Robert, 1892, 80), and Schedius who is crowned like Orpheus himself, Paus. 10.30.7-8. The status of wearing a 'crown' (στέφανος) typically signifies a completed initiation, cf. Harrison, 1903, 592 f. (for initiatory crowning by various kinds of στέφανοι, compare Emp. B 112.6 DK; Ar.*Ra*.330; Ath.9.409f; Plut.*Alex*.2.6). Thus, for example, Hippolytos, who is described by Euripides as an Orphic initiate, *Hipp*. 952-54, was called στεφανοφόρος in some renderings of the tragedy.
15. Such as Marsyas who is teaching a youth to play the flute, Paus.10.30.8, and Palamedes and Thersites who are playing dice, 31.1; compare Pi.*Fr*.130, where the blessed in the underworld delight themselves with various activities, e.g., playing draughts and music.
16. See especially Malten, 1913, 46 ff.; some of the references are *Orph.Fr*.222; D.S.1.96.5; Pl.*Grg*.493a-b, cf. *Phd*.107c-8c.

(τελευτήσασιν) they have what *they call initiations* (τελετὰς καλοῦσιν)[17] that *deliver* (ἀπολύουσιν) us from evils in the beyond. But terrible things await those who have neglected to sacrifice^{M}' (364e-365a).

As regards the rites of purification, it was the custom in Orphic initiation to rub oneself with 'mire' (βόρβορς) or 'mud' (πηλός), in order to 'wipe off' (ἀπομάττειν, περιμάττειν) pollution.[18] Thus, one who arrives in Hades 'purified' (κεκαθαρμένος) and 'initiated' (τετελεσμένος) will 'dwell with the gods'(μετὰ θεῶν οἰκήσει), while the one who is 'uninitiated' (ἀμύητος) and 'unsanctified' (ἀτέλεστος) will 'lie in the mire' (ἐν βορβόρῳ κείσεται, Pl.*Phd.*69c).[19] The same happens to other kinds of wrong-doers, according to Aristophanes' comedy *The Frogs* (*Ra.*145-51),[20] whose description, Robert takes to be a reference to the depiction of the punished in Polygnotus' painting.

> Diesseits der λίμνη [lake], also nach der Oberwelt hin, befindet sich der tiefe Schlamm mit dem πατραλοίας [parricide],und dem ἱερόσυλος [one who commits sacrilege], der βόρβορος πολύς [seas of filth] und das σκῶρ ἀείνων [ever-rippling dung] der Frösche.[21] (1892, 83)

Pausanias himself actually sees the ἱερόσυλος of Polygnotus' painting oppose, and thus indirectly reflect, the attitude of the 'pious' (εὐσεβής), which was characteristic of the painter's own time (10.28.6); and, in *The Frogs*, the initiated, who have acted with piety,[22] dance in the 'meadows' (λειμῶνες, 449) in the same underworld as those who are being punished (145-60).[23] In addition, this underworld is demarcated by the 'lake' (λίμνη), both in Pausanias' interpretation of the Delphic painting and in Aristophanes (*Ra.*137; 187), where Xanthias is told to run 'around the lake' (τὴν λίμνην κύκλῳ, 193), since, as a slave, he is not

17. As for the pun made with the words, τελεταί ('initiations') and τελευτήσαντες ('deceased'), see later p.137.
18. Compare references in Rohde, 1925, 2, 406, and the late, but explicit, reference to Orphic ritual pratice, Harp. s.v. ἀπομάττων (48), with the famous example of Aeschines and his mother, reproached by Demosthenes for their participation in mystic initiation, cf. D. 18.259 = *Orph.Test.* 205, identified as rites of Sabazios by Strabo, 10.3.18. Sophocles already seems to be familiar with a similar custom , *Fr.*34, which also reminds us of Heraclitus' ridicule, B 5 DK, as mentioned above, p.117.
19. Plato refers to those who 'long ago' (πάλαι) intimated a hidden meaning in these words and 'established the mysteries' (τελετὰς καταστήσαντες, *Phd.*69c). Undoubtedly, Plato here thinks of the Orphics, cf. Linforth, 1941, 170; H.S.Long, 1948, 25; Graf, 1974, 100, n.30.
20. Likewise D.L.6.39 and Plot.*Enn.*1.6.6; Aristid.*Or.*22.10.
21. Referring to Ar.*Ra.*145-46; 274; Paus. 10.28.6. Robert further draws attention to Pl.*Phd.*69c; *R.*363d; Plut. *Fr.*6,2, cf. op.cit.
22. Cf. ὅσοι μεμυήμεθ' εὐσεβῆ τε διήγομεν τρόπον, 456, referring specifically, in this context, to those who have shown a pious attitude towards strangers, cf. 457; 147.
23. Compare Plut. *Fr.*178.

allowed to participate in the mysteries proper. The 'initiates' (μεμυημένοι, 158), on the other hand, Xanthias will find close beside the road 'just at Pluto's gate' (ἐπὶ ταῖσι τοῦ Πλούτωνος θύραις, 163), i.e., at the House of Hades. A 'breath of flute-playing' (αὐλῶν πνοή) heralds their coming (313),[24] as they are about to tread the dance in the 'meadow' (λειμῶν, 326). Hence, the lake, the meadow, and even the House of Hades, do not, in this context, merely refer to the underworld *post mortem*, but also to its *ritual double*, established *pre mortem* as a part of mystic initiation. Insofar as this ritual actually frames the timeless realm of the beyond, it explains why those who were not initiated were nevertheless, as it is implied, also playing their part in it. That the guilty and polluted were indeed visible in the scenario, is even pointed out in *The Frogs* by the following exchange of words between Xanthias and Dionysus at the brink of the underworld:

Di.: What have you there?
Xa.: Nothing but filth (βόρβορος) and darkness (σκότος)
Di.: But tell me, did you see the parricides
And perjured folk he mentioned?
Xa.: Didn't you?
Di.: Oh, by Poseidon, yes. Why look! (Pointing to the audience)
I see them now. (Ar.*Ra*.273-76)[25]

Thus Dionysus mockingly relates the audience to the wrong-doers of the underworld. That the world of the audience is referred to in terms of the *other* world can further be inferred, for example, from Aristophanes' Euripides-

24. It may be significant in this respect that the art of flute-playing - referred to as 'the dark breath of (Athena) the revered daemon' (σεμνᾶς δαίμονος ἀερόεν πνεῦμα) - 'belongs to Bromius' (συνεριθοτάταν Βρομίωι, Telestes, *Fr*.1, PMG), being the cult-title of Dionysus as well as of his ritual attendants (cf. E.*Ba*.412-13; 446; 1249), since an Orphic hymn invokes the *kouretes*, who are daemons (*Orph.H*.38.14) being 'airy, soul-nourishing and ever-blowing breezes' (πνοιαὶ ἀέναοι, ψυχοτρόφοι, 22). The 'breath of flutes' (πνοὴ αὐλῶν) which is clearly related to the mystic rites of initiation in the *Frogs* (*Ra*.154; 313), may thus be esoterically associated with the immortality of the soul.
25. Compare, as a similar kind of reference, Asius, *Fr*.14 IEG 2, 46 (= Kern, 1922, 84), where it is said that a hero was stepping out of the mire, ap. Graf, 1974, 104. Thus, from the otherworldly meadow of salvation, the initiated looks upon the uninitiated 'here [on earth]' (ἐνταῦθα), as we read in Plutarch, *Fr*.178. The whole and relevant description goes as follows: 'in that place there are voices and dancing and the solemn majesty of sacred music and holy visions. And amidst these, he walks at large in new freedom, now perfect and fully *initiated* (μεμυημένος), *celebrating the sacred rites* (ὀργιάζει), *a garland upon his head* (ἐστεφανωμένος), and *converses with pure and holy men* (σύνεστιν ὁσίοις καὶ καθαροῖς ἀνδράσι); he surveys *the uninitiated , unpurified mob here on earth* (ἀμύητον ἐνταῦθα καὶ ἀκάθαρτον), the mob of living men who, herded together in mirk and *deep mire* (βορβόρῳ πολλῷ), trample one another down and in their fear of death cling to their ills, since they disbelieve in the blessings of the other world.'

quotation (Ar.*Ra*.1477): 'who knows if death be life and life be death?' (τίς οἶδεν εἰ τὸ ζῆν μέν ἐστι κατθανεῖν;);[26] and by the words 'up among the dead' (ἐν τοῖς ἄνω νεκροῖσιν), uttered by the chorus (420).[27] When Plato spoke of initiations of the dead (*R*.365a), he did not, at least not exclusively, refer to funeral rites, but also to some preparatory *ritual double* of what was later to happen 'physically'. The participants, referred to as 'the dead' (τελευτήσαντες), were, as expressed by the pun on τελευτήσαντες and τελεταί, none other than the participants in the ritual 'implementation' (τελετή) of this event.[28] Could it be that the audience (in *The Frogs*) was suggested to imagine itself in a role comparable to the ritual initiation by means of the theatrical staging of the underworld as well as by means of the pointing finger?

Be that as it may. In Orphic theology, it seems to be the case that it was actually the very constitution of living beings that was described by a metaphorical reference to death. According to Plato, for example, 'those around Orpheus' believed earthly life to be a punishment of the soul which was held fast (cf. ἵνα σῴζηται) in the 'body' (σῶμα, *Cra*.400c7-9), until it had paid for its sins, and Xenocrates seems to have equated this imprisonment with the deportation of the Titans to Tartarus (cf. Xenocrates, *Fr*.19; 20; Heinze, 1892,150 ff.), corresponding to the view, repeatedly referred to by Plato, that the 'body' (σῶμα) was a 'grave-monument' (σῆμα) for the soul (*Cra*.400c; *Phd*.62b; *Phdr*.250c; *Grg*.493a).[29] Empedocles, whose poems are clearly related to the framework of Orphic discourse, saw life on the earth as being really an existence in Hades (cf. Burkert, 1972, 134, n.80), and in the *Gorgias* dialogue, Socrates apparently follows Euripides' idea that perhaps life is death and death is life (*Grg*.492e).[30] The configuration of σῶμα and ψυχή as entities of death is transposed, in Orphic theology, to entities of life *as death*. Actually, σῶμα is generally used as a word for 'body' in Classical times (and not only for 'corpse' as in the epics), while ψυχή attains, as we have seen, a meaning compatible with our Christian notion of 'soul' (from being merely a 'memory image' in the epics). In Orphic and Pythagorean discourse, however, it is actually the states of life and death that are inverted, so that life is metaphorically, yet sincerely, described as death, and death as life. Surely, the inversion still draws on the deep-rooted notion of the

26. See Rogers, the *Loeb* edition, *c* ad loc.; and Ar.*Ra*.1082.
27. Sommerstein, however, is not inclined to think so, ad loc., 1996.
28. Compare Plut.*Fr*.178, in which it is stated that 'the verbs *die* (τελευτᾶν) and *be initiated* (τελεῖσθαι), and the actions they denote, have a similarity'.
29. Contrary to what is almost unanimously believed, this 'doctrine' is rather Pythagorean than Orphic and probably originates from Philolaus, Philol. B 14 DK, compare Clem.Al.*Strom*.3.3.16 f.
30. Cf. immediately above; likewise, Heraclit. B 62 DK; see also Dodds, 1951, 152, and Graf, 1974, 41, for further comments on the referential symbolism.

value of life, which is, however, transferred to death as being *the real life*, whereas life, as we know it from our mortal point of view, is merely a death, that is, a pale existence in the dark world of ignorance.[31] While in Platonic discourse, the 'exercise in death' (μελέτη θανάτου, Pl.*Phd*.81a) may, as a philosophical practice, generate the light of real being, it is in Orphic discourse the rites of purification that exempt man from life's imprisonment which is the penalty for ancestral, or Titanic, sin, as it were, namely in the form of deportation to the dark void of Tartarus.

The point of ritual symbolism here seems to be that those who neglect these rites remain in the impure condition of life *as death*. Thus, in the underworld, that is to say in a world *beyond* time, the *uninitiated* on Polygnotus' painting are destined to do repeatedly what they neglected to do *in* time, namely to carry *water* for ablution in the ritual of purification (cf. Harrison, 1903, 614; Graf, 1974, 106 f.; 115; 127), or, as in the Platonic reference, they are buried in mire (cf. *Phd*.69c), failing to have accomplished, as it may be inferred, the Orphic rites of ἀπομάττειν.

According to the Hieronymian tradition of Orpheus' *theogony*, there was, in the beginning of everything, water and then 'mud' (ἰλύς, *Orph.Fr*.57), or 'matter' (ὕλη, *Orph.Fr*.54)[32], whence the earth later solidified. Thus in this context, water probably symbolized the pure state of being, whereas in the impure state of life, the soul was held back in 'mud'.[33] Not surprisingly therefore, these elements reappear as the means of purification in respect of which mud may, more precisely, symbolize the 'garment' of flesh[34] that the initiates wipe off in order to escape, not only the immediate state of life, but also the earthly condition of metempsychosis.[35] By way of ritual imitation,[36] this condition is evoked as well

31. This is most explicitly stated in Plato's famous myth of the cave, Pl.*R*.516d ff.; Porph.*Antr*.62.8-9; see also Turcan, 1956, 136 ff., who claims that the word κρυερός shifts from being an adjective of *Hades* to being an adjective of *life*. Similarly in Plut. *Fr*.178, ap. note 25 above.
32. See West, 1983, 183, n.13, who suggests 'mud' (ἰλύς) for 'matter' (ὕλη) in *Orph.Fr*.54, supporting Zoëga's emendation.
33. That 'mud' signifies impurity is confirmed, e.g., by Ar.*Ra*.146; Heraclit. B 13; B 37 DK.
34. Cf. Plut. *Moralia* 415c; 591f; *Fr*.178; see also Burkert, 1972, 121, n.5.
35. See especially Graf, 1974, 135; Parker, 1983,281. Hence, in the account of Plutarch, Timarchus heard a voice informing him about the rules of metempsychosis during his katabasis in the cave of Trophonius. Among other things, the voice told him that 'in the stars that are apparently extinguished, you must understand that you see the souls that sink entirely into the body; in the stars that are lighted again, as it were, and reappear from below, you must understand that you see the souls that float back from the body after death, shaking off a sort of *dimness* (ἀχλύς) and *darkness* (ζόφος) as one might shake off *mud* (πηλός)', *Moralia*, 591f. As for the astral symbolism, see below, p.175, n.12. The bathing in πηλός and βόρβορος, on the other hand, Plutarch sees as some sort of magic self-mortification, *Moralia*, 166a, introduced by singers, 166b, who we may

as abandoned, as is also the mechanism in Bacchic mysteries, in which *ōmophagia* initiates the habit of vegetarianism (cf. above, p.115).[37] Heraclitus equates the bathing in blood with the bathing in mud (B 5 DK) and thus confirms, by way of ridicule, that the two activities were indeed closely related. By means of sacrifice (ritual slaying) and purification (ritual washing), both addressed the topic of salvation from bodily existence and prepared the souls' dwelling among the gods as the end of life.

This complex of mythical and ritual symbolism became an eschatological concern for the philosophers. Plato, for instance, did not suppress his fascination with 'those men who established the mysteries'; rather than being 'unenlightened' (φαῦλοι), as Socrates puts it, they 'had a hidden meaning' in what they said (*Phd.*69c). Still, although Plato himself often clothed his thoughts in a veil of myth,[38] he clearly condemned the automatic solution of ritual. The only way 'initiation' (τελετή) and 'purification' (καθαρμός) could be regarded as processes of improvement was in the sense of being philosophical practices (cf. *Phd.* 69d; *Phdr.*249c-d). Hence one should not rely on magic spells and acts of redemption as prescribed by the 'Ορφικά. But the relationship between philosophy and esoteric theology is a complex one. Often Plato made his point about initiatory rites metaphorically and by circumlocution rather than by denying them explicitly, and in some respects the Orphics themselves drew heavily on metaphorical references. Let us also bear in mind that among those of the philosophers (mainly to be counted among the Pythagoreans) who contributed actively, albeit by pseudepigraphical writings, to the corpus of *Orphika*, there could very well have been some of Plato's noetic opinion.

quite safely identify as Orphics.

36. See Douglas, 1966, 161 ff.

37. As we know sexual abstinence to have been part of the βίος ὀρφικός (as when, for example, Hippolytos rejects the passion of Phaedra and declares himself to have kept his body 'pure' (ἁγνός), E.*Hipp.*1004), it is indeed possible that Orphic initiation also included some rite of sexual defilement which was consequently succeeded by abstinence and purity. We may bear in mind, for example, that the wife of Archon Basileus, a high priestess of Dionysus, had a sexual experience with the god in the Anthesteria festival, D.59.76; Arist. Ath.3.5; Harrison, 1903, 534 ff.; Kerényi, 1976, 243 ff.; see also above, p.123, n.46. From the Dionysus' temple 'in the lake' (ἐν λίμναις), however, we have an inscription, in which the priestess on behalf of the other female participants confesses: 'I fast and am clean and abstinent from all things that make unclean and from intercourse with man [...]', ap. Harrison, 1903, 537; see also Burkert, 1983, 234 f., who shows that the Anthesteria festival was related to the Dionysian cycle of death and resurrection, op.cit. 232; cf. D.S. 3.62.6. The sexual body denoted, of course, the cycle of birth, and therefore constituted an object of asceticism for the Orphics, cf. Parker, 1983, 281 ff.

38. See my article on this subject, 1998.

Different contexts of discourse may have influenced each other and created a potential of meaning that went beyond the explicit frame of orientation.

In the ritual setting of the meadow, demarcated from the world of ordinary life by the lake, the dead gathered and awaited their fate. Whether they chose the life of a philosopher or the sweet song of Orpheus,[39] the paths of logos and mythos were intertwined. Yet they reached beyond the horizon of Homeric discourse, and they addressed with increasing fervour the end of *this* life, an end which was at the same time the truth and reality of *the other*. This is, in short, what separates the Orphic notion of ψυχή from the Homeric one, and confronts the praise of Panhellenic life with a praise of esoteric death.

39. For reference, see Pl.*R*.617e ff.

X. *Imitatio Mortis*

a. The context of the gold plates

On thin plates of gold, excavated in various places of the ancient Greek world, such as in Thessaly, Crete and Southern Italy, the individual's salvation in the afterlife was being addressed by short pieces of textual inscription. Günther Zuntz divided these texts into what he believed were three, thematically independent groups, A, B and C (1971, 286), of which only A and B need concern us here. However, although it will be useful to maintain Zuntz' notation, the most recent find of the Pelinna text-group (Γ) actually seems to provide a link between the other groups and perhaps finally prove that all the texts belong to the same, overall context of Bacchic mysteries as a part of Orphic discourse.[1] Importantly enough, they also belong to a funeral context, since they have been found in tombs together with inhumed corpses, and what makes them especially interesting to the present investigation is that a textual testimony of eschatology is directly embedded in a cult practice directed towards death. It is a matter of dispute, however, how we are to understand this obviously crucial relation. It is generally agreed that the texts, including metrical as well as non-metrical lines, reflect some orally-transmitted tradition (Guthrie, 1935, 171 f.; Zuntz, 1971, 343 f.; Graf, 1993, 247). But what was the purpose of inscribing quotations from this tradition on the tablets? According to Guthrie, 'the dead man is given those portions of his sacred literature which will instruct him how to behave when he finds himself on the road to the lower world' (1935, 172). The problem with regarding the plates as magic charms, however, is that it leaves the immediate context of initiatory ritual unexplained. We are better off, I would say, regarding the texts and their role in the funeral as being liturgical. As Graf points out, 'one of the ways initiation conquers death and assures eternal life is by ritually performing death and resurrection' (1993, 248). From this angle of comprehension, it may not be decisive whether the texts addressed a situation previous to the actual funeral, or the funeral itself, if not perhaps both, for they might, in any case, confirm what was also being done ritually. In the following, I shall keep to this line of thought.

1. See Graf, 1993, 239 ff., and the list on 257-58. Further, Burkert, 1998, 387 ff., for a short overview.

The 'I' of the A group,[2] clearly corresponding with the 'you' of the B group (through the 'you' of the P group), addresses, among others, Persephone, 'Queen of the Underworld' (χϑονίων βασίλεια), and claims to 'come pure from the pure' (ἐκ κοϑαρῶν κοϑαρά, *Orph.* A1.1; A2.1; A3.1), claiming to belong to 'your blessed race' (ὑμῶν γένος ὄλβιον, A1.3; A2.3; A3.3), since 'I have paid the penalty for unjust deeds' (ποινὰν δ'ἀνταπέτεις'ἔργων ἕνεκ' οὔτι δικαίων, A2.4; A3.4). 'Happy and blessed one' (ὄλβιε καὶ μακαριστέ), the Queen answers, 'you shall be a god instead of a mortal' (ϑεὸς δ'ἔσηι ἀντὶ βροτοῖο, A1.8). These declarations are recognizable as issues of Orphic initiation, as it was represented in Pindar (*Fr.*133, cf. above, p.126 f.) and Plato (*Phd.*69c, cf. p.135). Thus by the phrase 'I flew out from the hard and deeply-grievous circle' (ἱμερτοῦ δ'ἐπέβαν στεφάνου ποσὶ καρπαλίμοισι, A1.6), the initiate must be referring to his or her alleged redemption from the cycle of births. Further, allusion to heroic apotheosis is made by reference to the chthonic power of μοῖρα and the κεραυνός[3] having overcome the initiate before his or her present state of being. But what exactly, we might ask ourselves, is this state of being? The 'you' of the groups B and P, reflecting the 'you' of A1.8, may give us some answers.

In the texts of the B group,[4] the initiate is apparently given instructions of how to enter 'the House of Hades' ('Αίδαο δόμοι) correctly. Beside the house and a white cypress, the person will find a 'spring' (κρήνη),[5] which he or she must avoid (*Orph.* B1.1-2; B2.1-2; B10.5) while instead approaching another spring 'from the Lake of Memory, flowing forth with cold water' (τῆς Μνημοσύνης ἀπὸ λίμνης ψυχρὸν ὕδωρ προρέον, B1.4-5; B2.4-5; B10.6). To the guards in front of this spring, the person must declare himself to be 'the child of *Gē* (Earth) and of starry *Ouranos* (Heaven)' (Γῆς παῖς καὶ Οὐρανοῦ ἀστερόεντος,

2. The A group consists of plates from Thurii (A1-4), 4th Century BC, and from Rome (A5), 2nd Century BC.
3. It is not explicitly stated that this thunderbolt actually belongs to Zeus. Yet West confidently takes it as a representation of Zeus' blessing, 1982, 19, referring to Burkert, 1960/61, 211. As we have seen above, however, the thunderbolt of Zeus represents his power to punish as well as to save by means of translocation, p.88. If translocation is the matter here, it may well be in the form of removal from the cycle of reincarnation, and therefore, eventually, a blessing.
4. The B group consists of plates from Hipponion (B10), 5th Century BC; from Petelia (B1), Pharsalus (B2) and Thessaly (B9), 4th Century BC, and from Eleutherna (B3-5), Mylopetra (B6) and Stathatos (B7), 2nd Century BC.
5. *Orph.* B1 and B2 disagree on whether the spring will be found to the left or to the right (cf. B1.1; B2.1).

B1.6; B2.6),[6] and, while claiming to be thirsty and perishing, ask them for the cold water of memory (B1.8-9; B2.7-9; B3-8; B10). By this act the person distinguishes him- or herself from the ψυχαί 'of the dead' (νεκύων, B10.4, Caratelli, cf. *Text ed.* p.205) who are 'growing cold' (ψύχονται) while 'descending' (κατερχόμεναι) at the first κρήνη. That this source is flowing with the 'water of forgetfulness' (λήθης ὕδωρ) should be safely inferred from its traditional opposition to the 'water of memory' (μνημοσύνης ὕδωρ).[7] If, furthermore, Fritz Graf is right in taking the participle ψύχοντες (of B10.4) to mean that these ψυχαί are 'refreshing themselves' by their descent,[8] the concluding myth of Plato's *Republic* might give us some reason to think that they did so, more precisely, *by drinking from the water*. The Platonic myth tells us that Er, who was presumed dead, suddenly recovered his senses and was able to give an account of his experiences in the world beyond, since, contrary to all the other ψυχαί who were about to sink into new oblivious incarnations, he was not allowed to drink of the water of *Lēthē* (Pl.*R*.621b).[9] By this prohibition, Plato may refer to the Orphic taboo. The person who is about to enter the House of Hades must avoid forgetfulness (*lēthē*) by evoking the memory (*mnēmosunē*) of his divine origin. Only then he will be able to escape the wheel of generation.

In this respect, we are unavoidably reminded of the ritual descent (katabasis) into the cave of Trophonius, where, as a preliminary obligation, the visitor had to drink the water from two fountains, namely the Waters of Forgetfulness (*Lēthē*) so 'that he may forget all that he has been thinking hitherto' (ἵνα λήθη γένηταί οἱ πάντων ἃ τέως ἐφρόντιζε), and the water of Memory 'which causes him to remember what he sees after his descent' (ἀπὸ τούτου τε μνημονεύει τὰ ὀφθέντα οἱ καταβάντι, Paus.9.39.8). Thus, when he returns from the cave, the priests set him upon 'the throne of Memory' (θρόνος Μνημοσύνης) and interrogate him about all he has seen and learned in the dark (9.39.13). The fountain waters, like the λίμνη of the gold plates (B1.4; B2.4; B1.9), demarcate the border between the world of light and life and the world of darkness and death. Yet through the ritual manifestation of internal memory, this *other* world becomes the object of desire, a world of immortality, free from the sorrows and

6. This *legomena* has, of course, the explicit meaning of placing the initiate within the οὐράνιος γένος of the gods (B1.7), as parallelled in A1.3; A2.3; A3.3, but might also esoterically refer to the double constitution of man, i.e., his earthly - and mortal - nature, on the one hand, and the heavenly - and immortal - nature, on the other.
7. See, for instance, Paus.9.39.8; Pl.*R*.621a.
8. Graf translates B10.4 (ἔνθα κατερχόμεναι ψυχαὶ νεκύων ψύχονται) as 'Dort erfrischen sich beim Abstieg die Seelen der Toten', cf. *Text ed.* p.205.
9. For the traditional background to this motif, see Nilsson, 1943, 4, n.3-4.

labours of life. The vision in the dark, like Er's vision in the meadows, concerns the knowledge of metempsychosis,[10] and both visions are undoubtedly instances of Orphic discourse. As for the specificity of context, however, it is worth noticing that in the case of Trophonius the experience of the initiate is due to the institution of an oracle.[11] Perhaps this aspect is even significant with respect to the general symbolism of drinking the water of *Lēthē* and Mnemosyne. If the point is that a person loses his or her capacities of the mind by the drinking of *Lēthē,* thus forgetting his or her present state of being, it is understandable why the Platonic myth, together with the Hipponion text (B 10), considers reincarnation to be the consequence of such drinking; the state of ψυχή is, in both cases, the state of *being in the beyond*. Let us not forget in this respect that the semantics of 'life' and 'death' had the potential of being turned into 'their' opposites (as we have seen above, p.137), so that the allusions of life became a metaphor for death, and *vice versa*. Hence, the ψυχαί that are growing *cold* by the water of *Lēthē* (B10.4) may directly refer to those of the souls that are following the path of reincarnation, but may also, if indirectly, refer to the oblivious ψυχαί of the dead[12] who, by the drinking of *warm* blood, are filled with the remembrance of life as represented in the Homeric *Nekuia*. Moreover, the sacrifice that Odysseus must conduct in order to summon the dead (*Od*.11.35 f.) is very much like the one with which the inquirer of the Trophonian oracle

10. Cf. Pl.*R*.614e ff.; Plut. *Moralia* 431c f.; 590a-f; cf.944d-e; see above, p.129.
11. As such the cult of Trophonius resembled the iatro-mantic complex of hero-cult, in respect of which the Arcadian springs of infliction and healing (also mentioned by Pausanias) seem to relate, at least thematically, to the springs of *Lēthē* and Mnemosyne. Compare especially the 'spring of cold water, above which a plane-tree grows' (πηγή [...] ὕδατος ψυχροῦ [...] ὑπὲρ αὐτῆς πλάτανος πεφυκυῖα[M], Paus.19.2-3), with the Orphic 'spring' (κρήνη) of 'cold water' (ψυχρὸν ὕδωρ) beside which grows a 'white cypress' (λευκὰ κυπάρισσος), *Orph*.B1.1-2; B.10.3-4; 7. That the Orphics were generally responsible for turning the phenomena of ἰατρομαντεία and ἥρως ἰατρός into a practice of soteriological initiation, as is suggested by Nestle, 1930, 98 f., is also supported, for example, by the concluding line of one of the Petelia texts: 'and they shall let you drink from the divine spring, after which you shall reign with the other heroes' (καὐτ[ο]ί <σοι> δώσουσι πιεῖν θείης ἀπ[ὸ κρή]νης, καὶ τότ' ἔπειτ'ἄ[λλοισι μεθ'] ἡρώεσσιν ἀνάξει[ς', B1.10-11). Another instance of relation between the Trophonius-oracle and Orphic discourse is pointed out by Dieterich (1913, 90) who compares the evocation of Τύχη ἀγαθή and δαίμων ἀγαθός with the Orphic hymns, 72 and 73, addressing Tyche and Daemon. Compare also above, p.126.
12. That existence in Hades seems to be generally associated with forgetfulness is testified, e.g., by Theognis (cf. 'Persephone brings forgetfulness to the mortals, while damaging their wit' (Περσεφόνην [...] ἥτε βροτοῖς παρέχει λήθην, βλάπτουσα νόοιο, 704, my own translation); see also Dieterich, 1913, 93; related to the water of *Lēthē*, cf. Epigr Gr. 204; see also Rohde, 1925, II, 382.

warrants a successful vision (Paus.9.39.6). An important difference is, of course, that in the latter case, it is the visitor who must *drink* as a preparation for the ritual encounter. Hence, this person, who could be an Orphic initiate, takes the position of a ψυχή who chooses the source of immortal existence while denying the other source, being the source of mortal life. Perhaps we could even go as far as suggesting that he abandons the Homeric 'scheme of being' in which the life-blood is a vehicle of death *as life* and therefore of life *as death*. In the scene of the Hipponion text, this warm state of life is turned into a cold state of oblivion that the ψυχή must stay clear of. The 'truth of life' that comes together with the blood in Homeric tradition is thus confronted with the 'truth of death' that comes together with the water of memory in Orphic tradition.

The visitor to the Trophonian cave returns to the surface feet first (Paus.9.39.11), thus imitating the state of death.[13] Like other participants in the Orphic rituals of katabasis, he thereby overcomes a state of being that is concomitant to the wheel of births. Born from the same 'mouth' (στόμα) as that into which he descended, he 'conquers death and assures eternal life [...] by ritually performing death and resurrection' (cf. Graf, 1993, 248). If this ritual is further parallelled by the katabasis described in the texts of the gold plates, as we have now gained some reason to believe (not least because of the link created by Pl.*R*.621b), it is reasonable to suggest that these inscriptions refer to a similar initiatory ritual of *imitatio mortis*.

As perhaps already hinted in the pun on τελεταί and τελευτήσαντες (cf. above, p.137), Plato may have precisely such a ritual correlate in mind when speaking of the Orphic priests 'conducting [the initiates] to the House of Hades in their tale' (εἰς Ἅιδου ἀγαγόντες τῷ λόγῳ, *R*.363d). Yet the possibility remains, of course, that this logos represented an overall mythical frame of interpretation that was meant to account for the preparatory arrangements as well as for the funeral process. In the event of the latter, the deceased was, at any rate, inhumed together with the gold plate, on which the *legomena* that the initiate had to *remember*[14] finally confirmed his or her status as a divine being who would never again return to an earthly body.

Even if this be the overall theme of the textual inscriptions, thus connecting the ritual of initiation with the ritual of burial in a twofold process, there are still further problems to be solved regarding the details of interpretation. What about

13. This obviously reflects the way in which a corpse is customarily carried out of the house in which death has occurred, Reiner, 1938, 40, n.5; compare Meier, 1949, 108f., who relates the symbolism of death in the Trophonian cult to the Jungian archetypes.
14. See, in this respect, especially B10.1, which can be taken to suggest precisely this interpretation.

the relationship, for instance, between 'I' of the A group and the 'you' of the B group? The answer lies, I think, in the context of interaction between this person and Persephone.

In Sicily, in the ruined necropolis of Kamarina,[15] some of the excavations between 1899 and 1903 produced a small teracotta-figurine of Persephone[16] (cf. *plate 7*). Of special interest in this respect is the little male figure surrounded by the arms and breasts of the goddess. Furnished with wings (as on the Hermes-lekythos from Attica, cf. above, p.83) he suggests the presence of an εἴδωλον, a deceased person. That he is not just any deceased, however, is clear from the fact that in his hand he holds a crown while stepping into (or out of) a circle in her lap. Now, the interesting part is that this iconographic representation and the text on the Orphic gold plate (A1) are clearly interrelated. Thus, in the text, the initiate claims to have 'flown off' (ἐξέπταν)[17] from the 'cycle' (κύκλος, A1.5) [of reincarnation]. Furthermore, he stepped into the longed for 'circle' (στέφανος, A1.6)[18] and 'slipped into the bosom of the underworld queen' (ὑπὸ κόλπον[19] ἔδυν χθονίας βασιλείας, A1.7).[20] The word στέφανος which can signify any kind of surrounding, or encirclement, is also, and regularly, used as a word for the *crown* which the initiate was to wear in order to signal the fulfilment of initiation.[21] That the mannikin in the Kamarina terracotta is only *holding* such a crown might then suggest that he is depicted in the middle of a ritual process and therefore not yet entitled to *wear* the token of its fulfilment. This is consistent with the texts on the

15. This was actually one of the places that Orpheus was believed to have undertaken a katabasis, *Orph. Test.* 176.
16. P. Orsi, that supervised the excavations, took the figurine to represent Aphrodite, but later comparisons rather suggest the identity of Persephone, cf. Zuntz, 1971, 175, who does not, however, offer any further interpretation. A photograph of the figurine is published in Zuntz, 1971, 24b.
17. The verb πέτομαι may also remind us in this respect of the activity attributed to the Homeric psyche, *Il.*16.856; *Od.*24.7.
18. Although Zuntz is suspicious of the reappearance of line 6 after line 7, differing only in ἀπέβαν (*I stepped out of*), which could be, of course, an erroneous rendering of ἐπέβαν (*I stepped into*, Al.6), it would actually make sense if the initiate claims to have stepped into as well as out of the circle.
19. The word κόλπος may refer to the 'bosomy' *fold* of the garment, cf. Lidell & Scott, s.v., or it may, as in Epigr Gr. 237.3, mean the *lap* - or *womb*- of the goddess in a figurative sense, cf. Lidell & Scott, s.v.
20. Compare Rohde's reference to the 'bosom of nightly Hades' Ἀΐδεω νυχίοιο [...] κόλπος, Epigr Gr. 237.3, and Clem.Al.*Protr.*2.18, which make it highly plausible that the bosom, and accordingly the circle, represent the underworld into which the initiate is making his katabasis.
21. See, for example, Plut. *Fr.* 178, *Loeb.*

gold plates which likewise represent the very act of initiation. Yet we may infer that such representations did, at the same time, constitute a confirmation of the actual, and previous, fulfilment of the ritual proper.

Another confirmation, in the form of a blessing (*makarismos*), is uttered by the goddess herself (A1.8), and is followed by the initiate, the 'I', saying that 'as a kid I have fallen into milk' (A1.9). The texts of the Pelinna tablets, beginning with a similar *makarismos*,[22] continue by addressing the initiate with: 'Bull, you jumped into milk' (ταῦρος εἰς γάλα ἔθορες, P1.3; P2.3), while later addressing a 'ram' (κριός, P1.5; P2.4). As we have seen above, the initiate into Orphic-Bacchic mystery cult was identified with the child of Dionysus, either in the form of a kid (cf. p.114) or in the form of a bull (cf.p.123, n.47) undergoing the process of death and resurrection. Hence, it is tempting to interpret the kid/bull/ram-in-the-milk metaphor as referring to sacrificial animals representing the god as well as the initiates.[23] As we have also seen, the former was slaughtered by the latter in a ritual of defilement that evoked the final purity of deliverance from life in the body. Where Pindar (*Fr.*133) and the A group have Persephone as the bestower of this salvation, another Orphic fragment (*Orph.Fr.*232) refers to Dionysus Lysius, and the Pelinna group to *Bakchos* (cf. Βά<κ>χιος) as the one who sets the initiate free (cf. ἔλυσε, P1.2; P2.2). Thus, the P group creates a link to the *bakchoi* of the B group (cf. B10.16), rendering their ritual identities, together with the A group, as 'the animal in the milk', and being further in accord with the A group in holding Persephone as the important addressee (P1.2; P2.2; A1; A2.1; A3.1; A2.6; A1.7).

Although the precise character of the ritual acts remains unknown to us in the case of the A group as well as the B group, we may nevertheless have gained enough courage by now to draw the overall lines of the initiatory process, and of its crucial elements, well aware, of course, that in so doing we might easily

22. Compare thus the words of Persephone 'Happy and blessed one, you shall be a god instead of a mortal' in A1.8 with the declaration in P1.2; P2.2: 'Now you have died and now you have come into being, O thrice happy one, on this same day' (νῦν ἔθανες καὶ νῦν ἐγένου, τρισόλβιε, ἄματι τῶιδε), which, according to Graf, excludes the ritual setting of a funeral taking place three days after the event of death. Thus we may suggest that we are dealing with the context of initiation. Moreover, the very word τρισόλβιος is suggestive of mystery initiation, cf. later p.198, n.20.
23. See especially Kerényi (1976, 203-5) who, for instance, refers to Firmicus Maternus saying that 'either they cooked me in a cauldron, or they cut my body up into seven pieces which they placed on the spits' (aut in olla decoquunt, aut septem veribus corporis mei membra lacerata subfigunt, 8.2). The child of Dionysus was likewise divided into 7 pieces, cf. *Orph.Fr.*210b: 'they divided the boy's body into seven portions' (ἑπτὰ δὲ πάντα μέλη κούρου διεμοιρήσαντο, my own translation).

stray into the field of over-interpretation.Yet I believe the process to be largely as follows. Suppose the participant in Orphic initiation to be a woman.[24] She then enters some kind of circle, a ritual circumference, that encompasses the underworld. Some specific manifestation of 'stepping down' (cf. καταβαίνω) may take place in this respect. Whatever the precise scenario of the τόπος below, often referred to as the meadows, it seems to be divided into two spheres by running water, or by a lake. From this lake, the water of Forgetfulness somehow demarcates a group of uninitiated people who are probably represented as living in the dark and ignorant world of earthly life as well as being punished in Tartarus (by way of a metaphorical double). Whatever the kind of presence ritually allotted to this group, it is to be avoided by the other group, of which our participant shall prove to be a member. This she accomplishes by drinking the water of Memory before reciting the *legomena* of her salvation, and by carrying out a sacrifice, in which she draws the blood of life as a final repetition of ancestral sin. Subsequently, she purifies herself by rubbing her body with mud and is finally pronounced to be βάκχη entitled to wear the *stephanos* as a sign of ritual fulfilment (*teletē*).

At that moment, when the cycle of births is brought to a close, and the end is about to meet the beginning, life becomes death, and death becomes life: βίος - θάνατος - βίος.

b. Memory

We should now be better prepared to understand the death suffered by Orpheus and Dionysus. As we have seen they share the fate of *sparagmos* in spite of which they survive through one part of their bodies, the head and the heart respectively.[25] In the investigation of Homeric discourse, we saw that the word for 'head', κεφαλή, and one of the words for 'heart', θυμός, occasionally appeared as synonymous with ψυχή (cf. above , p.44, n.1; p.46, n.8). In such instances, the 'head' and the 'heart' might therefore, like the psyche, refer to the deceased as an *image of memory*. In the discourse of Orpheus, however, the 'head' and the 'heart' seem to point quite differently to the *immortality* of the psyche, thus once again reminding us of the semantic inversion of 'life' and 'death' that

24. As several of the gold plates, in different places, are found together with female corpses, it should be safe to say that both sexes were eligible for initiation. Graf, 1993, 255 ff.
25. We may try to compensate for this somewhat crude comparison by admitting that the death of Dionysus is not a *real* death, although it may influence the general meaning of immortality, and correspondingly that the survival of Orpheus is not a *real* survival, although it may likewise influence the general meaning of mortality.

took place interdiscursively between Homer and Orpheus. Perhaps this is reflected in Aristocritus' rendering of a fragment in which Orpheus exhorts Musaeus to conserve in mind and heart all that is declared since the time of Phanes (cf. ταῦτα νόωι[26] πεφύλαξο, φίλον τέκος, ἐν πραπίδεσσιν[27], εἰδώς περ μάλα πάντα παλαίφατα κἀπὸ Φανητος', *Orph.Fr.*61); Musaeus must learn to contain in himself the wisdom of divine existence by the faculties of memory.

Thus, memory, in the religious sense, has a similar status in both Homeric and Orphic discourse, namely that of *sustaining the invisible.* Hence, ψυχή, the phenomenon which is not recognized by the senses, but only mnemonically, belongs to the realm of the invisible, as does the goddess, Mnemosyne, by whom it 'reappears'. In Homer, however, this realm is defined as ᾿Αΐδης, the House of Hades, in which the inhabitants have no power or will of their own. Their existence is, in some sense, solely due to epic commemoration. The power and the will lie in the invocation of the Muses, the mother of whom is no other than Mnemosyne herself (cf. Hes.*Th.*54 ff.; 135; 915 ff.). The poet simply *receives* inspiration from the past (cf. Pl.*Ion* 534b), and in this context, the *keeping* of μνήμη ('memory') is the keeping of *the past,* not by way of any continuity with the present,[28] but rather by way of keeping it *to itself,* that is, by way of recreation. In this sense, the Homeric recitation is a cult, and the techniques of memorization are ritual, or to put it differently: *the past becomes present in the ritual performance of a song that is only equal to itself.* Homer did not gain his knowledge from the world around him, but from the holy tradition of repeating the past through the mouth of those who had witnessed it themselves, the Muses (cf. *Il.*2.484 f.). He did not need the capacity of seeing, and yet he beheld a horizon that was beyond the reach of anyone's eyes. Thus, there are profound similarities between the singer and the diviner; both receive their inspiration from the Olympic world of Apolline authority (cf. *Il.*1.70; Hes.*Th.* 32; 38). 'Aède et devin', as Vernant puts it, '[sont] aveugles à la lumière, ils voient l'invisible [...] L'Histoire que chante *Mnèmosunè* est un déchiffrement de l'invisible, une géographe du surnaturel' (1965, 111; 116).

The relationship between the Homeric narrative and the ritual of its recitation

26. In Homeric discourse, νόος is, as we have seen, the power of the intellect that Persephone permits Teiresias to keep in Hades as a matter of exception, cf. *Od.*10.494, and above, p.72; thus contrasted, for example, by Thgn.704, p.144, n.12.
27. While νόος is mainly connotative of the head, πραπίδες which typically refers to the 'midriff', is connotative of the heart, cf. *LS*, s.v.
28. See thus Bakhtin's definition of the epic genre, 1981, 15 ff. It is a rule of this genre, he claims, that there is no gradual connection between the present world of the listeners and the world of the past which is represented as 'the source of all authentic reality and value', op.cit.18.

is thus one of the past being recreated in the present. The apparently comparable relationship between theology and cult practice in Orphic discourse pertains to an entirely different perspective. While in this context the present state of being, the sensible world, is surrendered to oblivion, the other state of being, which is the object of memory, is not one of any historical past, but the real and original state of divine existence that is recreated as a ritual state of being. For this, Mnemosyne is summoned. 'O blessed goddess, wake in the initiates the memory of sacred initiation, and ward off oblivion from them' (μάκαιρα θεά, μύσταις μνήμην ἐπέγειρε εὐιέρου τελετῆς, λήθην δ'ἀπὸ τῶν<δ'> ἀπόπεμπε[M], *Orph.H.*77.9-10). Presumably, the context of μνήμη here corresponds with the μνημοσύνη of the gold plates, which will enable the initiate to utter the *legomena* in front of the guards of the underworld. Thus, the creative power of Orphic ritual is not confined to the verbal repetition of the past, as conducted in the *theogony* tradition, but due also to the acts of purification by which the 'end' (τέλος) meets the 'beginning' (ἀρχή), namely in the innermost constitution of man, the immortal soul.

It would not be fair to say, however, that Homer did not, in some sense, recognize human immortality. Yet apart from a few exceptions, the epic psyche existed through the μνήμη of others, as the μνῆμα of song, while in Orphic ritual the μνήμη was internalized as a property of psyche itself. Between Homeric and Orphic discourse, psyche changed from being the *object* of - to being the *subject* of - μνήμη. For this, Orpheus himself can be seen as the mythical representation - thereby authorizing it discursively - insofar as his head, connotative of his νόος, carried the memory of its own singing across the frontier of death.

A similar distinction, as that between Homeric and Orphic discourse, was made by Plato between μνήμη and ἀνάμνησις. While μνήμη is the 'recollection' of the sensual past, of things becoming and passing in time, ἀνάμνησις is the memory of timeless being, i.e., the memory that takes place in the intellectual and thus divine part of the soul. As for comparison, in Orphic theogony tradition the world originates in 'Time without age' (Χρόνος ἀγήραος, *Orph. Fr.*66),[29] while

29. Chronus was further identified with Cronus in *Orph.Fr.* 68; compare the Rhapsodic tradition, *Orph.Fr.*60, and the Hieronyman tradition, *Orph.Fr.*54, in which Χρόνος ἀγήραος succeeds ὕδωρ ('water') and ὕλη ('matter'), or ἰλύς ('mud'), interpreted by West as Uranus and Ge, 1983, 183 f.; see above, p.138. The motif of 'time without age' is also found in Parsian religion as *Zrvan Akarana* (cf. Guthrie, 1935, 87; Cornford, 1957, 178; West, 1971, 30 f.), and in Phoenician and Vedic cosmogonies (op.cit. 29; 33). West further claims that the motif must have been present in the Protogonus-theogony, 1983, 87, from which the Eudemian theogony-tradition differs by placing the 'Night' (Νύξ) as the absolute beginning, cf. *Orph. Fr.*24; *Orph.Fr.*28; West, op.cit. 118; Guthrie, 1935, 79.

in Pythagorean discourse, Mnemosyne is defined as the 'symphonic' principle of the world that is 'eternally unborn' (ἀϊδίου ἀγενήτου, Porph.*VP* 31).[30] In this allegorical perspective, in which myth becomes theology, and theology verges on becoming philosophy, the individual souls are not supposed to find their identity in any model of the past, but in the transcendence of time. That the remembrance of autochthonous ancestors in the cult of heroes, implying their presence in the grave, had the potential of providing the same perspective, would contribute to explaining why the Orphics intervened in the tradition, and why, as a probable consequence of this intervention, Pythagoras and Epimenides were thought to have remembered their existence in previous lives (cf. above p.121). Proclus, at any rate, claims in his commentary on the opening of Plato's *Timaeus*, that the soul gains *katharsis* exactly through *anamnesis* of previous incarnations (*in Ti.*22e-23a [I, 124, 4]).[31]

Thus, it may seem that the head of Orpheus flows with the stream of the Meles-river (cf. *Orph.Test.*115) in order to unite with his father, the Thracian river(god), Oeagrus (*Orph.Test.*22-26; Guthrie, 1935, 63, n.2). At any rate, seen in the light of the oracular capacities, by which this head may, for instance, remind us of the head of Mimer in a Norse context,[32] it can be said to encompass the flux of time. In some sense, it thereby transcended time itself, as did the psyche of the dead in the epics, the difference being, however, that the head of Orpheus, contrary to the epic psyche, remained visibly in this world, bearing witness to the immortal authority of Orpheus. If this was recognized as a challenge to the discourse of Homer, this challenge was met, as it seems, by giving Homer the very name of Meles (as was done either in oral tradition as such or by Alcidamas specifically around 400 BC, cf *Hom.Hes.Gen.Ag.* 314). Thus, Homer was equated, or even identified, with the river that carried Orpheus down the stream, or should we say, carried it down the flux of time while itself being the eldest of traditions and in possession, therefore, of the highest authority (cf. above, p.109; compare Pl.*Ion* 536b). The same text ends by quoting an epitaph saying that: 'Here the earth covers the sacred head of divine Homer, the glorifier of hero-men' (Ἐνθάδε τὴν ἱερὴν κεφαλὴν κατὰ γαῖα καλύπτει, ἀνδρῶν ἡρώων κοσμήτορα, θεῖον Ὅμηρον, *Hom.Hes.Gen.Ag.*326). This adoration of Homer, clearly indicating his oracular aspect together with the manner in which he glorified hero-men (i.e., by way of epic commemoration), was explicitly compared to that of Hesiod whilst also, as I suggest, implicitly to that of Orpheus.

30. Compare *Theol.Ar.*81; 15, cf. Vernant, 1965, 130, n.84.
31. See also Vernant, 1965, 116.
32. Cf. Jan de Vries who derives *Mimir* from the Latin *memor*; 'remembering', 1977, 387; likewise, Lincoln, 1982, 19 ff.

If Orphic tradition was younger than Homeric tradition, as Herodotus was presumably right to believe (2.53),[33] the mythical similarities, mentioned above, only testify to the importance of their being also living and contemporary traditions in mutual contest. Thus a famous example of their rivalry, concerning a religious matter of the highest importance, will be given in the next and final part of this book.

33. When Herodotus speaks of Homer and other poets, referring undoubtedly to Orpheus and Musaeus, he obviously thinks of living persons from the past. Yet, that he was in fact rendering the names of discursive traditions (not actual persons, we might take it), and thus using in this respect the instrument of mythical legitimacy, is not very surprising, since it does not conflict with his intentions of trying the matter of probability in cases relevant to his prominent concern. Against the view of regarding Homeric tradition as older than Orphic tradition, see Böhme, 1986, 21 ff., whose main arguments, however, are not convincing.

Part Three

The Mystery

XI. Representing Tradition

In Classical times the word μυστήριον, surviving in English as 'mystery', referred to a rite that was secret. Yet the adjectives μυστικός/μυστηρικός, surviving in English as 'mystical', did not refer to the secrecy of practice but to the practice itself. In the following, we shall use the English words in the same sense. A mystical experience in an ancient Greek context therefore identifies an experience of the mysteries, the secret rites, and not necessarily some secret, or altered, state of consciousness, as of the type that has often been applied to the so-called 'mystic' of Christian and other traditions.[1] The 'mystic' in ancient Greek tradition, that is, the μύστης, was simply a participant in the mysteries. The label of 'a mystical experience' has caused some confusion, as if it were of universal application, addressing in general the excited openness of the human mind towards the presence of the divine.[2] However, detaching the notion of 'mystical' experience from any precise psychological content, we would still want to say of the Greek *mustēria* that they addressed the presence of the divine, albeit in a certain ritualized form which was, at the same time, regarded as being its constitutive part.[3] Mystery cults created a space of interaction between mortals and immortals, including rituals of communication, that were to be kept apart from ordinary life. Hence, mystery rites were secret in the sense that they were tabooed, 'forbidden to speak of' (ἄρρητος or ἀπόρρητος),[4] and this was the rule that Alcibiades was accused of having violated.[5] Not that the gestures, the dance, or the garments, by which he and his companions might have alluded to the

1. Cf., e.g., Rohde (1925, I, 293) and Kerényi (1944, 13). As Burkert, somewhat rhetorically, points out: 'If mysticism means personal introspection, the opening of a deeper dimension in the soul until a light shines forth within, then the Eleusinian Mysteries were precisely *un*-mystical', 1983, 248.
2. Concerning the phenomenological concept of 'mysticism', see Geertz, 1990, 13 ff.; Bilde, 1990, 50 f.; Smidt Hansen, 1990, 104; Sinding Jensen, 1990, 169.
3. See thus Sinding Jensen (op.cit.) and J.P. Schjødt (1990, 149 f.) for suggesting a general classification of 'mysticism' being a kind of ritualized communication.
4. See E.*Ba*.472; a distinction, however, must be made between the two concepts. In the words of Kerényi: '[d]ie griechische Sprache selbst macht einen Unterschied zwischen dem unaussprechlichen Geheimnis: dem *arrhēta*, und dem, was unter dem Gebot des Schweigens geheimgehalten wurde: dem *aporrhēton*', 1962, 37; likewise, Burkert, 1987, 9.
5. Cf. And.1.11-12; 16-17; Lys.6.51; the *aporrhēton* was not merely a taboo on *mentioning* the *arrhēta*, the unspeakable parts of the mysteries, but a taboo on representing them in any conceivable way.

Great Mysteries (the initiation-rites of Eleusis), were *unknown* to ordinary people (many of whom may already have been initiated), not that any secret was *revealed*, but rather that the *aporrhēton* was *profaned* by imitation outside the proper frame of ritual; this was what the taboo, enforced by severe punishment, was meant to prevent.

While some information, however scarce, has actually defied the rule of silence, we cannot escape the feeling that, as for the most crucial of matters, the initiatory rites of Eleusis have in fact succeeded in keeping their secrets. We learn from Aristotle that *experience* (cf. παϑεῖν) rather than *learning* (cf. μαϑεῖν) was the core of these initiations (*fr*.15).[6] But since they were famous for promising a better fate in the afterlife, how can we trust Hippolytus, the Church Father, when he revealed the crucial rite to be the presentation of an ear of corn (Hippol.5.8.39 f.), or Clement, the Alexandrian Church Father, when he referred to the handling of various items in a 'chest' (κίστη) and a 'basket' (κάλαϑος, *Protr*.2.18)? How and why could eschatological importance be ascribed to such simple acts? Surely, any answer depends on what we are looking for. If the dimension of eschatology was a matter of possible interpretations governed also by rules of other discourses, as we might believe was the case, and if the importance was, first of all, a matter of social identification and stratification, we should not expect to uncover a specific secret, but rather satisfy our curiosity with some overall reconstruction of semantic relations that the initiates must at least to some extent have drawn on while at the mercy of frightening noises and strange happenings in the dark.

The popularity of the Eleusinian mysteries was perhaps unparalleled in the ancient Greek world. One of the sources that bears witness to this popularity, giving us, at the same time, the most comprehensive account of the overall framework of interpretation, is the *Homeric Hymn to Demeter*. The very fact that in this hymn the cult is praised in a mythological context over the length of 495 verses, shows that the Eleusinian tradition was considered a profitable matter to represent within the confines of Homeric discourse. Yet Homer had no discursive monopoly on such a representation. Since the cult became, at some point in time - between Archaic and Classical times - *a tradition of initiation*, it is not surprising that Orpheus was actually the one who was generally held to have established it.[7] Pausanias even intimates that the mysteries of Eleusis were

6. It goes without saying that this statement could have been polemic in the sense that Aristotle might not have recognized any 'theology' of the mysteries (such as was attributed to them in the Hellenistic times, cf. Cic.*Leg*.2.36; Epict.3.21.15) as being knowledge in the proper sense. Therefore it would not count as *learning*.
7. Cf. *Orph.Test*.102-4; the testimony of Theodoret (*Orph.Test*.103) may, in part, have built on Diodorus Siculus' claim that the rites, which Orpheus introduced in honour of

somehow reflected in the *Orphica* (1.37.4).[8] However, before delving too far into the actual, thematic differences between the Homeric and the Orphic discourse, we must concentrate for a moment on the question of dates.

The *Homeric Hymns* do not solely belong to Homeric discourse by way of plain, nominal reference, but also according to criteria of content, form and style.[9] Furthermore, as a genre they probably originated in the same *Sitz im Leben* as the epics, insofar as they may have been composed as 'preludes' (προοίμια) to the main epic recital.[10] Yet while the oldest of the hymns, including the *Hymn to Demeter*, are of the Archaic period, the youngest may even be from Hellenistic times,[11] and these probably had no immediate connection to any context of epic recitation. The hymns may thus have become a genre in its own right due to the fact that from the very start, they developed as a means of creating new poetic contributions that allowed the rhapsode to exhibit his compositional skill in a new and less restricted manner. At any rate, the genre seems to have invited poets of 'Homeric' orientation to praise divinities that were popular in respect of their chthonic qualities, e.g., Hermes, Dionysus and Demeter, thus representing counterparts to the Olympians who stole the show, as it were, in the epics. So the *Hymn to Demeter* should be appreciated in exactly this paradoxical relation and not as an independent voice of the Eleusinian cult. The hymn was not composed for recitation in the mysteries, but for recitation in the Homeric tradition. Still, the text gives an aetiological account of the cult that frames it as a tradition of its own. Even so, it is remarkable that Athens does not play any role in the story. Walton takes this fact to indicate indirectly the disapproval of Athenian dominance (1952, 107 f.; 113 f.). On this point, I tend to disagree with him. Although silence may admittedly be a way of suppressing unwanted issues

Dionysus and Demeter, were a copy of the Egyptian adoration of Isis and Osiris, 1.96.4; compare further the example of *interpretatio Graecae* in Hdt. 2.171, where Isis and Demeter are held to be the same goddess. See also Graf, 1974, 22 f.

8. According to the *Parian Marble*, Orpheus was the writer of poems about Demeter and Kore, *Orph.Test.* 221; and Pausanias refers to Musaeus as the author of a *Hymn to Demeter*, composed for the *Lycomidae*, 4.1.5; see Richardson, 1974, 77-86, for a commentary on the various versions of Orphic poems.
9. See especially Allen & Halliday, 1963, cv-cix; West, 1970, 300 ff.
10. Cf. Th.3.104; Pi.*N*.2.1-3; *Od*.8.499, schol.ad.loc.; compare h.Hom.2.1-3; 495; see also Lesky, 1957/58, 81; Richardson, 1974, 3 f. Thus, in h.Hom.6.19-20 the poet makes an appeal to the deity for victory in the poetic contest. However, the hymns that have survived may have developed as poems in their own right, since the length of, for example, the Hymns to Demeter and Aphrodite may not have been compatible with the genre of *prooimion*, cf. Nagy, 1990b, 353 ff.
11. Thus, the author of the hymn to Ares is supposedly Proclus, cf. West, 1970, 300 ff.

of identification, as has been exemplified above, there has to be supporting evidence as to the precise nature of such a suspicion[12] if it is to contribute positively to our investigation. It goes without saying that the Homeric hymn could have been intentionally archaic, thus only committed to account for the origin of the cult, but the range of silence still begs the question. Why is Eumolpus, ancestor of the Eleusinian Eumolpidae, mentioned while Keryx, ancestor of the Athenian Kerykes, is not?[13] Why is Triptolemus mentioned as one of those to whom Demeter reveals her mysteries, while his role of communicating cultivation to mankind is omitted? This heroic task was, after all, a motif of Panhellenic significance which would be likely to match the perspective of the epics.[14] If I am right, furthermore, in assuming that the editorial interests taken in Homeric tradition (cf. above p.101) and the Athenian participation in the administration of the Eleusinian cult were realized within the same overall orientation of Panhellenism,[15] it is hard to see why the author of the hymn would have wished to neglect the Athenian part of the tradition. The answer could be that the hymn was actually composed before Triptolemus was assigned his Panhellenic mission, i.e., not later than the early 6th Century BC,[16] and before the Athenian take-over of the cult administration.[17] If we agree with

12. If, however, we suggest that Walton is right, and, furthermore, that Graf is right in relating the Athenian administration to 'sophistic Orphism', cf. below p.160, n.23, we could actually assume the polemic to reflect the discrepancy between Homeric and Orphic discourse. Yet, I find it unlikely, for reasons referred to above, that the Orphics took part in the political ideology of Athens (cf. p.113, n.3). Still, the fact that the role of Eumolpus is downplayed in the Homeric hymns may suggest, after all, that Orphic influence, if present at the time of the hymn's composition, is deliberately suppressed, cf. Foley, 1994, 173.
13. About the priestly families of the Eumolpidae and the Kerykes, see further below, p.159 f.; and Richardson, 1974, 8.
14. See especially, Clay, 1989, 9 ff.; Foley, 1994, 176 f.
15. See in this respect, Nagy, 1990a, 36 ff.
16. See Nilsson, 1955, 417, and Graf, 1974, 125.
17. Cf. Richardson, 1974, 6f.; 10. However, there has been no general agreement as to the time when Athens took part in the administration of the *Eleusiniae*. Walton (1952, 112) finds the year of 590 plausible on account of some probable allusions in the laws of Solon (likewise Mylonas, 1972, 64, n.21), while Allen & Halliday (1963, 112, n.1) claim that the Athenian control must have been implemented even before 681; see further Foley who opts for a significant relation between Athens and Eleusis as far as back as in the Dark Ages, 1994, 170 ff. One question in this respect concerns what historical value we would want to draw from ancient references to Theseus' *synoikismos* (unification of Attica); Th. 2.15; Plut. *Thes.*10.3; *FGrHist* 10 Andron F 14, *FGrHist* 328 Philochoros F 107. In my view such references are primarily significant as testifying to the matter of mythical legitimation.

Richardson that Athens was not systematically involved until the middle of the 6th Century (op.cit.), it follows that the hymn was composed either before or at the beginning of the 6th Century.[18] The Orphic version of the myth[19] treats Triptolemus as a culture-hero and refers to the Eumolpidae as well as to the Kerykes. Thus, according to the same lines of argument, this mythical tradition must have been established some time after the Homeric hymn.[20]

The *temenos* of Eleusis was a cult-site that was far older, anyway, than either of the poetic traditions mentioned.[21] The earliest historical sources provide us with the glimpses of a cult of vegetation in honour of Demeter, the goddess of the corn.[22] It is likely that as such it was a tradition of local importance, until a decree from Delphi, probably in the fifth Olympiad (760 BC), made it a cult of Panhellenic obligation in response to the famine which devastated large areas of Greece. The cult was eventually adapted to a perspective of soteriology, and it is indeed tempting to compare this evolution with that change of context, according to which hero-oracles and Dionysian rites became elements in Orphic initiation. However incapable I am of proving it, I should like to suggest, and hopefully render plausible, that 'Orphism' was a Panhellenic movement of intervention in old traditions which were susceptible to being turned into eschatologically oriented rituals. Loosely organized by various poets and priests, 'Orphism' manifested itself in taking a discursive hold on different practices of chthonic adoration. Thus, the Eleusinian Demeter cult, in which the cycle of death and life was reassured, provided an obvious context for such intervention.

18. It is more difficult to opt for a *terminus post quem* but I am inclined to belief (with Richardson, 1974, 5) the genre of the epics to have preceded the genre of Homeric hymns, thus pointing to the 7th Century at earliest. I would not be surprised if the hymn was composed around the same time that the epics became written traditions.
19. Actually it seems that there were several poems of various periods, circulating under the names of Orpheus, Musaeus and Eumolpus, cf. Richardson, 1974, 77-88; still, we shall use the fragments, collected in Kern as *Orph.Fr.*43-44; 46; 48-53, 292, as belonging to one Orphic tradition. I very much doubt that the problem of internal differences, which is not treated here, should affect the generalizations given. Although the possibility remains that the poem of the *Berlin Papyrus* (*Orph.Fr.*49) was actually the Homeric hymn itself, adapted to Orphic discourse without significant alteration, cf. West, 1983, 24, the other references, given in *Orph.Fr.*50-53; 292, and related to *Orph.Fr.*49 via the name of Baubo, point to more substantial differences that allow us to assume that indeed Homeric and Orphic authority were in mutual opposition and associated with rival versions of the myth.
20. Another thing is that the hymn actually quoted some passages from the Homeric version, see Richardson, 1974, 81 f.
21. See especially Mylonas, 1961, 29 ff.
22. See especially Nilsson, 1955, 470, n.1-2.

Yet Orphic discourse never managed to dominate this tradition which therefore continued to be a tradition in its own right.[23] However, it became a battleground for different interests of representation, as comes to the fore, for example, in the clash between different accounts of the Demeter myth, as those being the product of, as well as authorized by, Homeric and Orphic discourse respectively.

From Classical times the hieratic duties, concerning the Great Mysteries, or the *Eleusinia* as they were also called, were divided between the Eumolpidae and the Kerykes. This division Foucart saw as a compromise between Athens and Eleusis, bestowing selected privileges of administration on the autochthonous family in each city (1914, 143 ff.).[24] Thus, the Kerykes were responsible for the part of the festival that took place in Athens, while the Eumolpidae[25] were responsible for the mysteries proper, that is, the part that took place in the Telesterion in Eleusis.[26] On closer inspection, however, the picture becomes somewhat murky. The eponymous ancestor, Eumolpus, did not exclusively belong to Eleusinian legend, but was also associated with an Athenian-Orphic context,[27] while the family of the Kerykes was not unequivocally of Athenian

23. Cf. Graf's comments on the earlier view that the Eleusinian Mysteries were simply a phenomenon of Orphism, 1974, 1 ff. While conceding the general rejection of this view, he warns against neglecting the actual interrelations between Orphic poetry and the tradition of Eleusis, op.cit. 8 ff. I certainly agree with him on that point; however, I cannot entirely follow his suggestion that the Orphic influence and the Athenian dominance (cf. the *aparchē*-inscription, IG 1^3 78, from about 422-18 BC) are part of the same overall strategy of adducing to 'themselves' the merits of civilization. If we take seriously the indications of controversy between Orphics and the ideology of the city-state, as pointed out by Detienne (1977, 166 ff.) and Vernant (1982, 51), we should perhaps be more hesitant to associate the Orphic taboo against ritual 'killing' (φόνος, cf. Ar.*Ra*.1032) with the legendary introduction of agriculture (as proposed by Graf, op.cit. 36 ff.).
24. The Kerykes (lit. the 'heralds') claimed themselves that they were of autochthonous origin in Athens, cf. Toepffer, 1889, 81, n.2; and although other sources refer to an Eleusinian genealogy, they seem, at any rate, to have been assigned Athenian duties from an early age, op.cit. 82 f.
25. The eponymous ancestor, Eumolpus, is mentioned as one of those among the Eleusinians to whom Demeter revealed the 'sacred rites' (ἱερά, ὄργια) not to be profaned, h.Hom.2.475 f.
26. Cf. Deubner, 1962, 71; only the hierophant (i.e., ἱεροφάντης, meaning: 'he who displays the sacred objects'), was thus allowed to enter the sacred room of Telesterion, the ἀνακτόρον = μέγαρον, Ael.*Fr*.10, cf. IG II/III^2 3811; IG II/III^2 3764; see further Toepffer (1889, 25 ff.) and Burkert, 1983, 276, n.8.
27. Eumolpus is even referred to as a writer of a hymn to Demeter, cf. Suid. s.v. According to Graf, 'Eumolpos gehört also zu den Autoritären für eschatologische Mythen, mithin in die Nähe der eschatologischen Dichtung, der Musaios und Orpheus angehören',

origin.[28] Furthermore, Malten has pointed out that one of the principal currents of mythical tradition had the rape of Demeter's daughter taking place in Argos.[29] Apparently, various references, corresponding perhaps to different local claims of authority, interfere with one another and create a picture of complex origin.

One major difference between the Homeric and the Orphic version of the Eleusinian myth of Demeter concerns genealogy. According to the Orphic story, Eleusis was inhabited by the 'aborigines' (γηγενεῖς) of Queen Baubo, her consort Dysaulus,[30] Triptolemus, Eubuleus and Eumolpus at the time of Demeter's arrival (Clem.Al.*Protr.*2.17; Paus.1.14.3). Of these persons, Homer refers to Eumolpus and Triptolemus, while the royal couple is exchanged with Metaneira and Celeus. The most crucial point of divergence, however, is perhaps that the attribution of *local origin* is passed over in silence by Homer. Thus, while the autochthonous character of tradition was explicitly referred to in the name of Orpheus, it was apparently suppressed in the name of Homer, the latter bearing witness, as it seems, to the Homeric strategy of bringing together different local traditions without being specific about any of them. Although Celeus is represented as being the rightful king of Eleusis, his name is also known to be an

1974, 19 f.; likewise, Töpffer, 1889, 36 ff. Thus Eumolpus is related to the discursive authority of Orpheus in Ov. *Met.* 11.92 f., and to Musaeus (whose oracles he edited, and whose son, Plato holds him to be, *R.*363c) in the *Parian Marble FGrHist* 239 A15; *Orph.Test.* 221. As for other connections between Eumolpus and Orpheus, see Kerényi, 1962, 35.

28. See, for instance, Paus.1.38.3; further discussed by Richardson, 1974, 8.
29. Malten takes the Νύσιον ἄμ πεδίον, which is found identically in Homeric and Orphic discourse (h.Hom.2.17 ≈ *Orph.Fr.*49, 5. 69, p.121, Kern) to be an erroneous rendering of Μύσιον ἄμ πεδίον in Argolis, 1909, 300. More importantly perhaps, he refers to various testimonies which place the *katabasion* of Kore in this area, cf., e.g., *FGrHist* 26 Conon F1.15; Likewise, Kern, *PW*, 4, 2727 ff.; 2753 ff. In Orphic discourse, however, the picture is not entirely unambiguous. Thus, Eleusis is given as the place of κάθοδος in *Orph.Fr.*49.120, cf. Malten, 1909, 434; 442; yet the hymn to Pluto only tells us that Eubulus (i.e., Pluto) abducts Kore 'to an Attic cave in the district of Eleusis, where the gates to Hades are' (ὑπ' Ἀτθίδος ἤγαγες ἄντρον δήμου Ἐλευσῖνος, τόθι περ πύλαι εἴσ' Ἀίδαο, *Orph.H.*18.13-15). Nothing precludes the meadow, from which she was taken, from being a place in Argolis. As we shall see later on, other points of reference suggest Argive tradition to be part of the Eleusinian complex of myth and cult, cf. below, n.31.
30. Baubo and Dysaulus (who is described as being αὐτόχθων by Asclepiades of Tragilus, *FGrHist* 12 F4) seem to belong quite specifically to, if not even being inventions of, Orphic mythology, see especially Kern, 1888, 498; *Orph.Fr.*53; *Orph.Fr.*49.89; Malten, 1909, 429 f.; Cook, 1965, II, 131; Graf, 1974, 159 f.

Argive patronymic name (Malten, 1909, 444).[31] The point of this transposed representation is likely to be that the Eleusinean myth is, first of all, considered a story of Panhellenic importance within the frame of Homeric discourse. Not so, however, in the Orphic discourse, by which the local tradition is emphasized as being local, albeit under the sway of Orphic authority.

In the Homeric hymn, it is Hecate and Helios who reveal to Demeter what has happened, after she has tried in vain for nine days and nights to find her daughter (h.Hom.2.54 ff.). In the Orphic version, Eubuleus and Triptolemus are the informants and accordingly they immediately benefit from her gratitude by receiving the knowledge of agriculture (Paus.1.14.3). Contrary to what we might have expected, initiation does not seem to be a theme of importance, if present at all, in the Orphic text.[32] Hence, referring to this fact, Graf claims that the main topic of concern was the cultural transition from the savage state of cannibalism to the developed state of agriculture (1974, 159 ff.).[33] Further, he uses this to support his main thesis, namely that the figure of Orpheus is incorporated as a cultural hero into Sophist theory in Classical times (op.cit. 38 f.; 161 f.). Be that as it may, I do not see why this motif should exclude the issue of initiation.[34] Rather, *teletē* constitutes the overall framework of interpretation, even as early as in Classical times. Surely, it begs the question of why in Homeric discourse the final gift of the corn (a motif that may be connotative of agriculture) is explicitly related to the introduction of mystery cult (h.Hom.2.471 ff.), whereas in early Orphic discourse such a relation seems absent.[35] It may be significant, however,

31. Further, the testimony given by Pausanias, which seems to imply the Orphic version, 1.14.3, also refers to an Argive tradition concerning the same mythical context, 1.14.2.
32. Neither does the *Parian Marble*, which dates from 264/3 BC and in which a similar account of the Orphic myth is given, mention any kind of mystery cult, ap. Graf, 1974, 161, n.20; see also Wilamowitz, 1959, II, 48 f. Thus, the silence should not, according to Graf, be explained by the possibility of inadequacy as to references given by Pausanias and Sextus, see the note immediately below.
33. Likewise Wilamowitz, 1959, II, 49. Graf further refers to Sextus Empiricus' quotation from an Orphic poem, arguably from 5th Century BC, which seems to be a 'Kulturtheoretisches Gedicht des Orpheus', 1974, 162. For complete fragment, see *Orph.Fr.*292.
34. If Graf is right in connecting the introduction of agriculture with the φόνος-taboo (1974, 36 ff., cf. above, p.160, n.23), which is, by the way, far from obvious, he must also disconnect the latter from the practice of initiation, and I do not see how this can be convincingly done (see above, p.117). I should find it more likely that mystery cult was a tacit and esoteric implication in every reference, even to the point of being the crucial context of meaning.
35. Yet in the famous *Berlin Papyrus* from the first Century BC (P. Berol. 13044 = *Orph.Fr.*49), into which verses of the *Homeric Hymn to Demeter* are inserted, we actually hear of Orphic 'initiations and secret rites' (τελετὰς καὶ μυστήρια, *Orph.Fr.*49.8).

that the Orphic story is not a story about Orpheus, but a story about Eumolpus, the descendent of Orpheus, and Triptolemus who were 'the first to sow seed for cultivation' (πρῶτον σπεῖραι καρπὸν ἥμερον, Paus.1.14.2).[36] If our task is, in turn, to evaluate the mythical, or legendary, significance of the figure of Orpheus in relation to the content of the poem, the issue of comparison which may put him on an equal footing with Homer is not the mere content itself, but rather the ritual context in which it is embedded. In this respect, the two discursive systems used different strategies in reaching for the highest representational authority: 'Homer' by representing the theme of Eleusinian tradition within the independent frame of recitation, 'Orpheus' by representing the same tradition in some association with the frame of τελετή ('initiation').[37] What I am striving to demonstrate here is that the ritual implications of each discourse seem to be omitted from the respective narratives. It was the mythical context that was focussed upon, not the rules by which it was currently governed. Thus precisely by revealing that Eleusinian tradition connects agriculture and the mystery cult, Homeric discourse may appear to have taken a step behind the authority of Orphic discourse. If, however, we take the myth ascribed to Orpheus to be of a relatively later origin than the one ascribed to Homer, it would also appear that Orpheus was making known a tradition that, in providing the context for his own practice of initiation, preceded the representation of both these aspects in the Homeric hymn. Better still, if we regard both poems diachronically as living traditions, each of these claims could be, and probably was, held synchronically from each point of view.

Thus, I find that Graf over-emphasizes the influence of Sophistic Orphism on the alternative and, in my view, competing version of the Demeter hymn. Furthermore, the question about Eumolpus' Athenian origin is of secondary importance. As I see it, primary Orphic interest focussed on the attempt to represent Eleusinian tradition as both autochthonous *and* Orphic, and the system of initiations that lay behind this representation was, I believe, strategically present as a tacit implication. Yet the autochthonous dimension was also transcended, if not at first hand by the Orphics then by the Delphic decree as early as 760. The Panhellenic interests that Homeric and Orphic discourse seem

36. We do not know much in detail about Triptolemus, but from Sophocles' lost play, called by the name of the hero and winning the theatre contest in 468, we are assured that he was a popular figure. Already from the middle of the 6th Century, he was thus pictured in his winged carriage bringing the cultivation of the seed to the whole of Hellas, cf. Graf, 1974, 125; see also Bianchi, 1976, plates 3; 5.1; 25; 26; 27 and 33. A few of these reliefs can be seen at the Museum of Elefsina (modern Eleusis), as well as *plate 12* showing Triptolemus between the two Eleusinian godesses.

37. See thus *Orph.Fr.*49.8.

to have taken in Eleusinian tradition in the wake of this development were not identical, as we shall see, rather they were in mutual opposition. The Homeric poet inserted a 'local' story in the Panhellenic frame of storytelling, whereas the Orphic poet added a local dimension to the esoteric, and in itself trans-local, frame of initiation.

XII. The Eleusinian Myth

Very truly, I tell you, unless a grain of wheat falls into the earth and dies, it remains just a single grain; but if it dies, it bears much fruit.

John 12.24-25

a. Correlations between myth and ritual

We are now ready to assess to what extent the Eleusinian myth, as represented by Homeric and Orphic discourse, may reflect the content of the Mysteries. Although the Homeric hymn does not contain any direct information about the Classical Eleusinian Mysteries, Martin P. Nilsson claimed that at least the overall significance of the cult practice was reflected in the narrative (1955, 474).[1] Thus, he suggested that the sequence of abduction and reappearance of Kore symbolized the storage of the seed corn in underground granaries, and further that the preservation of the stock may have been one of the main features of the cult (op.cit. 473). Nilsson's thesis is tempting insofar as the period of storage as well as the seasonal period through which Kore must stay in the underworld, amounts to one third of the year. However, as Burkert has pointed out (1983, 261), Kore returns in the spring, while the sowing takes place in the autumn (cf. h.Hom.2.401). Even more problematic, perhaps, is the reduction of the mythical narrative to mere allegory. It is true that in Hellenistic times the fate of Kore was intimately associated with the cycle of the grain,[2] but how old and how allegorical such an interpretation was, can only be a matter of speculation.[3] It is, on the other hand, immediately obvious why the myth of Demeter and Kore has been likened to the myths of Aphrodite/Adonis, Kybele/Attis, Isis/Osiris and Ishtar/Tammuz. In all of these stories, the motif of the death and resurrection of

1. An account of this narrative shall thus be given immediately below, *Chapter XIIb*.
2. References in Burkert, 1983, 260, n.19; 1987, 80; 158, n.85.
3. Indeed, there has been a great deal of guesswork in the attempts to define the phenomenological correspondence between the myth, the cult drama and the cycle of vegetation, cf. J.G. Frazer, 1912 , 5.1, 39 ff.; 225 ff.; Mannhardt, 1884, 1, 351 ff.; 2, 32 ff.; Harrison, 1903, 274; 1912, xvii. As to the precise allegorical translation, one must keep in mind that Kore must stay four months in Hades, while the grain sprouts only a few weeks after it has been sowed, cf. Burkert, 260; see further Otto, 1955, 320; Rohde, 1925, I, 292. Yet Nilsson's explanation would still meet the criteria of temporal correspondence.

the beloved victim seems to reflect the cycle of vegetation.[4] However, as Otto points out, the relationship between Demeter and Kore differs from the others in one respect: it does not constitute a liaison between lovers, but the loving bond between mother and daughter (1955, 318). Furthermore, Otto argues that it is not so much the sorrow as the wrath of the wronged mother that motivates the narrative (op.cit. 320 ff.).[5] The corn does not disappear from the field because of Kore's disappearance, but as a consequence of the mother's retribution (op.cit. 322). Otto draws the conclusion that Kore is not identified with the corn which is only introduced by Demeter after she has been reunited with her daughter (ibid.). Thus, 'Der Tod ist die Voraussetzung des Getreidewachstums', since '[d]ie Kornfrucht hat es ja vor dem Verschwinden der Persephone überhaupt nicht gegeben' (ibid.). This is, however, incorrect. In the hymn, we read that the Rharian field was once 'fertile corn-land' (φερέσβιον οὖθαρ ἀρούρης, 450) until Demeter hid 'the white grain' (κρῖ λευκὸν, 452).[6] Yet Otto may be right on one point, namely that the fate of Kore and the acts of the mother reflect above all else the relation between mother and child.[7]

Karl Kerényi, a close colleague of Otto, even claims that Demeter and Kore are two manifestations of one and the same goddess (1941, 172 ff.; 242 ff.; 1962, 137). This should not surprise us too much, since we have already dealt with the issue of divine identity between father and son, namely that between Zeus and Dionysus as Zagreus or 'the great youth' (cf. above, p.123 f.).[8] Kerényi goes further and applies this point to the process of initiation:

In der Identität von Mutter und Tochter erscheint die immer wieder Gebärende, die Mutter, in deren Gestalt und Schicksal der Myste eintrat, als dauerndes Wesen; das Kind ist das

4. Cf. Otto, 1955, 318, see also Jonathan Z. Smith, *ER*, s.v. 'Dying and Rising Gods', and note 2 above. I would like to add that in contrast to Dionysus, Adonis and others, Kore is nowhere said to suffer the fate of death. She is raped and married to the King of the Underworld, but that may be something slightly different. I would not wish to deny that the motif somehow implies the fate of death, but the distinction between what something *is* and what something is *parallel or similar to* may sometimes prove important, even in ancient myth.
5. Hence, Otto classifies the hymn together with the *Iliad* as *mēnis*-poems, ibid.
6. Compare further 306-8, and the mention of the 'meal' (ἄλφι), 209.
7. Herodotus makes the same emphasis, 8.65. Thus Demeter and Kore are often mentioned as simply 'the mother' (ἡ μήτηρ) and 'the daughter' (ἡ κόρη), cf. Nilsson, 1955, 470.
8. See thus Kerényi's own juxtaposition of the Eleusinian and the Cabeiric cults, 1962, 144. Further, Demeter and Kore are mentioned as 'the old' (ἡ πρεσβυτέρα) and 'the young' (ἡ νεωτέρα), cf. Nilsson, 1955, 470. Compare also Harrison (1903, 274; 479 f.; 652 f.) who deals with the motifs of the male and the female god as being represented at different ages while fundamentally being the same gods.

Zeichen davon, daß diese Dauer überindividuell ist: Fortsetzung und fortwärende Wiedergeburt in den Nachkommen. (1941, 200)

Hence Kerényi believes the archetype of womanhood to signify the crucial notion behind the mystery in Eleusis (1941, 207f.; 211 f.; 1961, 72 ff.).[9] The initiate (*mustēs*) finds himself in the scheme of procreation, which makes him experience death within the frame of continuous generation.[10]

To some extent, Kerényi's interpretation is actually based on the Homeric text (1941, 243), but his notion of the 'female archetype', by which he affiliates himself with Jung,[11] encumbers it, at the same time, with psychological implications that must be otherwise accounted for Without going into any discussion of this matter, I shall restrict myself to suggesting, along the lines of Kerényi's thesis, that myth as well as mystery in the Eleusinian tradition seems to deal with the divine relationship between mother and daughter as a relationship that implies the continuity of being beyond the border of death.

In trying to reach a closer understanding of the exact correlation between myth and ritual, and a closer view of the exact character of correlation between divine and human existence, it is time to take a look at the text itself. We shall

9. The double aspect of the woman as being born and giving birth may thus explain the doubling of the Eleusinian figure. Thus, on the Eleusinian relief (cf. *plate 12*), we might be tempted to interpret the position of Triptolemus between the two goddesses as presenting the condition of mortality. Although Kore does not exactly suffer the fate of death, the theme of division between Olympus and Hades surely evokes the human condition of life and death. That Triptolemus is depicted in the act of receiving his mission from the goddesses, may signify that life and death of the crops is a similar kind of cycle.
10. According to Jung, this may even be the continuous generation of the collective unconscious of which *anima* (the 'female archetype') is the typical symbol, 1976, 67 ff.
11. Thus, Jung is co-writer of Kerényi's work on mythology (1941) and says of *anima*, the 'female archetype', that '[d]ie dem Bewußtsein präexistente Psyche (z.B. beim Kind) hat einerseits Anteil an der mütterlichen Psyche, anderseits ist sie auch ein Hinüberreichen in der Psyche der Tochter' (op.cit. 224), and further that 'Demeter und Kore, Mutter und Tochter, ergänzen ein weibliches Bewußtsein [...] und erweitern damit das engbegrenzte und in Zeit und Raum verhaftete Einzelbewußtsein zu einer Ahnung größerer, umfänglicher Personlichkeit' (ibid.), namely *anima*. However, in contrast to Jung, Kerényi is not inclined to locate this archetype of the psyche in the psyche itself, but in the historical sources, where it appears as a self-identical type, cf. 1961, 54 f; 68 ff. The difference amounts to that between psychological and historical subject matters, whereas analytically, both angles operate from similar methods of reduction and generalization. Further, they are compatible as theories of universal, human consciousness. Although the angle taken in the present book is different insofar as it is directed towards human communication rather than human imagination, I do not wish to discredit the views of Kerényi and Jung on any general level.

restrict ourselves to accounting for the Homeric myth, since in this case we have the whole version before us, whereas the Orphic myth, to which we shall later return sporadically, has only survived in a form that is too fragmented to support any detailed interpretation.

b. The Homeric myth

The immediate reaction of Demeter to the screams of her daughter is somewhat odd: it is as if she anticipates what is going on from the very beginning. Although she only hears the echo of a cry, she immediately abandons herself to sorrow by covering her face with a black veil (h.Hom.2.40 f.).[12] While later, when reporting the episode to Helios, she says that 'with my eyes I saw nothing' (οὐκ ἴδον ὀφθαλμοῖσιν, 68), the words may imply that from the mother's epichthonic point of view, Kore was no longer visible insofar as she had been carried away to Hades, the hypochthonic realm of invisibility (2-3). Be that as it may, it is obvious that Demeter does not know exactly what has happened and searches for nine days and nights with torches in her hands in order to find the girl. It is remarkable, however, that she does this without enjoying the sustenance of nectar and ambrosia (48-49). It seems that by mourning over her daughter *as if she has died* (which, of course, she has not), the goddess denies herself the privilege of immortality. In any case, when Helios reveals to her what has happened with Zeus' full approval, she takes yet another step away from the realm of the immortals and departs for Eleusis in the figure of an old woman. In other words, she reacts in two ways as if she is submitting herself to the level of mortality (94-101). Even willing to become a nurse she is then brought to the palace of king Celeus (140 f.). However, when she crosses the threshold, seeing the child in the arms of queen Metaneira, she regains for a moment her divine appearance (187). Yet when Metaneira invites her to take a seat on the throne, she declines and bows her head (193 f.). Resuming her humble attitude she accepts instead the chair that Iambe brings her, and once more she abandons herself to mourning by hiding her face behind the veil and by abstaining from tasting any food or drink. However, by gentle teasing, Iambe succeeds in making the goddess smile and laugh (202 f.)[13] to the effect that Metaneira offers her a cup of wine (206 f.).

12. The gesture may even be suggestive of funeral lamentation and the following period of mourning, see especially Reiner, 1938, 43 f.; Alexiou, 1974, 41.; Richardson, 1974, ad loc.; A.*Ch*.11 f.; E.*Alc*.216; as for relevant comparisons in the Homeric discourse, compare *Il*.18.22-25; *Il*.24.93-94, cf. Reiner, op.cit.
13. As we shall later see, Orphic myth has a similar scene, in which Queen Baubo changes the mood of the goddess by some obscene gestures, cf. p.177. For the probable significance of Iambe's jests, see Wilamowitz, 1959, II, 52, n.2.

Demeter still refuses, telling her that wine constitutes an inappropriate drink for her, and instead bids the women to mix meal and water with soft mint (207-9). This 'draught' (κυκεών) she receives and thus introduces the ritual tradition (cf. ὀσίη, 211).

Metaneira asks her to become nurse for her child, Demophoön, and Demeter gladly accepts. Soon the child begins to grow 'like a divine being' (δαίμονι ἶσος, 235), since he is fed neither with mortal food nor at the breast but is anointed with ambrosia as if he were 'the offspring of a god' (ἀμβροσίῃ ὡς εἰ θεοῦ ἐκγεγαῶτα, 237).[14] Demeter breathes upon him, holding him in her bosom (cf. 178 f.), while at night she places him amongst the flames of the hearth. Her intention is to render the child immortal, but Metaneira, who spies on the goddess, becomes scared and spoils the process. Having earlier heard her own daughter's cry of fear, Demeter now recognizes the wailing of a mother, but this time, it is the goddess herself who is regarded as the violator (248 ff.). Demeter's anger, having previously been directed against the cunning of male gods, is now turned upon the foolishness of a mortal woman, and the goddess declares that mortals are 'ignorant' (ἀφράδμονες, 256)[15] of whether things that will happen to them are good or bad. She would have made Demophoön 'deathless and unaging' (ἀθάνατος καὶ ἀγήραος, 260), had not Metaneira interfered. Now Demophoön shall meet the *kēres* of death like everyone else. Yet she will allow unfailing honour to rest on him for all time, because he has laid in her bosom. Further, the people of Eleusis shall build her 'a great temple and an altar below it' (νηόν τε μέγαν καὶ βωμὸν ὑπ' αὐτῷ, 270), and she will teach them her 'rites' (ὄργια, 273), so that hereafter they may reverently perform them and, as she says, 'so win the favour of my heart' (ἐμὸν νόον ἱλάσκοισθε, 274).

Having uttered these words Demeter reveals her divine nature and turns away from the palace. Sitting in her new temple, she then causes a great famine by keeping the seed in the depths of the soil (306 ff.), and thus she would have destroyed the whole race of man and have robbed those who dwell on Olympus of their glorious tribute of gifts and sacrifices, had not Zeus taken pains to re-

14. We are reminded in this respect of the custom of anointing the corpse with honey as a means of preservation. In Nagy's view, the embalming may also imply beliefs in immortality, cf. 1983, 205 ff. and above, p.23. Further, Demophoön is also treated like a corpse in respect of being surrendered to the fire, cf. above p.32 ff. Actually, the boy is killed in the Orphic version of the myth, *Orph.Fr.*49, 100 f.; cf. Richardson, 1974, 81. The symbolism of death in the process of Demophoön's transition may thus be a theme that is, in both discourses, suggestive of transformation from a mortal to an immortal being. See further below, p.184 ff. However, the process is not fulfilled in the Homeric context.
15. It may be significant that the dead 'images' of the *Nekuia* are likewise described as being devoid of wit, cf. νεκροὶ ἀφραδέες, *Od.*11.476.

spond. However, she turns down his initial attempts to bring her back amongst the immortals (324 ff.). She will not - and we might add that in a sense she cannot - return to Mount Olympus since she behaves like a mortal woman whose daughter is dead. Only when Hermes brings back the girl from Erebus (337 f.), 'so that the mother may see her with her eyes' (ὄφρα ἑ μήτηρ ὀφθαλμοῖσιν ἰδοῦσα, 338-9 ≈ 349-50), does the goddess put aside her anger. Yet Kore, now called by the name of Persephone, must soon depart once more for the realm of the dead, since Hades has given her the seed of a pomegranate to eat. Even so, Demeter agrees to the arrangement that two thirds of the year Persephone will spend with her on Olympus (399-400),[16] while one third she will reside in the underworld. Hence, Demeter reestablishes the balance by letting fruit and corn sprout again in the land (453 f.; 471 f.), and eventually she instructs Triptolemus, Diocles, Eumolpus and Celeus how to perform the 'mysteries' (ὄργια, 476) 'which no one may in any way transgress or pry into or utter' (τὰ οὔ πως ἔστι παρεξίμεν οὔτε πυθέσθαι οὔτ' ἀχέειν, 478 f.). This done, she finally returns to the realm from which she came herself, the Olympic home of the immortals. The mortals, however, are left with a message:

> Happy is he among men upon earth who has seen these mysteries; but he who is uninitiate and who has no part in them, never has lot of like good things once he is dead, down in the darkness and gloom. (h.Hom.2.480-82)

Thus far, the Homeric representation of the myth. My suggestion is that it actually reflects the mystic context in a number of parallels: Demeter tends Demophoön with ambrosia, a token of immortality, while Hades nourishes Persephone with the seed of a pomegranate, a token of death. Demeter abandons the level of immortality, while trying instead to render a human child immortal. When this fails, her mind returns to Kore, who is hidden in the world below. As a countermove, Demeter hides the corn in the ground, and this makes it clear to Zeus that balance must be restored. Thus, when Kore returns from Hades, Demeter returns to Olympus, and vegetation returns to the fields. When failing to make Demophoön divine, Demeter gives up her mortal appearance, and when failing to bring Demeter back to Olympus from the human sphere, Zeus rescinds his approval of Kore's abduction to the chthonic sphere. Finally Demeter returns to her place in the Olympic pantheon, while Demophoön is destined to die as a

16. Kerényi interprets the tripartite division of the year as a distribution of three functions of the same goddess divided into Demeter, Hecate and Persephone, 1941, 160; 1962, 138; anticipated, according to Kerényi, in Hes.*Th.*411-14. I can easily accept Kerényi's point about the seasonal and regional division, but why this has to be due to a single, threefold goddess is beyond my understanding.

hero, and Persephone is destined to spend one third of each year with the King of the Dead. These parallels, it seems, belong to an interdependent play of relations between life and death, divine and human existence, and Olympic and chthonic powers. Tension (and hence the plot of the narrative) is created because at the outset the characters leave their proper domains, Kore by being transferred from the Olympic to the chthonic sphere, Demeter by abandoning the privileges of immortality, and Demophoön by being a mortal who receives them instead. This tension is again gradually resolved, when, at first, Demophoön resumes his earthly identity as a mortal, and when, at last, Demeter resumes her Olympic identity as an immortal, but between these two states, the balance is only restored because the divine daughter attains a new and double identity as the Olympic maiden, Kore, on the one hand, and the Queen of the Underworld, Persephone, on the other.[17] Thus, the categorical interrelations have not been reestablished without change. Kore/Persephone becomes a permanent symbol of the exchangeability of the Olympic and the chthonic world, preceded by the intervening interaction between immortality and mortality, divine and human existence. Obviously, and significantly, the corn is part of a similar double insofar as it is hypochthonic while being a seed and epichthonic when rising as an ear.

The way in which the relation between these levels is affected by (the narrative of) their temporary confusion, reminds us of a ritual process. Undoubtedly, in this case it is a structural similarity that is, at the same time, a matter of esoteric correspondence. Yet before returning to the possible content of corresponding rituals, a few comments shall be made on the traditions of cult to which the text itself refers.

As exceptional for the Homeric discourse, the posthumous honours of Demophoön - denoted as everlasting τιμή (263), not as the usual κλέος - undoubtedly refer to the hero-cult.[18] Since the katabasis of Kore has already brought us into the confines of a chthonic universe, this is not very surprising. However, it may be significant that although he becomes an object of local cult adoration, Demophoön does not, strictly speaking, become immortal. In this respect, the perspective of the hymn, exemplified by the fate of heroic Demophoön, accords with the overall perspective of the epics. The hero-cult is eventually given its due representation in local tradition but by being carefully phrased in the opposition between mortality and immortality.

The same distinction reappears, albeit implicitly, in respect of the mysteries

17. Cf. Kerényi, 1962, 138.
18. See Nagy, 1983, 201 ff.

that Demeter instructs the people of Eleusis to perform secretly (473 ff., anticipated already in 273 ff.). It is nowhere implied in the hymn that those who become initiated in these mysteries will become immortal. They will be 'blessed' (ὄλβιοι),[19] but when they die they will still go to the dark world below, and in the light of the epic perspective, this means a frozen world of remembered images.[20] It may not be as bereft of consolation as Achilles described it to Odysseus, nor merely a world of seeming insofar as a new path of continuity between life and death seems to have been established. Orphic afterlife, however, implying immortality of the soul, seems to be as far from the perspective as ever. Thus, the *Homeric Hymn to Demeter* is not only Homeric in respect of style and context, but also in respect of the basic line of eschatology.

19. Compare S.*Fr*.753 N ap. Richardson, 1974, 311; Pi.*O*.2.68 ff., and below, p.198.
20. The hymn seems to concern itself with the same theme of Hades as the realm of invisibility insofar as Kore's katabasis and anabasis are described from the mother's point of view, as visual disappearance (cf. οὐκ ἴδον ὀφθαλμοῖσιν, 68) and visual reappearance (cf. ὀφθαλμοῖσιν ἰδοῦσα, 338 f. ≈ 349 f.).

XIII. The Eleusinian Cult

To see God only, I goe out of sight:
And to scape stormy days, I chuse
An Everlasting night.
John Donne, Hymn to Christ

The overall scheme of sequential correspondence between the myth and the initiation process in Eleusis seems to be obvious enough.[1] Problems begin to arise when we set out to relate in more detail the content of the myth to the secret features of the cult. Exactly how adequately the initiates engaged in an imitation of the mythical drama, we simply do not know. Yet as a discursive frame of orientation, the mythical narrative should still warrant a coherence in our interpretation of what we actually know of the ritual practice.[2]

On the 19th Boedromion (September/October), the fifth day in the Greater Mysteries,[3] a 'procession' (πομπή) of ritual participants took place on the sacred road from Athens to Eleusis. Although there are some conflicting sources to the matter, I shall here opt for the general suggestion that this *pompē* included various citizens as well as the priests, the priestesses (carrying the sacred objects, *hiera*), the ephebes (escorting the icon of Iacchos) and the initiates.[4] Later, in the

1. Cf. Burkert, 1987, 77.
2. Clay warns against putting too much faith in the suggested correspondences between myth and cult, 1989, 202 ff. and opts for interpreting the Homeric hymn on its own narrative account. Yet, while the hymn may in some way have influenced the content of the ritual process, the same should be equally probable *vice versa*. For further comments on this problem, cf. below , p.174.
3. The mysteries of Eleusis were divided in the Lesser Mysteries, the first step of initiation which took place at Agrai near the centre of Athens, and the Greater Mysteries, which started in Athens and ended in Eleusis where the two final and secret stages of initiation took place. The structure and content of these festivals will not concern us here; cf. Mylonas, 1961, 224 ff.
4. Clinton (1988, 70) points to the fact that Plutarch mentions the 20th Boedromion as the day when the Athenians 'brought out Iacchos' (cf. Plut. *Camill.*19; Phoc. 28), whereas the inscription, IG II^2 1078, gives the 19th as the date of the *pompē* including the escorting of the *hiera*. Thus, Clinton suggests that the initiates did not arrive, together with Iacchos, until the 20th. If this be the case, it implies that the afternoon of arrival immediately preceded the first night of initiation, which leaves no time for rites of abstention

'yard' (αὐλή) before the *Telesterion* (initiation hall), a nightlong ritual, the παννυχίς, was enacted in honour of Demeter. Since the procession as well as the subsequent events on the *temenos* (the consecrated temple area) included the carrying of torches, it would be reasonable to see it as a symbolic representation of Demeter's search for her daughter.[5] Due to the chronology of mythical events it is unlikely that the *pannukhis* was related to the other danced performance[6] of the 'secret ritual acts' (μυστηρικὰ δρώμενα).[7] Rather, the *pannukhis* reflected a *mimēsis* of Demeter's mournful search which was not yet an object of the mysteries proper.[8] The parallel between the arrival of the initiates at Eleusis and Demeter's arrival at the same place - thus marking the *end* of her search - may instead persuade us to suggest that the *teletai* had their parallel in her actions while staying *at* Eleusis.

Supposedly, the participants were not introduced to the secret part of the 'initiation' (τελετή) before the 20th. More precisely, it has been suggested that on the night between Boedromion 20 and 21 some mystic performance reflected the mythical drama.[9] It is, however, doubtful that the building of the Telesterion

(see immediately below). However, more problematic is that we then have to regard the great Iacchos procession (cf. Hdt. 8.56; Plut.*Them.*15) as distinct from the procession of sacred officials and citizens (Clinton's reference (ibid.) to IG II^2 1006 is inconclusive). I believe the solution to be either that Plutarch was not very precise about the date, or that he was thinking of the night of arrival (i.e., the night between Boedromion 19 and 20). For regarding the 19th as the date of arrival of the initiates, cf. especially Mylonas, 1961, 253 ff.; Burkert, 1985, 287.

5. Cf. Richardson, 1974, ad loc.47; cf. also Proclus, who thought that a ritual wailing of the *mustai* reflected Demeter's mourning, in *R.* 125, 20. Further, the nine days of the search (cf. h.Hom.2.47) might reflect the length of the Mysteries (from the 15th to the 23rd), cf. Richardson, op.cit., but then the correspondence shifts to a level of criteria that do not follow the same type of similarity between certain acts. In the following we shall concentrate on possible correlations between representations of such acts.
6. See especially Burkert, 1983, 288.
7. Unless Clinton's suggestion is correct, cf. above, n.4, which I doubt very much, see especially And.1.11-12; 16-17; Th.6.28.1; Plut.*Alc.*22.4; Rohde, 1925, I, 289; Kerényi, 1941, 190.
8. The fact that Proclus does not regard the ritual imitation of Demeter's lament as *aporrhēton* in itself (cf. *In R.*1, 125 ff.) could thus be seen in favour of the suggestion that it reflected Demeter's immediate response to hearing Kore's faint cry and her subsequent search, but not her attitude while staying at Eleusis, cf. the testimony of Clement, *Protr.*2.16, cf. immediately below.
9. Cf. Foucart, 1914, 349 ff.; Deubner, 1909, 84; Mylonas, 1961, 262; see Aristid. *Or.*19.422d, and the δρᾶμα mentioned by Clement, Clem.Al.*Protr.*2.12.

would have been suitable for a successful reception of any dramatic staging.[10] Whatever happened that night, the *mustai* probably prepared themselves in the daytime by fasting and purification, by covering their faces and by the drinking of kykeon, the consecrated draught. Since in these acts we recognize a similarity in the content and sequence of the mythical events concerning Demeter's staying at Eleusis, it should be reasonable to assume that the following part of the initiation corresponded with Demeter's nightly nursing of Demophoön rather than with some composite dramatic representation of the complete narrative. However, during the night of the 20th, the initiates only went through the first part of the initiation (the τελετή), while for the final rites (the ἐποπτεία) by which they would become *epoptai*, i.e., 'those who have seen', they had to wait yet another year.[11] This concluding initiation took place on the night of Boedromion 21 and probably represented in some simple form the reappearance of Kore/Persephone.[12]

Having thus outlined the probable frame of an overall correlation between myth and cult, we shall look in more detail step by step at the process in myth

10. See thus Wilamowitz' comment on Clement's testimony, 1959, II, 473. Yet Mylonas still wants to propose 'that the story was developed in and out of the Telesterion, around the very landmarks supposed to have been consecrated by the actual experience and presence of Demeter', 1961, 262 f. The rites were still kept secret, according to Mylonas, by the wall that surrounded the *temenos* area. Compare, however, the doubts expressed by Farnell, 1921, 3, 181 f.; Nilsson, 1955, 662 f.; Kerényi, 1962, 40; Graf, 1974, 128. From the testimony of Plutarch, cf. *Moralia* 81d, we must infer, according to Graf, that the crucial rites were confined to the initiation hall, op.cit. 131 ff. Even if one looks at the various expansions of the Telesterion from the time of Pisistratus to the Roman period, it is difficult to imagine how a mythical drama could be staged 'in and out' of the hall. Although we may assume that initiation in some early form took place under the open sky, that is, before the erection of the Telesterion (cf. Allen & Halliday, 1963, 111; Burkert, 1983, 277), this does not enlighten us any further as to the nature of the subsequent performance.
11. Cf. Nilsson, 1955, 655 f.; see, for example, Pl.*Smp*.210a.
12. Cf. Otto, 1955, 330 ff.; Burkert, 1983, 286. Compared with Plutarch's equation of death with initiation (cf. *Fr*.178), the twofold structure of dying that he refers to in *The Face on the Moon* seems to fit the scheme of Eleusinian initiation rather neatly. Thus, while Plutarch speaks of the first death 'in the earth that belongs to Demeter' (ἐν τῇ <γῇ> τῆς Δήμητρος), he speaks of the second death 'in the moon that belongs to Persephone' (ἐν τῇ σελήνῃ τῆς Φερσεφόνης, *Moralia*, 943b). Although the metaphors allegedly recall Pythagorean soteriology rather specifically, the Orphics may very probably have been responsible for implanting a similar structure in the Eleusinian context. Hence, the first night of initiation belongs to Demeter, while the second belongs to Persephone. This is, at any rate, what we shall take as a guide-line for our structuring and interpretation of the complete process of initiation in Eleusis.

as well as in ritual. Clement, who is one of our most important informants on the Mysteries,[13] refers to the mythologem of Demeter sitting at the Eleusinian Callichorus-well in grief, and says that it is forbidden for the 'initiates' (μυούμενοι) to engage in this sorrow 'until the present moment' (εἰσέτι νῦν), lest they shall not seem to 'imitate' (μιμεῖσθαι) it as 'those who have fulfilled their initiation' (τετελεσμένοι, *Protr.*2.16). If I am right in taking this statement to mean that the mimesis of Demeter's grief *at* Eleusis refers to a ritual act that the *mustai* must wait to perform until the right moment comes when it will constitute a secret part of their initiation, it follows that the fasting and the covering of faces, which must form part of this mimesis, constitutes the introductory sequence of the mystic acts proper. Thus, Kerényi connects the verb μυεῖν, 'to initiate', with μύειν, 'to close', typically: 'eyes and mouth' (1944, 21), and claims that '[d]ie Mysterien beginnen für den Mystes, indem er als Erleider des Geschehnisses (μυούμενος) die Augen zuschließt, auf die eigene Dunkeltheit gleichsam zurückfällt, ins Dunkel eingeht' (op.cit. 22).[14] This ritual introversion, which may have consisted in hiding the initiate's head in a cloth as we see it on some iconographic representations, may very well be the *mimesis* of Demeter's own introversion, accompanied by fasting and ending with the drinking of *kukeōn* which are the elements included in what Clement claimed was the 'formula' (σύνθημα) of the Eleusinian Mysteries (*Protr.* 2.18).[15] However, the covering of the head may at the same time be a ritual of separating the initiate from the world of ordinary mortals, submitting him to the solitude of mystic experience in the dark. Thus,

13. We cannot know for sure whether or not Clement was initiated in the Eleusinian Mysteries. The rites, of which he gave a detailed account, could have been the rites of Alexandrian Mysteries (cf. Nilsson, 1955, 659), in which he had been either initiated or about which he was at least well informed. In any case, we should safely assume a large degree of correspondence with the two cults in honour of Demeter and therefore put some faith in Clement's references, however misguided some of them might be. Nilsson notes specifically that the *kalathos* mentioned in Clement's *sunthēma* was a feature in the Alexandrinian cult, op.cit.; this is also pointed out by Burkert who rightly doubts, however, that the Alexandrian public would 'accept something Alexandrian as 'Eleusinian'', 1983, 270.
14. Cf. Frisk, *GEW*, s.v. μύω. Yet there is some confusion as to what the μύησις refers to, cf. Clinton, 1988, 69, n.8. Typically, it has been associated with the introductory rites at Agrai, preceding the twofold initiation, τελετή and the ἐποπτεία, in Eleusis, cf. Nilsson, 1955, 655 f.; also Kerényi, 1962, 62. Still, the closing of the eyes, correlating with the covering of the face, does indeed seem to signify some preliminary rite in its own right, even if being a part of the τελετή, and as such it was probably thought of as a μύησις.
15. Thus 'I fasted; I drank the draught' (ἐνήστευσα, ἔπιον τὸν κυκεῶνα). Compare also the apparent relation between the myth, cf. h.Hom.2, 50; 129; 200, and the selected fasting, mentioned as an obligation in the Eleusinian Mysteries by Porphyrius, *Abst.*4.16.

in this case the ritual seems to resemble myth with a significance that also follows from its own structure. Conversely, it may said of the Homeric hymn that it resembles the ritual only insofar as the structure of performances is translatable into a scheme of events that fits the narrative purpose.

It may be worth considering in this respect that Clement did not seem to interpret the ritual undertakings in the light of the Homeric hymn, but in the light of an Orphic poem (cf. *Protr.*2.16-17), of which he gives a short paraphrase and one minor quotation. Since Orphic discourse was generally a discourse of ritual concern, we must suppose that the text at hand had a direct bearing on the initiation process, although we must at the same time expect it to be equally committed to the rule of secrecy as was the Homeric hymn. Yet different ways of speaking indirectly about the unmentionable may well happen to lead us on the track of basic meanings of the relevant context. Intriguing in this respect is Clement's reference to the role of Baubo.[16]

In the Orphic context, this 'nightly daemon'(δαίμων νυκτερινή), as she is called (*Orph.Fr.*53), assumes and combines in one person the roles that are divided between Metaneira and Iambe in the Homeric hymn. Being the Queen of Eleusis she receives Demeter as a guest in the palace and offers her a 'draught' (κυκεών) of wine and meal.[17] When Demeter declines, Baubo teases her by uncovering her 'genitals' (αἰδοῖα)[18] and revealing thereby the child of Iacchos in

16. Baubo also figures in the 'Orphic quotations of the Homeric hymn' (cf. *Orph.Fr.* 49) and therefore leads us to believe that we are actually dealing with some genuinely alternative version of the Eleusinian myth. We must keep the possibility in mind, however, that we may be dealing with some misguided rendering, confusing Homeric and Orphic tradition, cf. above p.161 ff., especially p.162, n.35.
17. Thus, the reference already departs from the Homeric 'draught' in that it includes the very ingredient that Demeter refused (in the Homeric hymn) as being improper for her: the *wine*.
18. Cf. Clement's paraphrase, *Protr.*2.17; see Cook, Zeus, II[1], 132, fig.79, and *plate 11* in this book, as for an iconographic representation that is undoubtedly related to this motif; thus Nilsson identifies a similar terracotta figure, also from Priene, as Baubo, cf. 1955, plate 45.3; see further Burkert, 1983, 285, n.53, who interprets the sexual disclosure as a reference to the taboo on eating beans (suggestive of a child's head, Iacchos in this case, and the female womb); some support for this thesis can, perhaps, be drawn from Paus.1.37.4. However, I see no other trace in Clement's rendering of the Orphic context that makes this symbolism plausible. Rather, a comparison should be made with the Egyptian tradition, reported by Herodotus, 2.59-60, and Diodorus, D.S.1.85, due to which female worshippers show their genitals to Osiris, incarnated in the bull-god. A reverse motif, to which Burkert draws attention are the Phrygian Mysteries in which, according to Clement, Zeus tore off a ram's testicles and threw them into the *kolpos* of Demeter, to atone for his sexual violations, *Protr.*2.13; cf. Burkert, 1983, 283.

her bosom (or rather 'below her breasts' (ὑπὸ κόλποις), 2.18). Pleased at the sight, Demeter now accepts the drink, and this - Clements says - is 'the hidden mysteries of the Athenians' (κρύφια τῶν 'Αθηναίων μυστήρια[M], 2.17). Apart from the discrepancies between the two versions, the overall structure is the same insofar as *fasting* and *introversion* in both cases turn into *disclosure* and *drinking* of *kukeōn*. Yet in the Orphic version we are given some information about the content of the teasing, while such information is absent from the Homeric version. Surely, Iambe's endeavours to please Demeter plus the vision of Metaneira with the child in her arms could be regarded as a divided parallel to the composite Orphic motif, supported by the fact that Baubo combines the role of Iambe with that of the queen. However, the revelation of Baubo's female and motherly nudity causes Demeter to react with delight, whereas in Homer the sight of mother and child makes her react with sorrow. This could be taken to mean that the sexual motif of 'the child in the lap' is suppressed in the Homeric hymn in favour of various other representations of woman and child as, for example, Metaneira's and Demeter's nursing of Demophoön. What I am suggesting here is that these various motifs concerning 'the child in the lap' may all indirectly, i.e. cryptically, refer to the process of initiation. The reason for hazarding this conclusion is not merely that Clement also happens to hold this view, but above all that the discovery of the same motif is a central element in Orphic initiation (as we have seen above p.120; 146). True, Persephone rather than Demeter typically occupies the role of a nurse in the Orphic context, but the crucial factor may be that the very role of the divine 'nurse' (κουροτρόφος)[19] constitutes in all instances the process of esoteric initiation, giving the initiate the role of the child.[20] That the mysteries of Eleusis are the mysteries of Demeter *and* Kore/Persephone may be reason enough for dividing the 'ritual' roles *between* them, just as the *mustai* were probably identified with the role of Demeter as well as with the role of Persephone (cf. later p.188). Furthermore, let us not forget Kerényi's thesis that in fact Demeter and Kore, mother and daughter, were two

19. Cf. Richardson, 1974, 24; 155 f.; Price, 1978, 171f.; 199 ff. Compare, for example, the initiation of Epimenides, D.L.1.114-115, according to Orphic or Pythagorean custom, cf. *GDI*.5039.14; Porph.*Antr*.60.6; *Abst.* 4.16; *Orph.H*.51-53.
20. Here, it must be relevant to refer to Parmenides' much-discussed journey to the heavenly realm of the goddess who will tell him the truth. If the journey is described by metaphors of initiation (Guthrie, *HGP*, II, 10 ff.; Burkert, 1969, 5 ff.), which I find no reason to doubt, then the 'I' of the text, the '*kouros*' in the lap of the goddess, is highly suggestive of an Orphic or Pythagroean initiate, cf. Guthrie, *HGP*, II, 2; Burkert, 1969, 21; Coxon, 1986, 15 ff.

aspects of one and the same goddess.[21] However, it may be premature to stress this issue of identification, be it between Demeter and Kore, or between the goddess and the initiate. In myth the goddesses participated in the world of human conditions, whereas in the ritual the *mustai* participated in the world of divine conditions. If indeed the cult was to some degree myth repeated by way of human acts, we may further suggest that the *mustēs* assumed the role of the human child, Demophoön, while some mystagogue, be it the priestess of Demeter or some other cult administrant, took up the role of the divine nurse.[22] Thus, on the one hand, thc iconographic motif of the initiate, seated on a goat's fleece with a cloth over his head (cf. *plate 8 + 9*, also Bianchi, 1976, plate 51), reminds us of Demeter in the palace;[23] on the other hand, it may also reflect the nursing of Demophoön in the hearth insofar as a woman, a ritual nurse standing behind the initiate, holds a torch to his hand (*see plate 9*; also Bianchi, 1976, plate 49). However, even for the artist in the time of the Roman Empire, the taboo on any depiction of the true mysteries was probably respected; he may have alluded only to some aspects of the initiation ritual and not to any concrete ritual as such, that is, in any directly recognizable manner. Yet we are getting ahead of ourselves. Before commenting on the nocturnal 'rite of fire', we must take a look at the acts immediately following the fasting and the drinking of *kukeōn*.[24]

As drinking succeeds abstinence, so disclosure succeeds concealment (behind

21. Thus, while Iacchos appears as a child in the 'bosom' (κόλπος) of Baubo in the Orphic myth, cf. Clem.Al.*Protr.*2.18 = *Orph.Fr.*52, he appears in the 'bosom ' (κόλπος) of Demeter in Sophocles, *Ant.*1115. Further, Strabo takes him to be the daemon of Demeter, cf. Str.10.468. See Burkert, 1983, 279.
22. This might be what is hinted at in the hymn speaking of 'nurses and handmaids much less skilful' (h.Hom.2.291) who are taking over from Demeter.
23. This part of the ritual should probably be regarded as an 'enthronement' (ϑρόνωσις), cf. Burkert, 1983, 266 f.; cf. h.Hom.2.195 f., of which we also know that it was an introductory part of the Orphic *telete*, cf. Suidas; *Orph.Test.*223d; see also Kerényi, 1976, 210-17, as for the Bacchic context. The fact that Demeter rejects the royal throne in favour of a simple wooden chair may point to an intended inversion of the real, albeit camouflaged, hierarchy between the goddess and the mortal queen, thus making the corresponding 'enthronement' a part of the liminal or marginal phase of the ritual process, where the normal, hierarchal positions are temporarily abandoned (cf. Turner, 1977, 96 f., following the structural scheme of Van Gennep, 1909, 212 ff.). Hence, the queen is seated as an old woman, while the *mustēs* is seated as a divine being.
24. I shall not comment further on the drink apart from referring to Kerényi's not much believed suggestion that the actual, ritual draught included a hallucinogen, cf. Kerényi, 1962, 100; discredited by Burkert, 1983, 287. Obviously the meaning of the draught was related to the overall agrarian significance of the cult, Deubner, 1909, 72 ff.; see thus Theophrastus' reference to the moistening of the barley grain with water for use in sacrifice, ap. Porph.*Abst.*2.6, and further below, p.182 f.

the veil), and the corresponding feature in the cult was very likely to be the following disclosure of Demeter's sacred 'chest' (κίστη).[25] Obviously, Baubo's role in Orphic myth carries sexual connotations,[26] and in *Lysistrate* (1182-84), Aristophanes imparts sexual meaning to the *kistē*.[27] The symbol that represents and probably unites the chthonic aspect of these sexual allusions may be found in the figure of the snake, lying in the female lap as depicted on sepulchral reliefs (cf. Küster, 1913, 67)[28] and on Roman reliefs which represent the mystic scenario of Eleusis (cf. *plate 8 + 9*). On the latter, the snake appears uncoiling from the *kistē* through the folds of the garment of either Demeter or Persephone and is touched by the initiate.[29] As we have already seen (p.123), a similar rite seems to have taken place in the Bacchic cult, where it (secretly?) summoned the offspring of the bull, i.e., Dionysus in the form of a snake. Correspondingly, Baubo's sexual disclosure reveals Iacchos who was, at least in Classical Times, associated with Bacchus/Dionysus. Further, the phallic aspect of the snake[30] was in itself

25. Thus, the whole *sunthēma* rendered by Clement runs as follows: 'I fasted; I drank the draught; I took from the *chest* (κίστη); having done my task, I placed in the basket, and from the basket into the chest', *Protr*.2.18.
26. This is already hinted at in her name, cf. Wilamowitz, 1959, II, 52, n.1; Graf, 1974, 168. Further, the chthonic sphere was often associated with the female womb or bosom, thus, the 'bosom of nightly Hades' ('Αΐδεω νυχίοιο ...κόλπος, Epigr Gr. 237.3) presumably alludes to the bosom of the divine nurse, be it Persephone, cf. above p.178, Demeter or Baubo, cf. above, n.21; and the hollow altar used in the hero cult, the so-called *eskhara*, was another word for the vagina. Lastly, it should be noted that Dysaulus, the spouse of Baubo, is intimately associated with Hades himself, thus establishing another implicit association between Baubo and the Queen of the underworld.
27. Further, according to Burkert, the sacrificial pig, which formed part of the Eleusinian sacrifices and which was referred to by Aristophanes as the χοῖρος, was associated with the female genitals, 1983, 259; see also Cook, *Zeus*, II[1], 132, fig.79, and *plate 11*.
28. Thus, it may not be an over-interpretation to see the female vagina as symbolizing a 'channel' (cf. the note above on the double meaning of ἐσχάρα) between the world of darkness and the world of light (as actualized in giving birth, cf. also below, y?), and in this case a channel whence the snake appears, cf. Küster, op.cit. 65; Rohde, 1925, I, 35.
29. This may indeed remind us of Clement's description of Bacchic initiation, in which a serpent (being the epiphany of a god) was 'being pulled through the bosom of the initiates' (διελκόμενος τοῦ κόλπου τῶν τελουμένων, Clem.Al.*Protr*.2.14), cf. above, p.123, n.46. It is rather obvious that the word κόλπος, translated above as 'bosom', must refer more specifically to the 'fold of the garment', which the initiates wear, cf. Lidell & Scott, s.v. κόλπος. That Clement's way of putting it may, however, carry a somewhat more intimate sexual association is not to be ruled out on this account.
30. Cf. Eitrem, who accounts for the chain of associations between 'death', 'phallus' and 'serpent', 1909, 31. Thus, Burkert finds the snake to serve as a symbol of 'phallic

suggestive of Dionysus' chthonic domain. Thus, in Bacchic initiation, most likely under the reign of Orphic *teletē*, a veiled boy was led by a ritual 'nurse' towards a 'winnowing basket' (λίκνον) which contained a phallus.[31] As we know from comparisons between various iconographic representations, the *liknon* and the *kistē* were used for similar purposes, and in Orphic discourse they specifically served to carry the surviving part of the divine child.[32] Yet in Bacchic initiation they were also used to hide the phallus, obviously a representation of the divine being's fertile power.[33] Now, as we find a snake winding around the *liknon* as well as the *kistē*, we shall perhaps regard it as an epiphany of the content by way of synecdoche. Having no personal nature on its own, it may manifest the chthonic power of death, sexuality and rebirth - in other words, the continuity of being. Hence, when on the Roman reliefs we see the writhing body of the snake leading from the *kistē* to the lap (or *kolpos*) of the goddess, we have gathered enough evidence by now to suggest that also in this context it represented the mystic power of sexuality (specifically phallic, I would assume) which is responsible for the cycle of births. Hence, the combination of male and female sexuality may have been exactly what Baubo and the mystic *kistē* revealed.[34] Actually, the 'sacred objects' (τὰ ἅγια) that Clement pretended to strip

impregnation', 1983, 152, and suggests that it 'arouses both a fear of death and a secret sexual fascination', op.cit. 269. It should not pass unnoticed, however, that the snake was also, and quite prominently, associated with *healing*, as in the cult of Asclepius, and *nursing*, as in the cult of Hygeieia, cf. *LIMC* V[1] 557; V[2] 381.8-10; 382.16-19. Yet it may also have been the chthonic powers that were invoked in this respect.

31. Cf. Burkert, 1987, 58 (figure 6), cf. 95.
32. Thus, the *liknon*, referred to in myth, corresponded with the *kistē* associated with ritual, Cf. above p.123 n.46; *Orph.Fr.*199; Kerényi, 1976, plate 88; 89; Bianchi, 1976, plate 18; cf. Guthrie, 1935, 112. Whereas in myth the part of the body in question was the heart, we also have a vase-painting which shows the mask of Dionysus lying in the *liknon*, cf. Kerényi, op.cit. plate 89.
33. See further, *plate 10*; Kerényi, 1976, plate 135 = Bianchi, 1976, plate 85; compare also Clement's reference to the genitals of mutilated Dionysus in the *kistē* of the Cabeiric rite, *Protr.* 2.16, which, if we trust Clement's account, must have been under Orphic influence in this respect, see above p.112, n.2.
34. Thus on the famous fresco of the *Villa of the Mysteries* at Pompei a cloth seems to be lifted from the sex of a winged female figure (*Aidos*, 'Shame'?), who at the same time pulls back from the sight of something exposed in a *liknon*, when a servant removes the veil from it (cf. Bianchi, 1976, plate 92 = Kerényi, 1976, plate 110; a large, coloured and very detailed reproduction can be found in LA VILLA DEI MISTERI, La Liberia dello Stato Roma, 1947). What the *liknon* contained may be revealed on a mosaic from Djemila-Cuicul in Algeria showing a female figure who tries to avoid the sight of a huge phallus exposed when a veil is removed from the *liknon* by a Bacchic servant; see comments in Burkert, 1987, 95, together with figure 7, ibid. (Present in the middle of the

bare (cf. ἀπογυμνῶσαι) can be divided into a male and a female group, the former consisting basically of cakes and fruits and a 'serpent' (δράκων), the latter of spice, a lamp, a sword and a woman's comb. The serpent, Clement takes to be 'the mystic sign' (ὄργιον) of Dionysus Bassareus, while the second group he takes to be 'the unutterable symbols' (ἀπόρρητα σύμβολα) of the earth goddess.[35] More specifically, he regards the comb as 'a euphemistic and mystic expression for the female genitals' (εὐφήμως καὶ μυστικῶς εἰπεῖν, μόριον γυναικεῖον[M], *Protr.* 2.19). It goes without saying that the information given by Clement has to be taken with a grain of salt. Still, the other testimonies allow us to believe that he was at least on the right track. At least it seems safe to claim that the content of the *kistē* carried allusions to the male and the female genitals.[36] Further, when Clement said, according to the formula (the *sunthēma*), that the *mustēs* was 'working' (ἐργασάμενος, 2.18)[37] with something from the *kistē* before placing [it] in the *kalathos*, we may be dealing with a ritual act similar to the one that may have been hinted at in the iconographic representation of the initiate touching a snake in the 'fold' (κόλπος) of the goddess. If we do not believe Clement's description to be exhaustive, which, considering the range of circumstances, would be inadvisable, then what could these symbolic representations be? There are a plethora of possible answers.[38] A correlate to the Indian *Lingam* and *Yoni*, representing the male and the female members, is possible.[39] As for a more specific suggestion, however, Burkert has proposed that a pestle and mortar,

mosaic was Orpheus!). On a teracotta (cf. *plate 10*) we behold a similar scene with a winged figure, Aidos (cf. Bianchi, op.cit.36), fleeing from the revealed phallus.Intriguing in the comparison between this relief and the 'Villa painting' is that in both cases the veil seems to be connected somehow with the winged woman as if it revealed her sex simultaneously as revealing the content of the basket. Again the *liknon* of Bacchic cult may correspond with the *kistē* of the Demeter-cult, and the painting of the Roman *Villa* may allude to a confrontation between the male and the female sex.

35. The precise rendering 'Ge Themis' due to an emendation of Wilamowitz, cf. *Loeb*.
36. See also Burkert, 1983, 270, n.21, in further support of this.
37. Lobeck replaced ἐργασάμενος with ἐγγευσάμενος, which would be consistent with Clement saying that the initiate 'ate from the tympanon' (ἐκ τυμπάνου ἔφαγον, *Protr.* 2.14) in the Anatolian Demeter cult. Yet Theoprastus' use of 'ἐργασία' in relation to producing what seems to be a *kukeōn* (cf. Porph.*Abst*.2.6) favours the text as it stands in the *Loeb* edition; see the note below.
38. See references in, and critique by, Nilsson, 1955, 658 f.
39. As for these symbols of male and female sexual energy, cf. Zimmer, 1972, 142. Intriguing in this respect is the parallel, demonstrated by O'Flaherty, between Shiva, who is intimately associated with the lingam, and Dionysus, especially in respect of the erotic dance, which seems indeed a relevant topic for further comparison between the two, 1980, 138 ff.

used for 'working' with the first grain, tangibly related the cycle of vegetation to the cycle of human fertility. Thus the precise undertaking could have been to 'grind the wheat, at least symbolically, in order to help in producing the next kykeon [...] The sexual associations of stamping and grinding are obvious' (1983, 273). Although there is some evidence found in Theophrastus,[40] I take Burkert's suggestion to be an inspired guess but little more than that. Yet as for the symbolic reference there cannot be much doubt. The disclosure pointed to the regenerative capacity of the sex. That this capacity was, at the same time, connected with the realm of death,[41] as the serpentine figure may lead us to suggest, can also be safely inferred from the Homeric hymn. I find it quite plausible therefore that the secret theme of the disclosure was the nature of this connection. This, however, Clement may have failed to comprehend.

Stripping bare, not only the contents of the chest, but also his own head that was hitherto veiled in darkness, the *mustēs* thus participated, according to the wording of Clement, in 'such initiatory rites that belong to the night and the fire' (ἄξια μὲν οὖν νυκτὸς τὰ τελέσματα καὶ πυρὸς[M]', *Protr.*2.18). The fire from torches,[42] which is the fire Clement is thinking of here, is apparently not a reference to the preceding *pannukhis*-ritual but rather relates to the night between Boedromion 20 and 21. Presumably then, this is the time and occasion for the *teletē*, the main *aporrhetic* initiation of the *mustēs*, as implied on various reliefs.[43] However, an Athenian inscription as early as from the 5th Century BC (IG I² 6 = LSCG 3.108) speaks of the Keryx, who chooses only one young *mustēs* to be initiated 'from the hearth' (ἀφ' [ἑστίας μυομέ]νο, IG I² 6.107).[44] Here, the hearth

40. Thus Theophrastus speaks of the 'the tools with which they worked' (τῆς ἐργασίας ὄργανα), i.e., produced a mixture of barley and water. Further, these instruments 'afforded a divine assistance to human life' (θείαν τοῖς βίοις ἐπικουρίαν παρασχόντα), and were 'concealed with the taboo of mentioning them' (κρύψαντες εἰς ἀπόρρητον), ap. Porph. *Abst.*2.6. Further on, Theophrastus mentions the cakes made of the first fruit as an offering to the gods. Surely, we might be tempted to relate these cakes to those which Clement claimed to find in the *kistē*.
41. Thus Burkert sees the act of grinding as 'an act of destruction', suggesting 'the basic human themes of aggression', op.cit.
42. That Clement is thinking of torch fire is inferred from his related, rhetoric appeal to the *dadoukhos*, 2.19, cf. further Butterworth's translation in *Loeb* of the sentence mentioned above, 2.18.
43. Cf. *plate 9* and plate 44.2 in Nilsson, 1955, I; also comments, in Burkert, 1985, 288.
44. See especially Clinton for other textual testimonies, 1974, 98-116, and a general discussion of specific rites concerning the 'hearth-initiate'. Clinton claims that this representative participant simply 'offered prayers or sacrifices on behalf of all the initiates and perhaps also on behalf of the city, and in so doing assumed on this occasion quasi-sacerdotal functions', 1974, 99. I would be reluctant to accept, however,

must mean the city hearth, and the child may thus have been chosen as a representative of the people as was Demophoön in the myth.[45] Yet even if we believe this initiation to have been part of the mysteries carried out in the Telesterion, we are not justified, however tempting it may be on account of Demophoön's 'initiation', to think of a sole, exclusive fire ritual. The veiled *mustēs* who, seated on the throne, suffers the 'fire initiation' on some reliefs, also appears as engaged in other acts on other reliefs and apparently occupies, in all instances, a middle and central role in the initiation process as such. Thus on the Lovatelli urn, the 'nursing mystagogue' holds a *liknon* over the head of the initiate. Surely, various elements that may have been carried out separately in the ritual were thus mixed in one simultaneous scenario in the iconographic representation, but if indeed the fire initiation was exclusively performed for one selected child, it would seem unlikely that this motif was being conflated with elements of the ordinary process rather than simply being omitted from the depiction.[46] As I see it, nothing argues against the possibility that a chosen infant was brought along for extraordinary initiation together with the older *mustai* who were also exposed to flaming torches in a 'fire ritual' signalling the overall, nursing process of Demeter.[47] In the Homeric version of the myth, this process failed because of human intervention, leaving Demophoön the heroic glory instead of immortality. In the Orphic version, however, the child was actually killed (*Orph.Fr.*49.100-1).[48] How are we to evaluate this discrepancy? Actually, our previous investigations have prepared us to give at least one possible answer. If we read the Orphic text as an esoteric reference to Orphic ritual, which I take to be an option for serious consideration in every instance of Orphic discourse, then 'the death of the child in the care of the nurse' may correspond to the 'death and resurrection' in the process of Orphic initiation (as shown in *Chapter VIIIa*). Further, the disclosure of Iacchos in the lap of Baubo (reminding us of the initiate in the lap of Perse-

that such functions alone should adequately explain the mentioning of the *hearth*. We must at least be wary of a possible symbolic connection between this initiation 'from the hearth' and Demeter's nursing of Demophöon *in the hearth*.

45. I follow here the suggestions in Burkert, 1983, 280 f.
46. Unless, of course, Heracles, whose initiation is probably featured on the Torre Nova sarcophagus, was the single, chosen one.
47. It is true that the line, 107, in the inscription mentioned above speaks of exclusiveness (cf. Μὲ εν[αι ἐσιέναι μεδέ]να πλὲν το ἀφ'[ἐστίας μυομέ]νο), but it seems to address a special case of preparation and payment administered by the Keryx in Athens before the Mysteries, not the context of the Mysteries as such.
48. Referring to a similar version in Apollodorus, 1.5.1, Richardson claims this to be the original story, 1974, 81.

phone, cf. *plate 7*),[49] may point to the initiated as having achieved resurrection and no longer being part of the state of mortality, since he has escaped the *kuklos* (*Orph.*A1.5), the wheel of births (*Orph.Fr.*229-30). He is killed, but only in order to become immortal, since the nurse who kills him is not a human nanny but the divine mother of chthonic offspring. Thus, Hippolytus would have us believe that in the night of torch fires, the hierophant announced a divine birth with the words: 'The Mistress has given birth to a sacred boy, Brimo to Brimus' (ἱερὸν ἔτεκε πότνια κοῦρον, Βριμὼ Βριμόν, Ref.5.8.40),[50] the 'strong one', as the informant takes it. Who would that boy be? Iacchos-Dionysus, Plutus ('Wealth'), the initiate or some or all of them at the same time? We cannot know for sure.[51] But, if, in any case, we take the lowered torch to signal a 'fire ritual', corresponding to Demeter's hiding Demophoön in the hearth, we are supposedly dealing with an *imitatio mortis*, a symbolic sacrifice of the flesh, or even funeral,[52] in which the initiate is being purified. On the Roman reliefs, we see that close to the feet of the *mustēs* an animal is being sacrificed on the altar.[53] The question is whether or not these two 'fire rituals' were somehow connected, and if so, in what sense? Burkert suggests that the 'mystery pig' (cf. Ar. *Ach.*747; 764), which was sacrificed in the preliminary rites, was to die 'in place of the initiate himself' and 'had the character of an anticipatory sacrifice of a maiden' (1983, 259). Further, he suggests that a ram would be killed and skinned during the mysteries proper, and that this was 'attested as a sacrificial victim for Kore' (op.cit. 282). This latter sacrifice in 'the great fire', Burkert relates to the 'theme of infanticide' and claims that the ram's skin, on which the *mustēs* was sitting, 'could only have come from

49. The eschatological scene of the 'meadow' (λειμών), in which the purified rejoice in Bacchic initiation, is thus described as 'the flowering bosom' (εὐανθεῖς κόλποι) in Ar.*Ra.*372 ff., and used as a metaphor for the female sex in E.*Cyc.*170 f. See also above, p.180 f.
50. Ap. Burkert, 1983, 289, from whom the interpretation is taken.
51. Hippolytus' testimony, if at all trustworthy, may even have referred to the *epopteia* in the next night of second-year initiation. Yet the context of criss-cross identifications probably applies not only to various names but to various sequences of the overall mystic process as well, cf. Burkert, 1983, 288 ff.; 1985, 288. Some relation between other cults, under the Orphic hegemony, of 'nurse and child' may certainly have exerted its influence, such as the cult of Rhea and the 'megistos kouros' in Crete, as referred to in E.*Ba.*120-35; see also above, p.112; 122.
52. Thus, Demophoön is anointed with ambrosia, cf. h.Hom.2.237, as is the corpse of the dead, cf. the tending of Sarpedon, *Il.*19.38, cf. 18.345 ff.
53. On the Lovatelli-urn, cf. *plate 8*, a pig is being slaughtered, while on the sarcophagus from Torre Nova, cf. *plate 9*, a libation is poured over meat which is being roasted over the burning altar.

[such] a sacrifice' (ibid.).[54] Given the plausibility of Burkert's suggestions, it still begs the question whether this sacrifice was thought to relate the fate of the *mustēs* to that of Kore or to that of the 'burning child', or, perhaps, to both. Having said that, I find the assumptions a bit far-fetched. Why the double sacrifice of a substituted animal? And why is it that the Roman reliefs show only the remains of the ram, while they show the actual process of sacrificing the pig? In itself the act of killing in honour of the Eleusinian goddesses included a manipulation of mortality, a control over life and death, which was probably thought of as significant and somehow related to other uses of the fire. A further conclusion, I would not wish to make.

As for the content and chronology of mystic events between the first and the second night of initiation, we know very little for certain. For instance, what about the 'sacred encounters' between the hierophant and the priestess which Asterius, the Bishop of Amaseia in Asia Minor, said took place in the Eleusinian Katabasion? According to Asterius' account, the torch fires were extinguished during this 'sacred marriage'[55] (*hieros gamos*) and the initiates were left in the dark believing that their 'salvation' (τήν σωτηρίαν) might depend on what went on between the two.[56] Although it would be unwise, I think, to dismiss the notion of 'hieros gamos' as applicable to one or other of the ritual events, we cannot know when and how these events were supposed to take place.[57] What perhaps

54. Further, the decorations at the corners of the Telesterion were ram's heads (cf. ibid.) and on the Roman relief we find a ram's horns depicted at the heels of the initiate, cf. *plate 8 + 9*.
55. The expression is Burkert's, cf. 1983, 284, but 'hieros gamos', which is the Greek equivalent, is generally used as a term for an intimate encounter in mystery cult.
56. Cf. Asterius Hom.10, Migne.
57. While Foucart puts some faith in Asterius' late testimony, 1914, 479 f.; 495 f., Mylonas denies its validity on the grounds that there is no archaeological evidence of a Katabasion, by which Asterius must have meant a subterranean chamber, 1972, 314; likewise Kerényi, 1962, 110. Whether by Katabasion the bishop could perhaps also have alluded to the Plutonion outside the Telesterion (also denied by Mylonas, ibid., n.74), or to a 'bridal chamber' (παστάς), like the one used in other mysteries as, for instance, the Anatolian cult of Demeter (cf. Clement, *Protr.*, 2.14) or the Orphic cult of Ge in Phlya (cf. Harrison, 1903, 535, n.3) or even to the Anaktoron, the private chamber of the hierophant, does not concern us here, but Mylonas' refusal may, in any case, be too hasty, cf. Harrison, op.cit. 536; Deubner, 1909, 85, and Burkert, 1983, 282 f.; 284, n.47. Even if there was no exact room or space into which the couple were literally 'descending', 'the darkness of the sealed room may well have evoked a sense of nearness to Hades', as pointed out by Burkert, op.cit. 280. If any notion, or exact enterprise, of katabasis was relevant to the Eleusinian Mysteries, which some testimonies actually suggest (cf. Luc. *Cat.*22; and further Foucart, 1914, 401), it would, however, have been likely to include not only the priest and priestess but the initiates

can be said is that the confrontation between male and female sexuality, anticipated already in the disclosure of the chest, produced a divine child with whom the *mustēs* was somehow associated or related. Thematically, however, this takes us as far as the *epopteia* and presumably therefore up to the second and final night of initiation.

This must have been the night in which the initiates were left in utter darkness, exposed to frightening effects - including a disquieting noise[58] - until a 'marvellous light' (θαυμάσιος φῶς) shone forth (cf. Plut. *Fr.*178).[59] This light probably came from the fire that the hierophant had made in the Anaktoron and now exposed to the blinking eyes of the initiates by opening the door to the surrounding hall of the Telesterion?[60] In the glow of the fire, the hierophant

as well. The Telesterion, closed to anyone but the *mustai* and the mystagogues, might have been immediately suggestive of the underworld.

58. Cf. Plut. *Moralia* 943c; see the comment in Graf, 1974, 133 f.; 137. Perhaps this θόρυβος had its parallel somehow in the Corybantic rites at the initiatory cave, cf. above p.125. Somebody, probably the mystagogues, thus scared the *mustai* in order to keep them awake; see the suggestions in Burkert, 1987, 93. If we take the figure of Iacchus in E.*Ion* 1074 ff., to be representative of the role of the initiate (which the comparison between LSCG 15.42 and Clem.Al. *Protr.*2.18 may entitle us to), then 1077 could very well point to this part of the rite. Similar initiatory methods are known from various primitive societies, cf. Eliade, 1958, 31 f.; 35; see also Schjødt, 1992, 11, as for a phenomenological typology. It is also worth mentioning that, when Timarchus was descending into the oracular crypt of Trophonius, 'his first experience was of profound darkness; next, after a prayer, he lay a long time not clearly aware *whether he was awake or dreaming* (εἴτ' ἐγρήγορεν εἴτε ὀνειροπολεῖ). It did seem to him, however, that at the same moment he heard a crash and was struck on the head, and the sutures parted and released his soul' (*Moralia*, 590b); compare thus this death-metaphor with the cases of asphyxia, in Plut. *Moralia*, 563d, and Pl.*R.*614 ff., which are, reversely, suggestive of initiatory experience. The connection between darkness, death, initiation and sleep is, moreover, explicitly stated in Plut.*Fr.*178, which describes it as the context of the release of the soul; compare further with the similarity of the interrelated representations of death, sleep and darkness in Homer, cf. above p.75, n.22; p.79, n.35; p.91.
59. Compare also Plut.*Them.*15.1.119d and Ar.*Ra.*155; further the 'πολλῷ πυρὶ' in Hippol. *Haer.*5.8; as for the comparable mysteries of Isis, see Apul.*Met.*11.23 (p.285), in which the initiate declares that 'about midnight I saw the sun brightly shine' (nocte media uidi solem candido coruscantem lumine); and the comments in Graf, 1974, 131 ff. We can thus quite safely assume that the effect produced by the sudden disclosure of a source of light was a traditional element in the Mysteries, most probably in the night of *epopteia*.
60. Cf. Plut.*Moralia* 81e, compared with IG II/III^{2} 3764; 3811; see further Burkert, 1983, 276, n.8; 291, n.82.

allegedly showed an ear of corn,[61] representing either the life of the new-born child, called by the name of Plutus or Brimus (cf. Richardson, 1974, 28; Burkert, 1983, 289 f.), or the life of the daughter returning from the world of darkness (cf. Otto, 1955, 332 ff.; Kerényi, 1967, 96 ff.). If, however, the return of Kore was announced by the Hierophant's stroke on a bronze gong, as reported by Apollodorus of Athens (*FGrHist* 244 F 110),[62] we should not forget that the crucial demonstration (*deiknymena*) seems to have happened in total 'silence' (σιωπῇ).[63] The *mustēs* (take it to be a boy here) became an *epoptēs* after having simply experienced with his own two eyes the vision of 'the holy' in front of him. What he saw, we cannot know for sure. Yet, that Persephone, the female child, must have played a central role in this event, remains, I believe, beyond any doubt. Being not only the one who returns to the surface of the earth, but also the one who must descend periodically below it, as Queen of the Underworld, she combines as well as separates *the light and the dark*. Perhaps, what the *epoptai* were then made to believe, was that this 'double' had its equivalent in some way to the fate of human beings. Whether or not there was any independent revelation of Persephone's return from the void of darkness, it may have been parallelled by, or even involved in, a similar returning of the initiates,[64] if we accept that they themselves were suffering a katabasis. Actually, we have several indications that the process of mystery initiation was indeed experienced as a journey through the realm of darkness.[65] Hence, it is reasonable to think of the initiates as *psuchai* who 'went down' like Kore to confront the invisible reality of Hades.[66] Subsequently then, by illuminating this realm of darkness, and thereby

61. See in this respect, Hippol. *Haer.*5.8 (p.162, 59), and his use of the word θαυμαστός in relation to the ear of corn. See Burkert, 1983, 290 f.
62. Compare Pi.*I.*7.3; E.*Hel.*1346.
63. Cf. Plut. *Moralia* 81e; Hippol.*Haer.*5.8 (p.162, 60); Tert.Valent. 1 (p.541); Clem.Al.*Protr.*2.19; compare h.Hom.2.478 f., which opts for understanding this silence as being equal to the *arrhēton*, the taboo on talking about the holy revelation.
64. Cf. Strabo, 10.3.9: 'the secrecy with which the sacred rites are concealed induces reverence for the divine, since it imitates the nature of the divine, which is to avoid being perceived by our human senses' (ἡ κρύψις ἡ μυστικὴ τῶν ἱερῶν σεμνοποιεῖ τὸ θεῖον, μιμουμένη τὴν φύσιν αὐτοῦ φεύγουσαν ἡμῶν τὴν αἴσθησιν).
65. Cf. above, n.57 and Plut.*Fr.*178.
66. Cf. Eliade, 1958, 16: 'Darkness is a symbol of the other world [...] the world of death', and his account of the Eleusinian death-symbolism specifically, op.cit. 110 ff.; compare especially Plut.*Fr.*178; however, Eliade seems to conflate the semantic relationship between, on the one hand, darkness, katabasis and death, with, on the other, the general phenomenological suggestion that 'there is always the idea of a death to the profane condition', op.cit.15. True, the initiate has departed from his former status in life and society, but the *imitatio mortis* of mystery initiation should not be taken in any

supplanting it, a final exposition of 'the great fire' (cf. ὑπὸ πολλῷ πυρί) (which had been used earlier in a manipulation of mortality, cf. above p.186) marked the anabasis and survival (which I take to be suggestive of each other) of the initiates, as well as of Kore. Thus, in Aristophanes' *The Frogs*, we hear the chorus sing:

Now haste we to the roses,
And the meadows full of posies,
Now haste we to the meadows
  In our own old way,
In choral dances blending,
In dances never ending,
Which only for the holy
  The Destinies (Μοῖραι) *array*
O, happy mystic chorus, (ὅσοι μεμυήμεθα)
The blessed sunshine (ἥλιος) *o'er us*
On us alone is smiling,
  In its soft sweet light:
On us who strove for ever
With holy, pure endeavour,
Alike by friend and stranger
  To guide our steps aright (*Ra*.449-459)

The expression in verse 455, μόνοις γὰρ ἡμῖν ἥλιος ('the sun for us alone'), refers to the status of the initiated as compared to that of the uninitiated. Although Aristophanes is probably speaking of the Lenaean rituals, he provides a context of initiatory dances in the meadows, which might have applied just as well to the Great Eleusinia.[67] In Pindar, *Fr*.129+130, we find a similar reference to the light of the sun, shining exclusively for the just and purified souls, and, what is more, 'it shines for them in the night below[M]' (τοῖσι λάμπει τὰν νύκτα κάτω), namely 'in the meadows red with roses' (φοινικορόδοις ἐν λειμώνεσσι).[68] The underworld sun is a familiar theme of esoteric or mystic topography,[69] and this

metaphorical, but rather in a literal, albeit ritual, sense, see above p.145.

67. Cf. Graf, 1974, 43. Compare further *Ra*.145-60 with Plut.*Fr*.178, and above, p.135 f.
68. Further, in the *Argonautica* of Apollonius, Aethalides, the son of Hermes, is granted 'eternal memory' (μνῆστιν ἄφθιτον, A.R.1.643 f.), in contrast to κλέος ἄφθιτον (*Il*.9.413), and thus for him the sun will always shine, A.R. 1.643 ff. In the context of Orphic discourse this implies immortality; compare also Apul.*Met*. 11.23 (p.285); 11.24 (p.286), which support the suggestion that the mysteries of Isis were to some extent modelled on the Eleusinian Mysteries, cf. Burkert, 1987, 97 f.
69. See especially Kingsley, 1995, 51 f., on this point, and compare, for instance, Plut.*Fr*.178 with Plut.*Them*.15.119d.

may even have been the kind of sun Orpheus was believed to worship,[70] related, as it might have been, to the Thracian sun-gods, Zalmoxis and Sabazios (the Thracian-Phrygian name of Dionysus) who were a source of influence behind Orphism as well as of Greek mystery cults in general.[71] A similar theme may be found in Egyptian mythology insofar as the Egyptian sun-god survives the journey through the underworld at night to rise anew on the horizon in the morning.[72] In fact, Horus, the offspring of Osiris and Isis, was associated with this morning sun as being 'a child of light',[73] which may further tempt us to regard the ancient identification of the pair, Dionysus and Demeter, with the pair, Osiris and Isis - together, of course, with their divine child - as being actually due to one overall, Mediterranean 'mythology' of regeneration. Compare thus the procession from Athens to Eleusis,[74] accompanied by torches[75] and the ritual cries of ἴακχ'ὦ ἴακχε (cf. Ar.*Ra*.316 f.; Hdt.8.65), in which, Iacchus, according to Aristophanes, represents 'the light-bringing star of nightly initiation' (νυκτέρου τελετῆς φωσφόρος ἀστήρ (*Ra*.342)![76] Now, Plutus (the child-god of 'wealth') was also associated with a star and was called the truest light of men (cf. Richardson, 1974, 318, ad h.Hom.2.489). In other words, 'the divine child' of the Eleusinian Mysteries was, as Richardson puts it, identified 'with the light itself' (op.cit. 28).[77] However, insofar as Aristophanes and others were apparently free to allude to this, it could not in itself have denoted a central part of what was considered as being *aporrhēton*. Rather, it was the precise nature of

70. See Macr.1.23.22.
71. See especially Thomsen, 1949, 128; Pettazone, 1954, 84 ff.; Voigt, *Roscher*, I.1, 1031 f.; Toepffer, 1889, 31 f.; Linforth, 1918, 23-33; Eliade, 1983, 151. See further Strabo, 7.3.5, for the legendary connection between Zalmoxis and Pythagoras.
72. See further Pettazzoni's account of the widespread, and eschatologically significant, theme of the underworld journey of the sun, 1954, 92 f.
73. See, for example, RÄR, 309.
74. From Classical Times there was a Iaccheion in Athens, from which a wooden icon of Iacchus was fetched and brought to Eleusis together with the *hiera* from the Athenian Eleusinion; see in this respect Rohde, 1925, I, 284; Graf, 1974, 49, n.43.
75. Kerényi offers an etymological interpretation of the name *Iakchos* which is at least worth considering here, namely that it is related to the fire of sacrifice by the Cretan *i-wa-ko,* 1976, 77.
76. See especially Kerényi, 1976, 78, and Richardson, 1974, 27 f., who are probably right in regarding this motif as pivotal to the secret context of the Mysteries, albeit represented in an official and therefore inadequate way.
77. The Christian parallel to this symbolism is well-known, and emanated from the mouth of Jesus, according to John: '*I am the light of the world* ('Εγώ εἰμι τὸ φῶς τοῦ κόσμου), whoever follows me will never walk in darkness but will have the light of life', John 8.12; likewise, 1.5; 9; 9.5; 12.46.

relations between the gods and goddesses at work *in* the mystery proper, and, most importantly, their significance *in and for* the very act of *epopteia,* that was taboo. My suggestion is that the birth of a divine child, concomitant with the reappearance of Kore, formed a central part of this taboo, and that the genetic as well as amorous relations on the part of the divinities involved constituted an important background for appreciating this. Thus, we are brought back to the discursive implications of tradition which may be the only historically passable route into the core of the mystery.

XIV. Between Discourses

a. The relational structure of a secret

In the *Bacchanals*, Teiresias teaches Pentheus that in human life two powers are in command:

> [...] divine Demeter -
> Earth is she, name her by which name thou wilt; -
> She upon dry food nurtureth mortal men:
> Then followeth Semele's Son [Dionysus]; to match her gift
> The cluster's flowing draught he found, and gave
> To mortals [...] (E.*Ba*. 275-80)

Short of an explicit relationship between these 'powers', Demeter and Dionysus, the tradition of the Eleusinian Mysteries nevertheless indicates its presence in a number of ways. One instance can be found in the Homeric hymn. After having turned down a cup of wine - arguing that it is improper for her - Demeter instructs Iambe and Metaneira to prepare a draught which contains barley meal (h.Hom.2.207-9). Hence, by this gesture Demeter can be seen to oppose her own attributive element, the barley, to that of Dionysus, i.e., the wine. In the context of concrete ritual, namely on the last day of the festival in Eleusis, the cry of ὕε - κύε, meaning 'flow' and 'conceive',[1] indicates a similar double of 'wet' and 'dry' (cf. E.*Ba*.275-80 above). It is probable that the heavenly rain was thereby evoked to meet the fertility of the ground, suggestive perhaps of intercourse between the male and the female god. In the Orphic hymn, Baubo reveals in her bosom the infant Iacchus, identified, in Classical times, with Dionysus.[2] Whether or not the birth of Dionysus, or perhaps of Iacchus, was associated with the preceding Lesser Mysteries,[3] the motif as such may have been significant at some point in

1. See especially Kerényi, 1967, 141 f.; Burkert, 1983, 293, n.89.
2. Cf. S.*Ant*. 1115 ff.; E. *Ion* 1074 f. *Ba*. 725. Iacchus also shares with Dionysus the tauromorphic aspect, cf. Graf, 1974, 51, n.5; iconographic correspondences, op.cit. 61. As for a general view of Iacchus as 'die eleusinische Sonderform des Dionysos', ibid., n.10a; Burkert, 1983, 279, n.23; further Strabo who reports him to be 'the first leader of the mysteries and the daemon of Demeter[M]', 10.3.10, and the Orphic Hymn, 42, in which Dionysus is called 'redeeming Iacchus' (λύσειος Ἴακχος, 2-4). In Orphic mythology, Iacchus occurs as the name of the child of Zeus and Persephone, Kerényi, 1951, 237; Graf, op.cit. 75, n.57.
3. Cf. St.Byz. s.v. Ἄγρα, commented by Graf, 1974, 68; see also Deubner, 1909, 70. These Mysteries (*ta mikra*) took place at Agrai near Athens and were possibly held in honour of Dionysus, whereas the Greater Mysteries (*ta megala*) were held in honour of Demeter

the course of Eleusinian initiation. As a matter of comparison, Clement intriguingly refers, in his account of the Anatolian Mysteries of Demeter, to the Orphic theogony, where Zeus impregnates Demeter with Persephone,[4] and later Persephone with the tauromorphic Dionysus.[5] Clement adds with contempt that by meeting her in the form a 'snake' (δράκων), Zeus thus reveals his true nature (cf. ὅς ἦν, ἐλεγχθείς, *Protr.* 2.14).

Notwithstanding his moral judgement, Clement may be partly right. Do we not sense a pulse of extension and contraction in these shifting identities of the gods? Zeus and Dionysus are united in Zagreus, in Kabiros, in the Great Youth (*megistos kouros*), appearing as the snake and the bull in perpetual metamorphosis. The divine daughter is separated from her mother, yet reunited with her in Eleusis, even perhaps to the extent that they assume the position of one and the same goddess, as Kerényi suggests (1941, 167 f.).[6] A pair of gods, announced in the anonymous form of τὼ θεώ,[7] or ὁ θεός and ἡ θεά,[8] were worshipped in Eleusis.[9] 'Man wußte sehr wohl', Nilsson writes, 'daß ὁ θεός Hades-Pluto und ἡ θεά Kore-Persephone war' (1955, 471). Yet can we really be so sure about that? May ὁ θεός not be suggestive also of Zeus and Dionysus and may ἡ θεά not be suggestive of Demeter as well as of Persephone? The 'continuity of being' as expressed through the presence of father-child/mother-

and Persephone. That some reference to the birth of Dionysus, or Iacchus, may have been a part of the Lesser Mysteries is suggested by various iconographic material. Graf discusses the matter at length, op.cit. 67 ff. (commenting especially on the *pelike* from Kerch, cf. Nilsson, 1955, plate 46), concluding that no secure correspondence between the motif of the birth of Orphic Dionysus-Zagreus, child of Persephone and Zeus, and the Lesser Mysteries can be established, op.cit. 77.

4. This genealogy also occurs in the Orphic version of the Demeter-myth, *Orph.Fr.*49.18; Foucart takes the hypothetic 'hieros gamos' of the mystery night to symbolize the intercourse between Zeus and Demeter, 1914, 475.
5. Cf. above, p.123; an Orphic hymn (30.6-7) associates this 'unspeakable' (ἀρρήτος) union between Zeus and Persephone with the generation of Dionysus-Eubuleus (identified as Iacchus in *Orph.H.*42.2-4).
6. Kerényi cites the occurrence of the plural Δαμάτερες, referring to the two great goddesses of Eleusis, as an example, ibid.
7. Cf. Nilsson, 1955, 470.
8. IG II ^{2} 2047-48.
9. On the fragments of the Lakrateides' votive relief (cf. Kerényi, 1967, 153) from the 1[rst] Century BC, the inscriptions, ΘΕΩΙ and ΘΕΑΙ, denoting dedications to a male and a female god, both unnamed, are still legible. (On the left side of the pair, Triptolemus and Pluto are named); see also Mylonas, 1961, 238. As for similar inscriptions on the Lysimachides relief, see Thönges-Stringaris, 1965, 53 + Beilage 14, 2 (156); Nilsson, 1955, plate 39, 3. The anonymous dedications may very well demonstrate the *aporhetic* significance of the Eleusinian 'pair of gods', cf. Kanta, 1979, 59.

child, is that not the continuity in which mortals also have their lot?

Referring to the festival of Lenaea, Heraclitus claims that Hades and Dionysus are one and the same god (B 15 DK). The Orphic *Book of Hymns* presents a phonetic link between Eubulus, which is a name for Hades (or Pluto, *Orph.H.*18.12), and Eubuleus, which is a name for Dionysus (*Orph.H.*19.8; 30.6; 42.2). Futhermore the name of Pluto (cf. *Orph.H.*18) is inevitably associated with Plutus, Demeter's Cretan child (cf. Hes.*Th.*966-72; *Od.*5.125 ff.), who is, as we have seen, highly significant in the Eleusinian context as well (cf. h.Hom.2.489).[10] Here, the child of wealth (Plutus), the child of strength (Brimus),[11] and the child of light (Iacchus) may be several aspects of one and the same, namely the son of Demeter *as well as the son of Persephone* (cf. Arr.*An.*2.16.3).[12] In other words, Dionysus is significantly present, while at the same time not directly spoken of, as a child in Eleusinian initiation.

Apart from being closely associated with the new born child, Dionysus is also associated with the King of Death. Yet it seems as if the latter, Pluto or Eubulus, is transformed into the former, Plutus and Eubuleus, through several instances of sexual intercourse by which Hades is in turn associated with Zeus.[13] In Homeric discourse, Zeus remains Olympic while approving of Hades' chthonic intervention. In Orphic discourse, on the other hand, Zeus couples with Demeter, and subsequently with Persephone, in his own chthonic epiphany as a snake. The outcome of these chthonic encounters, both Orphic and Homeric, is the

10. See especially Richardson, 1974, ad loc. (316 ff.), and above, p.185; 188; 190.
11. See Foucart, 1975, 479; Burkert, 1983, 289, n.73. Brimo, the mother of Brimus (cf. Hippol.Hear.5.8), is not only one of Demeter's many names in the mystery cult (cf. Clem.Al.*Protr.*2.13), it also occurs as a name of Persephone and Hecate, cf. *Roscher*, I.1, 820 (Roscher); Kerényi, 1962, 99; Burkert, 1983, 289, n.77.
12. Further references *Roscher* II.1 2-3 (Stoll); Burkert, 1983, 289, n.72; and above, p.192, n.2. On a *pelike* from Kerch (cf. Nilsson, 1955, plate 46), the birth of Dionysus is depicted as a counterpart to the birth of Plutus. More important, however, they are thematical correlates, see also above p.185. See Deubner, 1909, 85; as for other similarities, Cook, *Zeus*, III, 84, Abb.27; see also comments in Graf, 1974, 67 ff. Thus, while Eubuleus - associated with Iacchus - identifies the child of Persephone (*Orph.H.*30.6-7; 42.2-4), Eubulus identifies the child of Demeter (*Orph.H.*41.8), also associated with Iacchus (S.*Ant.*1115; Str.10.3.10).
13. This is, for instance, suggested in the scholion on Pl.*Grg.*497c, ap. Foucart, 1975, 475, n.2. The mythologem of abduction further shows a frequent correspondence between Hades and Zeus, cf. Sowa, 1984, 138. They are even identified in a fragment by Euripides, ap. Clem.Al.Str.688 (= E.*Fr.* 912 N); cf. Harrison, 1961, 480; Pluto is praised as the chthonic form of Zeus in *Orph.H.* 18.3; 41.7, and while Eubulus may be used rather exclusively of Hades, Eubuleus, which is one of Dionysus' appellatives, is used of the chthonic Zeus, Farnell, 1921, 3, 144; Mylonas, 1961, 238.

generation of new life. This, I believe, was in all its simplicity the crucial motif which the Eleusinian tradition adopted, the motif that was symbolized by the ear of corn: *life from death*, the seed from the dark, growing into the world of light.[14]

Thus, it is tempting to suggest that the Eleusinian mystery cult was basically a manifestation of the 'cycle of births', not necessarily in the sense of metempsychosis, but in the sense of life's ongoing generation. The perspective of Orphic myth, however, allows for another interpretation. Zeus and Demeter beget a daughter, with whom the father begets a son. The succession is like a reproduction of the divine pair itself,[15] and their union does not so much generate the new life of independent beings but rather multiplies the aspects of those who *are* already - as well as the relations between them. The male god comes to carry the aspects of both father and son,[16] while the female god comes to carry the aspects of mother and daughter.[17] Interrelatedly, the chthonic Zeus is associated with the underworld king as well as with the divine child, for whom Demeter and Kore, transformed into an underworld queen, share the role of nurse.[18] Thus, in the mythologem of the Orphic nurse, holding Iacchus in her bosom, we may see the most crucial Orphic impact on the Eleusinian Mysteries: *Baubo the nocturnal daemon*.

It is exactly the revelation of this motif that is absent from Homeric discourse. The chthonic mediation between life and death, fulfilling for the individual initiate the continuity of being, is precisely, and more or less exclusively, part of Orphic theology. From the Homeric perspective, the initiation at Eleusis rather concerned the cycle of life and death, the collective dimension of genetic continuity. The jesting of Iambe, alluding perhaps to diction mediating the dimension of epic fame, is opposed to the disclosure of Baubo's bosom, as the

14. Thus, Demeter's intercourse with Iason, impregnating her with Plutus, took place in 'the thrice-ploughed fallow' (νειῷ ἔνι τριπόλῳ, Hes.*Th.*971).
15. Thus, in Orphic discourse, Zeus, the begetter, is the beginning and end of everything. This, the initiate must remember, cf. above p.124 f.
16. See above, p.122 f.; 166.
17. As for the regeneration of Demeter herself, Kerényi writes: 'Die Göttin wird Mutter, sie zürnt und trauert wegen der Kore, die ihr aus ihrem eigenen Wesen geraubt wurde, und die sie zugleich auch wiedererhält - in der sie sich selbst wiedergebiert. Die Idee der wurzelhaft-einen Urmutter-Urtochter-Göttin ist zugleich diejenige der Wiedergeburt', 1941, 174. Kore is also called *protogonos kourē*, 'the firstborn girl', Paus.4.1.8, by which name she parallels the Dionysus *Protogonos* of the Orphic theogonies.
18. In this motif, we may also notice a doubling of the same divinity that transcends the difference of sex insofar as we put faith in Hippolytus' rendering of the *legomena*: 'Βριμὼ Βριμόν', i.e., Demeter's [Brimo's] birth of the male child, Brimus.

voice is opposed to the body, as myth is to ritual. Still, neither Homer nor Orpheus won the monopoly of representing the tradition of Eleusis. As a discourse in its own right, myth as well as ritual, this tradition mediated not only between Olympic and chthonic powers, but between Homeric and Orphic discourse as well.

b. The Eleusinian eschatologies of Homer and Orpheus

In a way, the discourse of the Eleusinian mystery tradition was the discourse of no one but Demeter. Actually, she resembled the authority of Homeric poetry, or rather the Muse, by being the original communicator of tradition, and she resembled Orphic theology, or rather Orpheus himself, by specifically introducing rites of initiation. Yet Demeter installed no single, mediating author to represent her discourse as being a legitimate one. She revealed her mysteries to Triptolemus, Eumolpus and various others, but not to any one author beyond the scope of myth. Certainly, the family line of the Eumolpidae were continuously provided with the authority to exercise the duties of their ancestor, but not with the authority to speak of it. Indeed, tradition *was* spoken of and most importantly within the authorized frames of Homeric and Orphic discourse, but both groups of representatives were forbidden to openly reveal what was, in fact, experienced by thousands once a year. Being a discourse with no human voice at its centre, the mysteries of Demeter were dispersed in various contexts of representation, by which they reflected a complex of tradition that was itself being disseminated in opposing systems of authorial representation (as exemplified by the competing authorities of Homer and Orpheus). Each being an important contributor to the persistence of mystery initiation, none was empowered to possess and express the true content of revelation. While many a representative of tradition, as well as its later adversaries, each had a word to say, the final word rested on the lips of Demeter, and this was of necessity a word of silence. Ancient Greek religion seems to have drawn one of its last breaths in the dark room of Eleusis.

However, the Eleusinian cult was not, at least not primarily, a cult of the word, but a cult of 'the sight'. In the Homeric hymn this is stated as the issue that separates the initiated from the uninitiated:

> Happy (ὄλβιος) is he among men upon earth who has seen these mysteries; but he who is uninitiate and who has no part in them, never has lot of like good things once he is dead, down in the darkness and gloom. (h.Hom.2.480-82)

It seems to be implied by way of negation that the privilege of the initiate actually transcends the fate of death, namely insofar as he is blessed in a way that, in contrast to the uninitiated, will comfort him in the dark House of Hades.

Nothing, however, suggests immortality of the soul, let alone the condition of metempsychosis. One is forced to ask what else would immortality be if not this implied continuity of consciousness! However, the dead in the *Nekuia* as well as in the *Deutero-Nekuia* also exhibited signs of such mental continuity, but this continuity was confined to the memory of the individuals' lives and therefore, in a certain sense, defined as a strictly epic continuity (p.59). The composer of the Homeric hymn may have wanted to say something similar by way of a few, carefully-chosen words: The experience of the mysteries, including the climax of a wonderful vision, is precisely the 'part' that the initiate 'takes with him' to the grave (as opposed to the 'not partaking' (ἄμμορος, 481) of the uninitiated). In Homeric discourse, death reflects the wonder of life, if only by a vision of what lies beyond it. From the perspective of Homeric discourse, the Eleusinian *epopteia* probably framed and fulfilled this vision of life in the light of a divine presence. Still, the notion of life thus envisioned was more likely to be one of life 'surviving' in collective commemoration, and, of course, in generations to come, than it was one of earthly life reduced to 'seeming'. Life viewed as a preamble to death which was, in turn, viewed as the essence of being, was far from the perspective of Homeric discourse, nor is anything of the kind suggested by the wording of the hymn.

A fragment of Pindar, however, offers a different approach:

> Blessed (ὄλβιος) is he who has seen these things (ἐκεῖνα)[19] before he goes beneath the hollow earth; for he grasps the end of life (οἶδεν μὲν βιότου τελευτὰν) in apprehension of the god-given beginning (οἶδεν δὲ διόσδοτον ἀρχάν)[M]. (Pi.*Fr.*137)

These lines speak not only of the privilege of 'having seen' (ἰδὼν) but also of having insight (cf. οἶδεν). The initiate has seen for himself that life is an 'image' (εἴδωλων) 'that remains alive, for it alone cometh from the gods' (ζωὸν λείπεται αἰῶνος· τὸ γὰρ ἐστι μόνον ἐκ θεῶν , *Fr.*131b). So far, Pindar's statement looks more like an interpretation of Homeric eschatology than a denial of it, but the important change of perspective appears in comparison with fragment 137 insofar as 'the end of life' or 'that which remains *alive* or *everlasting* (αἰῶν)' is recognized as a 'god-given beginning'. The important point about this phrasing is that it does not seem to draw its inspiration from the context of Homeric discourse. In fact, it is Alcmaeon, who provides us with the closest parallel by saying, according to Aristotle, that men 'die because they cannot connect the beginning with the end' (ἀπόλλυσθαι, ὅτι οὐ δύνανται τὴν ἀρχὴν τῷ τέλει προσάψαι, Arist. *Pr.*916a35 = Alkmaion B 2 DK). The dominant discursive

19. The ἐκεῖνα undoubtedly refers to the Mysteries of Eleusis.

context, within which such eschatology was formulated, was, as we have seen (cf. above p.124 ff.; 139 f.) the tradition of Orpheus. Death is seen not merely as a memorized repetition of a life once lived, but rather contains the principle of life which, cleansed of earthly existence, begins again in the realm of the beyond. Initiated into this knowledge, the soul *does not die* in the epic sense of wandering off to the House of Hades, cooled by the spring of 'forgetfulness', but ends the cycle of *life as death*, drinking the pure water of 'memory', which connects this end with a new beginning. That Pindar was not unfamiliar with such an eschatology is further indicated, I would say, by his reference to the redemption from metempsychosis in the second *Olympic Ode*, 2.68 ff., in which context he speaks of ψυχή as the continuous, and obviously autonomous principle of life that survives death on an individual level.[20] Thus Pindar, who can neither be reduced to a voice of Homeric nor Orphic discourse, nevertheless serves as a link between Homeric and Orphic eschatology.

Returning to the specific context of Eleusis, we might take note of what Burkert has regarded as a paradox, namely that

> in the perspective of 'religions of salvation', concern and doctrines about the soul should be the very centre of interest; yet in the evidence there is hardly even a faint indication of this, whether in the mysteries of Eleusis, Dionysos, Meter, Isis or Mithras. Ancient mysteries were a personal, but not necessarily a spiritual, form of religion. (1987, 86 f.)

Surely, Burkert is correct in saying that we do not find any such doctrine.[21] The question is, however, whether we should expect to find one, and also, what exactly Burkert means by 'a spiritual form of religion'. If, by spiritual, Burkert simply refers to a constituent concern for the fate of ψυχή, then at least Orphism was spiritual. As for the religious tradition of Eleusis, I agree, we find no independent evidence of that. However, the characteristic feature of the Eleusinian Mysteries was exactly that, while independent of any other authorization than their own, they depended heavily on representation by

20. Compare the fragment of Sophocles, 753 N ap. Richardson, 1974, 311, in which 'the thrice blessed' (τρισόλβιοι) among mortals are contrasted with the rest who can expect nothing but evil things after death. The number 3 may remind us of esoteric numerology as related to metempsychosis, cf. above p.127, especially Pi.O.2.68 ff. Yet, there is not much to qualify in what way and to what extent Sophocles might have shared a view of eschatology associated herewith, and although he may indeed have been influenced by Orphic discourse, as we know Pindar was, we shall not pursue the matter any further here.
21. However, some indication, albeit late, of the implicit importance of the notion of ψυχή is found in Procl. *in R*.2, 108. 17-20: συμπαθείας (αἱ τελεταὶ) εἰσὶν αἴτιαι ταῖς ψυχαῖς περὶ τὰ δρώμενα ('the initiations make the souls sympathize with the ritual acts').

others. Therefore, the question that may be asked of mystery cults in general, may also, in the specific context of Eleusis, be asked of the different contributors to its eschatology, in which case we end up with different answers. My point is that the significant silence of Eleusis provided room for such heterogeneity.

So there *was*, and there *was not*, a spiritual concern at stake in the Eleusinian Mysteries, and although the initiation was certainly a personal matter for each of the initiates, it may be fair to say that the ritual processes both *were*, and *were not*, a 'personal form of religion'. With regard to the Homeric discourse, the unavoidable death and everlasting honour of Demophoön was indeed the fate of one person, yet it also signified what we may call a 'collective form of religion', not only by referring to the context of the Eleusinian hero-cult, which was thereby given a Panhellenic voice, but also by referring to the context of the mysteries in the light of notions such as 'mortality' and 'glory'. From the viewpoint of the hymn, participation in the mysteries *was* a personal comfort, it was a wondrous vision which probably gave some substance to the divine character of the memory image, implicated as it may have been by the envisioned exchangeability of sleep and death. Yet nothing suggests that this 'psychic' substance continued a 'new life' of its own after death. The privilege of the initiate was to behold the divine condition of continuity, namely that nothing simply disappears. However, this might not mean anything save that the initiated would never be forgotten, and probably also that the memory on the part of generations to come was in a certain sense, revealed in a silence of truth, conditional on the very cycle of life. Nothing in the Homeric representation forces the Eleusinian Mysteries into a category of 'personal religion'.

It is otherwise in the context of Orphic discourse. Here, Demophoön was not doomed to the general condition of mortal existence, but rather saved from it by a ritual of purification that was fulfilled. Killed by his divine nurse, Demophoön was initiated into a continuity of being that parallelled the fate of the divine child, Iacchus or Dionysus. Demophoön *became* a divine child, and from the viewpoint of Orphic discourse, the Eleusinian *mustēs* was inclined to believe the same of himself. In Orphic discourse, mystery initiation was indeed a matter of 'personal religion'.

Conclusion

By emphasizing the discrepancy between the Homeric and the Orphic notion of ψυχή as central to the general and profound difference between a negative and a positive eschatology, it may seem that I have created a puzzle rather than solved one. So be it. The aim has been to get behind imposed stereotypes of religious beliefs. Hopefully, the selected studies of Homeric, Orphic and Eleusinian discourse have provided us with some idea of how different, yet also interrelated, various attitudes towards death seem to have been in Ancient Greece. As suggested from the beginning, these attitudes - as well as the relationship between them - can be viewed as deriving their structure both from imitation as well as opposition, and they seem to have evolved (to the extent of their exhaustion) due partly to external changes, partly to the internal work of religious tradition permeated as it was with - what one might be inclined to think of as - an agonistic mentality of the Greeks. However, it would not be fair to leave the perspective of discontinuity completely unmitigated by those traces of semantic continuity that certainly appear as well. How explanatory they are, I am not sure. Yet my suggestion is that insofar as this study has made them emerge above the heterogeneity of the texts, they may also have been actively present in antiquity, if not as a matter of conscious beliefs, then as a rule of discursive potentials. But what were these elements that combined the attitudes to afterlife in a chain of transformation leading from a negative to a positive concern? What were the limits, τὰ ἔσχατα, to which the changing of interpretation was attached?

For a start, we may suppose the chthonic twins of Sleep (*Hypnos*) and Death (*Thanatos*) to have been significant.[1] As we recognize them in the dominant mythologies of Homer and Hesiod they inhabit two neighbouring realms in the world beyond. In the *Iliad* they even make their visits to the world of mortals *together*. Thus, Hypnos is not only present when sleep occurs, but in the event of death as well.[2] The eschatological significance of this may become even clearer when compared to another, closely-related level of epiphany, on which we find the encounter between the dream (or the psyche) and the mortal person. Being

1. I am aware that this suggestion and the following extrapolations may bear some resemblance to the view of E.B. Tylor. See, however, p.44 f., for a critique of his arguments.
2. As is depicted, for example, in several vase paintings where the two brothers are about to carry a deceased youth away, cf. Pestalozzi, 1945, plate 37; plate 88; *LIMC* V² 248.593, V¹, ad loc.; VII² 617.15, VII¹, ad loc. Cf. also above, p.90, n.3.

individual representations of the realms of Hypnos and Thanatos, the dream and the psyche are, in turn, representative of different individual protagonists, comprising the categories of the immortals and the departed mortals. Coinciding as this overlapping is with the instantiation of epiphany, the epiphany coincides itself with the ritualized encounter between the level of mortality and the level of immortality. This may be the basic line of eschatology that, being already present in the discourse of Homer, inhabits the roots of what was to become a belief in immortality in the discourse of Orpheus. Yet in Homer, the relationship between the levels is not one of continuity but rather one of reflection, that is, of mutually exclusive reference. The visible and temporal world of mortality has its counterpart in the invisible and timeless world of the beyond, and it is from this world, accessed by the inspired state of poetic commemoration, that re-creation of the past takes place. Transformed into images of the lives they once lived, the dead are surrendered merely to the timeless fame of song. Thus being a mirror of life, the epic world is itself part of the beyond whence it defines life as the final and farthest limits of existence. In this sense, the eschatology of the Homeric epics is essentially a negative eschatology. Yet the narrative is also positively born from, as well as driven by, information from the beyond. As Homer receives knowledge from the Muses, so the heroes, Achilles and Odysseus, for example, receive knowledge from the dead. The end of life is an instance of spatial rather than temporal exclusion, or it is both, we might say, as two sides of the same coin, interconnected in the referential House of Hades, the real dwelling place of Homeric poetry itself.

This *other* world, present and repeatedly represented by a divine memory, is fostered behind the blind eyes of Homer and transmitted to the anonymous inspiration of subsequent singers. Initially authorized by the Muses, Homer becomes himself the authority for the repetition of song. And it is *his* memory, the memory of the dead (in both senses), that is challenged by the head of Orpheus which continues to sing even beyond the limits of death. Here, a crucial step is taken, on several interrelated levels, from the land of the living to the land of the dead. As Orpheus is born from a Muse, while not explicitly inspired by one, his first and most prominent successor even incorporates this very authority in his own name, Musaeus. In Orphic discourse, the relationship between mortals and immortals is one of continuity rather than one of reflection; hence the interest in representing hero-cults within the context of soteriological initiation, namely insofar as Homer's collectivized reflection of the vital image is here being confronted with the localized, and therefore individualized, preservation of the vital power itself.

In general, the notion of the hero was a notion of ambiguity. In the context of the cult of the dead, the deceased became potential objects of heroic adoration, associated with the vital power of the earth and thus even with some kind of immortality. Although this meaning potential of chthonic religion was indeed dissented from by way of neglect in the epic universe of Homer, neither were the Panhellenic heroes of the past merely ordinary mortals, nor were they in reality to be kept apart from extra-linguistic claims of descent. The exclusiveness of epic reference was always potentially challenged by reference to the ritualized and inhabited depths of the earth. The dead were represented, not merely by song, but also by the land. This was something which the Orphics apparently knew how to use to their advantage, shifting, for instance, the contact between the living and the dead from an extrinsic to an intrinsic dimension, focussing on actualization by doing, rather than by hearing. In this way, the commemoration of ancestors, or heroes, became a model for self-identification, as, for example, in the ritual of incubation where the relation between the dream and the psyche met a frame of interpretation that differed significantly from the orientation of the Homeric epics. Memory of the beyond was internalized, representing the pure and divine origin of ψυχή, now a principle of conscious continuity, capable of dreaming, that is, of gaining access to the beyond of its own accord. The initiated became a hero himself in the story of his own life. Yet the real life was due to the remembered state of origin, whereas life in the body was a sinful and unreal state of being that had to be washed away with the element that represented it, i.e., the mire of earthly existence. Thus, in an Orphic ritual which represented life as death and death as life, the initiate was being prepared to meet his or her physical death as the beginning of a new, purified state of being. In this sense, Orphic eschatology was a positive eschatology.

While the Olympic gods are predominant in the world of Homeric discourse, the chthonic powers are predominant in the world of Orphic discourse, demarcating a difference of orientation towards the epichthonic and the hypochthonic spheres of activity. However, the regenerative power of the earth was a source of influence that was, in turn, abandoned by the Orphics insofar as they offered a final redemption from the grievous cycle of life. It was otherwise in the chthonic tradition of Eleusis where Demeter and Kore, mother and daughter, were worshipped as a double goddess of the earth, representing the cycle of life. Developing from a cult of vegetation into a Panhellenic institution of mystery initiation it became profoundly involved in, while not reduced to, the competing traditions of Homeric and Orphic discourse. In the former, the goddesses were praised as embodying the balance between Olympic and chthonic powers under the sway of Zeus, whereas in the latter, they were active as autonomous chthonic nurses implementing the esoteric transformation from mortal to eternal life. However, if we are right in suggesting the presence of a secret and intimate relation between, on the one side, mother and daughter, and, on the other, father and son, this relation can be taken both ways, equally open as it might have been to symbolizing the cycle of generations and the continuity of individual being. What was commonly agreed upon, respecting the constraints of secrecy, was merely that the initiates improved their fate by experiencing the sacred. Whatever they got from the blind eyes of Homer or the singing head of Orpheus, the Eleusinian Mysteries made them *behold the end of life in silence*. In this legislated blind alley, with all internal differences resolving in the same darkness, ancient Greek religion took the final step beyond its own limits.

Technicalities

Greek words which also happen to be adopted by way of general convention will occasionally be given in idiomatic English, such as 'psyche' for ψυχή. Otherwise, transcriptions will follow the standard of *LS* and be marked by italics, which in this case would make *psuchē*.

When nothing else is mentioned, translations of Greek texts are taken from the latest edition of the *Loeb Classical Library* or of translations mentioned below in *Text editions*.

Quotations of ancient sources will be marked with an M when they represent modified versions of standard translations.

All abbreviations for ancient authors and works refer to the standards in *LS* and *OLD*. References to text editions which are not mentioned in *LS* or *OLD* are due to the index below.

Text editions

Arnobius = Arnobii Adversus Nationes, Libri VII, *Corpus Scriptorum Ecclesiasticorum Latinorum*, ed. A. Reifferscheid, Wien. 1875

Asius, *Fr.*, *Iambi et Elegi Graeci*, 2, ed. by M.L. West. Oxford. 1972

Asterius, Hom.10: *J.P. Migne, Patrologia Graeca* 40.324, ed. by C.Datema. Leiden. 1970

Clem.Al. *Strom.* = 'Stromata', ed.Stählin et al., *Die griechische christliche Schriftsteller*, 2. Leipzig. 1906

DK = Diels, Kranz: *Fragmente der Vorsokratiker*, red. og overs. af H.Diels & W.Kranz, I (1906), II[I] (1907), II[II] (1910), Berlin Koerte (Menander).

Emp. (Translation taken from G.S. Kirk, J.E. Raven & M. Schofield, 1983)

Euripides - Iphigenia in Tauris, ed. with intr. and com. by M. Platnauer. Oxford. 1967

Euripides - Alcestis/Hippolytus/Iphigenia in Tauris, transl. by Philip Vellacott, Penguin Classics 1974

Firmicus Maternus - L'erreur des Religions Païennes, ed. R. Turcan. Paris. 1982

Herodotus. The Histories. Trans. by A. de Sélincourt, rev. with intr. by A.R. Burn. London. 1972

Fragmenta Hesiodea, ed. by R. Merkelbach and M.L. West. Oxford: At The Clarendon Press 1967

Hom.Hes.Gen.Ag. = 'Of the Origin of Homer and Hesiod, and of their Contest', *Hesiod, The Homeric Hymns and Homerica*, Loeb

IEG = Iambi et Elegi Graeci II. Ante Alexandrum Cantati, ed. by M.L. West. Oxford 1972.

LSCG = *Lois Sacrées des Cités Grecques*, ed. by F. Sokolowski, Paris: Édition E. De Boccard, 1969

Heraclit. (Translation taken from K. Freeman,1952)

Nauck = *Tragicorum Graecorum fragmenta*, ed. by A. Nauck. Leipzig. 1889

The New Testament and other early Christian writings. Bart D. Ehrman, New York & Oxford, 1998

N.T. = *Novum Testamentum.*

*Orph.*A; B; P = Gold Lamellae (cf. the survey in Zuntz, 1971, 286, and Graf, 1993, 257-58); P1-2 refers to the edition in Graf, 1993, 241; B 10 refers to the edition in Cole, 1980, 225; otherwise, Zuntz, 1971, 300-348. Translation of *Orph.*A; B taken from K. Freeman, 1952. Other editions used: by G.P. Caratelli in 'Test e Monumenti', *La Parola Del Passato*, 29, Napoli, 1974; by B. Merkelbach in 'Bakchisches Goldtäfelchen aus Hipponion', *Zeitschrift für Papyrologie und*

Epigrafik (ZPE), 17, Bonn, 1975; by M.L. West in 'Zum neuen goldblättchen aus Hipponion' ZPE, 18, 1975, and F. Graf's translation in *Orpheus. Altgriechische Mysterien*, ed. by J.O. Plassmann, München, 1982, 168-69

Orph.Derv. = *Studies on the Derveni Papyrus*, ed. by A.Laks & G.W. Most. Oxford: Clarendon Press, 1997. *Col.*I-VII in reconstructed Greek (by Tsantsanoglou, 93-95); complete translation of columns I-XXVI, 10-22. All columns are also published in reconstructed Greek in ZPE 47, 1982

Orph.H. = *The Orphic Hymns*, ed. and translated by A.N. Athanassakis A.N, Missoula, Montana, 1977

Orph. Test. = Pars Prior Testimonia Potiora, p.1-79, *Orphicorum Fragmenta*, ed. by O. Kern,
Dublin & Zürich: Weidman. 1922

Pherecyd.Syr. (F, Schibli = *Pherecydes of Syros*. H.S. Schibli. Oxford: Clarendon Press, 1990)

PMG = *Poetae Melici Graeci*, ed. by D.L.Page. Oxford: Clarendon Press. 1962

Pseudo-Plato, Axiochus, ed. by J.P. Hershbell. Society of Biblical Literature: Texts and Translations, 21. Graeco-Roman Religion Series, 6. 1981: Michigan: Edwards Brothers

Xenocrates = *Xenokrates - Darstellung der Lehre und Sammlung der Fragmente*, ed. by R. Heinze. Leipzig. 1892

Tert. Valent. = Tertullianus, Liber Adversus Valentinianos, *Quinti Septimi Florentis Tertulliani - Opera Omnia*. II, Paris. 1844

Bibliography

Albinus, L. (1993) "Græsk shamanisme?" *Agora. Themata 6.* Institut for klassisk arkæologi og Institut for Oldtids- og Middelalderforskning.

Albinus, L. (1994) "Diskurs-begrebet i religionshistorisk kontekst - En nøgle til forståelse af religiøse transformationsprocesser i antikken", *Religionsvidenskabeligt tidsskrift*, 24. Aarhus, 13-38.

Albinus, L. (1997a) "Discourse Analysis within the Study of Religion - Processes of change in ancient Greece", *Method & Theory in the Study of Religion*, 9/3, 203-32.

Albinus, L. (1997b) *Oldgræsk dæmonologi fra beretning til begrundelse. En religionshistorisk undersøgelse*, Ph.D. Thesis, available at the Department of the Study of Religion, Faculty of Classics, University of Aarhus.

Albinus, L. (1998) "The Katabasis of Er", *Essays on Plato's Republic.* E.N. Ostenfeld (ed.). Aarhus Studies in Mediterranean Antiquity, vol. 2. Aarhus, 91-105.

Alexiou, M. (1974) *The Ritual Lament in Greek Tradition.* Cambridge.

Allen, T.W. (1924) *Homer: The Origins and the Transmission.* Oxford.

Allen, T.W. & Halliday, W.R. (1963) *The Homeric Hymns.* Oxford & Amsterdam.

Andronikos, M. (1968) *Totenkult.* Archaeologia Homerica, 3. Göttingen.

Ankermann, B. (1918) "Totenkult und Seelenglaube bei afrikanischen Völkern", *Zeitschrift für Ethnologie*, 50, 89-153.

Arbman, E. (1926-27) "Untersuchungen zur primitiven Seelenvorstellungen mit besonder Rücksicht auf Indien", *Le Monde Oriental*, I-II. Uppsala, 1924-28.

Athanassakis, A.N. (1977) *The Orphic Hymns.* Missoula, Montana.

Bakhtin, M. (1973) *Problems of Dostoevsky's Poetics.* Transl R.W. Rotsel. Ardis, US.

Bakhtin, M (1981) *The Dialogic Imagination.* M. Holquist & C. Emerson (eds. & transl.). Austin, Texas.

Bakhtin, M. (1994) The Bakhtin Reader. Selected writing of Bakhtin, Medvedev, Voloshniov, P. Morris (ed.). London.

Bengtson, H. (1960) *Griechische Geschichte.* München.

Bianchi, U. (1976) *The Greek Mysteries.* Iconography of Religions, XVII, 3. Leiden.

Bickel, E. (1926) *Homerischer Seelenglaube.* Schriften der Königsberger Gelehrten Gesellschaft. Berlin.

Bilde, P. (1990) "Paulus som mystiker", *Mystik - Den indre vej? En religionshistorisk udfordring.* P. Bilde & A. Geertz (eds.). Aarhus, 47-70.

Blinkenberg, Ch. (1919) *Hades' Munding.* Copenhagen.

Boas, F. (1940) *The Idea of Future Life among Primitive Tribes.* New York.

Bond, G.W. (1988) *Euripides - Heracles. Introduction & Commentary.* Oxford.

Bowra, C.M. (1964) *Pindar*. Oxford.

Boyancé, P. (1935) "Les Deux Démons Personnels dans l'Antiquité Grecque et Latine", *Revue de philologie, de litterature et d'histoire anciennes*, 9. Paris.

Bremmer, J. (1983) *The Early Greek Concepts of the Soul*. Princeton.

Bremmer, J. (1994) *Greek Religion*. Greece & Rome - New Surveys in the Classics, 24. Oxford.

Bruit Zaidman, L. & Schmitt Pantel, P. (1989) *Religion in the Ancient Greek City*. (Translated by P. Cartledge). Cambridge.

Burkert, W. (1960-61) "Elysion", *Glotta*, 39, 208-13.

Burkert, W. (1969) "Das Proömium des Parmenides und die Katabasis des Pythagoras", *Phronesis*, 14, 1-29. Bonn.

Burkert, W. (1972) *Lore and Science in Ancient Pythagoreanism*. Cambridge, Mass. (English edition, translated with revisions from *Weisheit und Wissenschaft: Studien zu Pythagoras, Philolaos und Platon*, Nürnberg, 1962).

Burkert, W. (1977) *Orphism and Bacchic Mysteries: New Evidence and Old Problems of Interpretation*. The Center for Hermeneutical Studies in Hellenistic and Modern Culture. Colloquy 28. Berkeley & California.

Burkert, W. (1983) *Homo Necans*. Berkeley, L.A. & London.

Burkert, W. (1985) *Greek Religion*. John Raffan (transl.). Cambridge, Mass.

Burkert, W. (1987) *Ancient Mystery Cults*. Cambridge, Mass. & London.

Burkert, W. (1993) "Bacchic Teletai in the Hellenistic Age", *Masks of Dionysos*, T.H. Carpenter & Ch.A. Faraone (eds.). Ithaca & London, 259-75.

Burkert, W. (1998) "Die neuen orphischen Texte: Fragmente, Varianten, 'Sitz im Leben'", *Fragmentsammlungen philosophischer Texte der Antike*. W. Burkert, et al. (eds.). Vandenhoeck & Ruprecht in Göttingen, 387-99.

Böhme, J. (1929) *Die Seele und Das Ich Im Homerischen Epos* (mit einem Anhang *Vergleich mit dem Glauben der Primitiven*). Leipzig & Berlin.

Böhme, J. (1935) "Hundt, Der Traumglaube bei Homer", *Gnomon*, 11, 466-73. Berlin.

Böhme, R. (1986) *Die Verkannte Muse*. Bern.

Calligas, P.G. (1986) *Early Greek Cult Practice*. Skrifter utgivna av Svenska Instituttet i Athen., 229-34.

Carpenter, R. (1933) "The Antiquity of the Greek Alphabet", *AJA*. 37, 8-29.

Carpenter, R. (1956) *Folk-Tale, Fiction and Saga in the Homeric Epic*. Berkeley.

Chantraine, P. (1964) *Homère: Iliade - Chant 23*. Paris.

Chantraine, P. (1968) *Dictionaire étymologique de la langue grèque - histoire des mots*. Paris.

Claus, D.B. (1981) *Toward the Soul: an inquiry into the meaning of psyché before Plato*. New Haven.

Clay, J.S. (1989) *The Politics of Olympus*. Princeton, N.J.
Clinton, K. (1974) "The Sacred Officials of the Eleusinian Mysteries", Transactions of the American Philosophical Society, 64/3.
Clinton, K. (1988) "Sacrifice at the Eleusinian Mysteries", *Early Greek Cult Practice*. Skrifter utgivna av Svenska Instituttet i Athen. Ed. R. Hägg, et al., 69-79.
Cole, S.G. (1980) "New Evidence for the Mysteries of Dionysos", *Greek, Roman and Byzantine Studies*, 21, 223-38.
Coldstream, N.J. (1976) "Hero-Cults in the age of Homer", *JHS*, 96, 8-17.
Coldstream, N.J. (1977) *Geometric Greece*. Cambridge.
Cook, A.B. (*Zeus*) *ZEUS - A Study in Ancient Religion*, i-II$^{1-2}$, Cambridge, 1914-40.
Cornford, F.M. (1912) *From Religion to Philosophy*. Cambridge [1991].
Cornford, F.M. (1957) *From Religion to Philosophy*. New York & Evanston.
Coxon, A.H. (1986) *The Fragments of Parmenides*. Assen & Maastricht.
Cunliffe, R.J. (1924) *A Lexicon of the Homeric Dialect*. Oklahoma, [1963].
Danforth, L.M. (1982) *The Death Rituals of Rural Greece*. Princeton, N.J.
De Waele, F.J.M. (1927) *The Magic Staff*. Gent.
Dietierich, A. (1913) *Nekyia - Beiträge zur Erklärung der Neuentdeckten Petrusapokalypse*. Leipzig & Berlin.
Detienne, M. (1963) *La notion de daïmôn dans le pythagorisme ancien*. Paris.
Detienne, M. (1977) *Dionysos mis à mort*. Gallimard.
Deubner, L. (1900) *De Incubatione*. Leipzig.
Deubner, L. (1909) *Attische Feste*. Hildesheim [New York 1969].
Dickinson, O. (1994) *The Aegean Bronze Age*. Cambridge.
Dietrich, B.C. (1967) *Death, Fate and The Gods*. London.
Dodds, E.R. (1951) *The Greeks and the Irrational*. London.
Douglas, M. (1966) *Purity and Danger. An analysis of the concepts of pollution and taboo*. London, [1991].
Dowden, K. (1989) *Death and the Maiden*. London & N.Y.
Dreyfus, H.L. & Rabinow, P. (1982) *Michel Foucault: Beyond Structuralism and Hermeneutics - With an afterword by Michel Foucault*. Brighton, Sussex.
Durkheim, E. (1912) *Les formes élémentaires de la vie religieuse*. [1960] Paris.
Ehnmark, E. (1948) "Some Remarks on the Idea of Immortality in Greek Religion", *Eranos*, 46, 1-21.
Eisler, R. (1923) *Orphisch-Dionysische Mysteriengedanken*. Hildesheim. [1966]
Eitrem, S. (1909) *Hermes und die Toten*. Oslo.
Eliade, M. (1951) *La Chamanisme*. Paris.
Eliade, M. (1958) *Rites and Symbols of Initiation. The Mysteries of Birth and Rebirth* (translated from the French by Willard R. Task). New York, Hagerstown, San Fransisco, London.

ER = *Encyclopaedia of Religion and Ethics*, J. Hastings (ed.). Edingburgh, 1908-26.
Fabian, J. (1979) "The Anthropology of Religious Movements: From Explanation to Interpretation", *Social Research - An International Quarterly of the Social Sciences*, 46, 4-35. New York.
Farnell, L.R. (1921) *Greek Hero Cults and Ideas of Immortality*. Oxford.
Felten, W. (1975) *Attische Unterweltsdarstellungen*. München.
Finley, M.I. (1979) *The World of Odysseus*. New York.
Focke, F. (1941) *Rite und Reigen*. Stuttgard & Berlin.
Foley, H.P. (1994) *The Homeric Hymn to Demeter. Translation, Commentary and Interpretive Essays*. Princeton, N.J.
Ford, A. (1992) *Homer: The Poetry of the Past*. Ithaca & London.
Foucart, P.F. (1914) *Les Mystères D'Eleusis*. Paris. [New York 1975].
Foucault, M. (1969) *L'archéologie du savoir*. Paris.
Foucault, M. (1977) *Language, counter-memory, practice. Selected essays and interviews by Michel Foucault*. D.F. Bouchard (ed.). Ithaca, N.Y.
Frankfort, H. et al. (1946) *Before Philosophy*. Harmondsworth, Middlesex [1954].
Frazer, J.G. (1912[3ed.]) *The Golden Bough - A Study in Magic and Religion*. Cambridge [1933].
Freeman, K. (1952) *Ancilla to the Pre-Socratic Philosophers*. Oxford: Basil Blackwell.
Frege, G. (1891/92) *Funktion, Begriff, Bedeutung. Fünf logische untersuchungen*. Göttingen [1969].
Friis Johansen, K. (1934) *Iliaden i tidlig græsk Kunst*. København: Povl Branner.
Frisk, H. (1961) *GEW* = *Griechisches Etymologisches Wörterbuch*. Heidelberg.
Fustel de Coulanges, N.D. (1864) *La Cité Antique*. Paris [1900].
Garland, R. (1985) *The Greek Way of Death*. London.
Geertz, A. (1990) "Introduktion: Mystik som et religionsvidenskabeligt problemområde", *Mystik - Den indre vej? En religionshistorisk udfordring*. P. Bilde & A. Geertz (eds.). Aarhus, 9-32.
Gordon, R.L. (1977) *Myth, Religion and Society*. Cambridge.
Graf, F. (1974) *Eleusis und die Orphische Dichtung Athens in Vorhellenistischer Zeit*, Versuche und Vorarbeiten, 33. New York.
Graf, F. (1992), "Nachworth", *Orpheus. Altgriechische Mysterien*. J.O. Plassmann (ed.), 161-75.
Graf, F. (1993) "Dionysian and Orphic Eschatology", *Masks of Dionysos*, T.H. Carpenter & Ch.A. Faraone (eds.). Ithaca & London, 239-58.
Guthrie, W.K.C. (1935) *Orpheus and Greek Religion*. Princeton, N.J. [1993].
Guthrie, W.K.C. (*HGP*) *A History of Greek Philosophy*, I-V. Cambridge, 1962-78.
Hack, R.K. (1929) "Homer and the Cults of Heroes", *American Philological Association*, 60, 57-74.

Hainsworth, J.B. (1968) *The Flexibility of the Homeric Formulae*. Oxford.
Harrison, J.E. (1903) *Prolegomena to the Study of Greek Religion*. London, [1961].
Harrison, J.E. (1912) *Themis*. Cambridge, [1977].
Hartog, F. (1988) *The Mirror of Herodotus. The Representation of the Other in the Writing of History*. Transl. J. Lloyd. Berkely, Los Angeles & London.
Havelock, E.A. (1963) *Preface to Plato*. Cambridge, Mass.
HDA = Handbook of Discourse Analysis, I-IV. T.A Van Dijk (ed.). London, 1985.
Henrichs, A. (1982) "Changing Dionysiac Identities", Jewish and Christian Self-Definition, B.F. Meyer & E.P. Sanders (eds.), vol. 3. Philadelphia, 137-60.
Hertz, R. (1905-6) "Contribution à une étude sur la représentation collective de la mort", *L'année Sociologique*, 10, 48-137. Paris.
Heubeck, A. (1989) *A Commentary on Homer's Odyssey*, vol.2. Oxford
Hild, J.A. (1881) *Études Les Démons - dans la littérature et la religion des Grecs*. Paris.
Horst, P.C. Van der (1942) "ΔΑΙΜΩΝ", *Mnemosyne*, 10.
Howard, A. (1996) "Speak of the Devils. Discourse and Belief in Spirits on Rotuma", *Spirits in Culture, History and Mind*. J.M.Mageo & A. Howard (eds.). New York & London, 11-27.
Hultkrantz, Å. (1953) *Conceptions of the Soul Among North American Indians*. Stockholm.
Hultkrantz, Å (1984) "Shamanism and Soul Ideology", *Shamanism in Eurasia*, Mihály Hoppál (ed.), I. Göttingen, 28-36.
Humphreys, S.C. (1981) "Death and Time" *Mortality and Immortality. The Anthropology and Archaeology of death*, S.C. Humphreys & H. King (eds.). London, 261-84.
Humphreys, S.C. (1983) *The Family, Woman and Death*. London.
Huntington, R. & Metcalf, P. (1979) *Celebration of Death*. Cambridge, Mass.
Hölscher, U. (1939) *Untersuchungen zur Form der Odyssee*. Berlin.
Hölscher, U. (1972) *Die Erkennungsszene im 23. Buch der Odyssee*. Wege der Forschung, 634. Darmstadt [1991].
Jaeger, W. (1947) *The Theology of the Early Greek Philosophers*. Oxford.
Jeanmaire, H. (1951) *Dionysos*. Paris.
Jeffrey, L.H. (1961) *The Local Scripts of Archaic Greece*. Oxford.
Jensen, J. Sinding (1990) "Mystikken som rituelt sprog", *Mystik - Den indre vej? En religionshistorisk udfordring*. P. Bilde & A. Geertz (eds.). Aarhus, 155-70.
Jensen, M. Skafte (1968) *Homerforskning*. Copenhagen.
Jensen, M. Skafte (1980) *The Homeric Question and the Oral Formulaic Theory*. Copenhagen.
Jensen, M. Skafte (1992) *Homer og hans tilhørere*. Copenhagen.

Jung, C.G. (1976) *Die Archetypen und das kollektive Unbewußte*, Gesammelte Werke, Bd. 9/1. Olten.

Kakridis, J. Th. (1949) *Homeric Researches*. Lund.

Kanta, K.G. (1979) *Eleusis*. Athens.

Kerényi, K. (1937) *Pythagoras and Orpheus*. Zürich [1950].

Kerényi, K. & Jung, C.G. (1941) *Einführung in das Wesen der Mythologie*. Zürich.

Kerényi, K. (1944) "Mysterien der Kabiren", *Eranos Jarhbuch*, 11. Zürich, 11-53.

Kerényi, K. (1951) *Die Mythologie der Griechen*. Zürich.

Kerényi, K. (1961) *Umgang mit Göttlichem*. Göttingen.

Kerényi, K: (1962) *Die Mysterien von Eleusis*. Zürich.

Kerényi, K. (1967) *Eleusis. Archetypical Image of Mother and Daughter*. New York.

Kerényi, K. (1976) *Dionysos. Urbild des unzerstörrbaren Lebens*. München & Wien.

Kern, O. (1920) *Orpheus. Eine Religionsgeschichtliche Untersuchung*. Berlin.

Kern, O. (1922) *Orphicorum Fragmenta*. Dublin/Zürich [1972].

Kessels, A. (1969) "Ancient Systems of Dream-Classification", *Mnemosyne*, 22, 389-424.

Kessels, A. (1978) *Studies on the Dream in Greek Literature*. Utrecht.

Kingsley, P. (1995) *Ancient Philosophy, Mystery and Magic - Empedocles and Pythagorean Tradition*. Oxford.

Kirk, G.S. (1962) *The Songs of Homer*. Cambridge.

Kirk, G.S. (1974) *The Nature of Greek Myth*. London.

Krarup, P. (1945) *Homer*. Copenhagen.

Kruyt, A.C. (1906) *Het Animisme in den Indischen Archipel*. S'Gravenhage.

Kübler, K. (1959) *Die Nekropole des 10. bis 8. Jarhhunderts*. Berlin.

Küster, E. (1913) *Die Schlange in der Griechischen Kunst und Religion*. Religionsgeschichtliche Versuche und Vorarbeiten.Vol. 13/2.

Kurtz, D.C. & Boardman, J. (1971) *Greek Burial Customs*. London.

Laks, A. & Most, G.W. (1997) "A Translation of the Derveni Papyrus", *Studies on the Derveni Papyrus*. Oxford.

Leach, E. (1976) *Culture and Communication*. Cambridge.

Lesher, J.H. (1992) *Xenophanes of Colophon. Fragments. A Text and Translation with a Commentary*. Toronto, Buffalo & London.

Lesky, A. (1957/58) *Geschichte der Griechischen Literatur*. Bern.

Lessing, G.E. (1769) *Wie die Alten den Tod gebildet habenx?*. Gesammelte Werke, 5. Leipzig [1855].

Lévy-Bruhl, L. (1918) *Les fonctions mentales dans les sociétés inferieures*. Paris.

LFE = Lexicon des Frühgriechischen Epos. Snell & Mette (eds.). Göttingen.

LIMC = Lexicon Iconographicum Mythologiae Classicae. Artemis Verlag, Zürich & München, 1981-97.

Lincoln, B. (1982) "Waters of Memory, Waters of Forgetfulness", *Fabula*, 23, 19-34.

Linforth, I.M. (1941) *The Arts of Orpheus*. The Philosophy of Plato and Aristotle. New York [1973].

Lloyd, G.E.R. (1987) *The Revolutions of Wisdom - Studies in the Claims and Practice of Ancient Greek Science.* Berkeley, L.A. & London.

Lloyd, G.E.R. (1990) *Demystifying Mentalities*. Cambridge.

Lloyd, G.E.R. (1996) *Aristotelian Explorations*. Cambridge.

Lobeck, Chr.A. (1829) *Aglaophamus - De theologiae mysticae graecorum causis.* Regimontii Prussorum.

Long, H.S. (1948) *A Study of the Doctrine of Metempsychosis in Greece - From Pythagoras to Plato*. Princeton, N.J.

Lord, A.B. (1968) "Homer as Oral Poet", *Harvard Studies in Classical Philology*, 12, 1-46.

Lord, A.B. (1960) *The Singer of Tales*. Boston.

Lowenstam, S. (1981) *The Death of Patroclus. A Study in Typology*. Königsheim.

LS = Greek-English Lexicon: Lidell & Scott (Jones & McKenzie). Oxford.

Lynn-George, M. (1988) *EPOS: Word, Narrative and the Iliad*. London.

Malten, L. (1909) *Der Raub der Kore & Altorphische Demetersage*, Archiv für Religionswissenschaft, 12, 285-312; 417-46. Leipzig.

Malten, L. (1913) "Elysion und Rhadamanthys", *Jahrbuch des Deutschen Archäologischen Institut*, vol. 28, 35-51.

Mannhardt, W. (1884) *Mythologische Forschungen aus dem Nachlasse*. Strasbourg & London.

Marzullo, B. (1952) *Il Problema Omerico.* Firenze.

Meier, C.A. (1949) *Antike Inkubation und Moderne Psychotherapie*. Zürich [1979].

Merkelbach, R. (1951) *Untersuchungen zur Odyssee*. München [1969].

Moore, C.H. (1916) *Religious Thoughts of the Greeks*. Cambridge.

Moszyński, K. (1976) "Slavic Folk Culture", *Vampires of the Slavs*. J.L. Perkowski (ed.). Cambridge, Mass. 180-87.

Mylonas, G.E. (1948) "Homeric and Mycenaean Customs", *Archaeological Journal of America*, 52, 56-81.

Mylonas, G.E. (1957) *Ancient Mycenae*. Princeton.

Mylonas, G.E. (1961) *Eleusis and the Eleusinian Mysteries*. Princeton, N.J. [1971].

Nagy, G. (1979) *The Best of the Acheans*. Baltimore & London.

Nagy, G. (1980) "Patroklos, Concepts of Afterlife, and the Indic Triple Fire", *Arethusa*, 13/2.

Nagy, G. (1983) "On the Death of Sarpedon", *Approaches to Homer*, 189-217, Rubino, C.A. & Shelmerdine, C.W.. (eds.). Austin.

Nagy, G. (1985) "Theognis and Megara: A Poet's Vision of His City", *Theognis of Megara. Poetry and the Polis* (22-81). G.Nagy and T.J.Figueira (eds.), 22-81.

Nagy, G. (1990a) *Greek Mythology and Poetics*. Ithaca & London.

Nagy, G. (1990b) *Pindar's Homer. The Lyric Possession of an Epic Past*. Baltimore & London.

Nagy, G. (1996) Poetry as Performance. Homer and Beyond. Cambridge.

Nestle, W. (1930) *Griechische Religiosität von Homer bis Pindar und Aeschylos*, I, Berlin & Leipzig.

Nietzsche, F. (1972) "Die Geburt der Tragödie aus dem Geiste der Musik", *Werke. Kritische Gesamtausgabe*, III[I]. Berlin & New York.

Nilsson, M.P. (1927) *The Minoan-Mycenaean Religion and its Survival in Greek Religion*. Lund [1968].

Nilsson, M.P. (1935) *Homeros*. Lund.

Nilsson, M.P. (1943) "Die Quellen der Lethe", *Eranos. Acta Philologica Suecana a Vilelmo Lundström Candita*, 1-7.

Nilsson, M.P. (1955[3 ed.]) *Geschichte der Greichische Religion*, I. München.

Nilsson, M.P. (1950) *Geschichte der Greichische Religion*, II. München.

Nock, A.D. (1972) *Essays on Religion and the Ancient World*. Oxford.

O'Flaherty, W. (1980) *Sexual Metaphors and Animal Symbols in Indian Mythology*. Chicago.

OLD = Oxford Latin Dictionary. Oxford.

Onians, R.B. (1951) *The Origins of European Thought*. Cambridge.

Otto, W.F. (1927) *Die Manen*. Darmstadt [1958].

Otto, W.F. (1955) *Die Gestalt und das Sein*. Darmstadt [1974].

Paasonen, H. (1909) "Über die ursprünglischen Seelenvorstellungen bei den finnisch-ugrischen Völkern und die Benennungen der Seele in ihren Sprachen", *Journal de la Société Finno-Ougrienne*, Helsinki.

Page, D.L. (1955) *The Homeric Odyssey*. Oxford.

Page, D.L. (1963a) *History and the Homeric Iliad. Berkeley* & L.A.

Page, D.L. (1963b) *Archilochus and the oral tradition*. Fondation Hardt. Pour L'Étude de L'Antiquité Classique, vol. 10, 119-64.

Parker, R. (1983) *Miasma*. Oxford.

Parry, M. (1971) *The Making of Homeric Verse*. Oxford.

Paulson, I. (1958) *Die Primitive Seelenvorstellungen des nordeuropäischen Völkern*. Stockholm.

Pêcheux, M. (1988) "Discourse: Structure or Event?", *Marxism and the Interpretation of Culture*. C.Nelson & L.Grossberg (eds.). Urbana & Chicago, 633-50.

Persson, A.W. (1931) *The Royal Tombs at Dendra near Midea*. Lund.

Pestalozzi, H. (1945) *Die Achilleis als Quelle der Ilias*. Zürich.
Pettazoni, R. (1954) *Essays on the History of Religions*. Leiden.
Petzl, G. (1969) *Antike Diskussionen über beiden Nekyiai*. Meisenheim.
Plath, D.W. (1964) "Where the Family of God is the Family: the Role of the Dead in Japanese Households", *American Anthropologists*, 67/7.
The Presocratic Philosophers. A Critical History with a Selection of Texts (1983), G.S. Kirk, J.E. Raven & M. Schofield (eds.). Cambridge.
Preusz, K.T. (1914) *Die geistige Kultur der Naturvölker*. Leipzig.
Price, T.H. (1978) *KOUROTROPHOS. Cults and Representations of the Greek Nursing Dieties*. Leiden.
Price, T.H. (1979) "Hero Cult in the Age of Homer and Earlier", *Arktouros. Hellenistic Studies*.
Puhvel, J. (1969) "'Meadow of the Otherworld', Indo European tradition", *Zeitschrift für Vergleichence Sprachforschung*, vol. 83. Göttingen.
PW = Paulys Real-Encyclopädie, herausgegeben von Wissowa, Kroll, Stuttgart, 1894-978.
Radcliffe-Brown, A.R. (1933) *The Andaman Islanders*. Cambridge.
Ravn, O.E. (1953) *Babylonske religiøse tekster*. Copenhagen.
Reinhardt, K. (1961) *Der Ilias und Ihr Dichter*. Göttingen.
Reiner, E. (1938) *Die Rituelle Totenklage der Griechen*. Tübinger Beiträge zur Altertumswissenschaft, 30. Stuttgart & Berlin.
Reverdin, O. (1945) *La Religion de la cité platonicienne*. Paris.
Richardson, N.J. (1974) *The Homeric Hymn to Demeter*. Oxford.
Richardson, N.J. (1993) *The Iliad: A Commentary*. VI: books 21-24. Cambridge.
Ricoeur, P. (1976) *Interpretation Theory - Discourse and the Surplus of Meaning*. Fort Worth.
Rohde, E. (1925[10ed.]) *Psyche - Seelenkult und Unsterblichkeitsglaube der Greichen*, I-II. Tübingen.
Roscher = W.H. Roscher - Ausführliches Lexicon der Griechischen und Römischen Mythologie. Hildesheim, 1965.
Rose, H.J. (1925) *Primitive Culture in Greece*. London.
Rowe, C.J. (1983) "The Nature of Homeric Morality", *Approaches to Homer*, Rubino, C.A. & Shelmerdine, C.W. Austin (eds.). Texas, 248-75.
Rubino, C.A. (1979) "A Thousand Shapes of Death", *ARKTOUROS. Hellenistic Studies*, 12-18.
Russo, J. (1992) *A Commentary on Homer's Odyssey*, III. Oxford.
RÄR = *Reallexikon der Ägyptischen Religionsgeschichte*. Berlin 1952.
Schadewaldt, W. (1944) *Von Homers Welt und Werk*. Stuttgart.

Schadewaldt, W. (1959) *Neue Kriterien zur Odyssee-Analyse.* Wege der Forschung, 634. Darmstadt [1991].

Schibli, H.S. (1990) *Pherecydes of Syros.* Oxford.

Schjødt, J.P. (1983) "Livsdrik og vidensdrik", *Religionsvidenskabeligt tidsskrift*, 2. Århus, 85-102.

Schjødt, J.P. (1990) "Mystikken og Den anden Verden. Et essay om problemerne ved en indplacering af mystik som en religionsfænomenologisk kategori", *Mystik - Den indre vej? En religionshistorisk udfordring.* P. Bilde & A. Geertz (eds.). Aarhus, 139-54.

Schjødt, J.P. (1992) "Ritualstruktur og ritualklassifikation", *Religionsvidenskabeligt tidsskrift*, 20. Århus, 5-23.

Schliemann, H. (1878) *Mykenae.* Darmstadt [1966].

Schmitt-Pantel, P. (1982) "Évergétisme et mémoire du mort", *La Mort, Les Morts, dans les Sociétés Anciennes*, 177-88. Cambridge.

Schnaufer, A. (1970) *Frühgriechische Totenglaube.* New York.

Schwartz, E. (1924) *Die Odyssee.* München.

Seaford, R. (1994) *Reciprocity and Ritual. Homer and Tragedy in the Developing City-State.* Oxford.

Segal, C. (1971) *The Theme of the Mutilation of the Corpse in the Iliad.* Leiden.

Sfameni Gasparro, G. (1996) "Daimôn and Tuchê in the Hellenistic Religious Experience", *Conventional Values of the Hellenistic Greeks.* (Studies in Hellenistic Civilization, 8). P. Bilde, T. Engberg-Pedersen, L. Hannestad & J. Zahle (eds.). Aarhus, 67-109.

Smidt Hansen, B. (1990) "Ramakrishnas mystik til belysning af mystik som generelt eller specifikt fænomen", *Mystik - Den indre vej? En religionshistorisk udfordring.* P. Bilde & A. Geertz (eds.). Aarhus, 93-105.

Snodgrass, A. (1971) *The Dark Age of Greece: An Archaeological Survey of the Eleventh to the Eighth Centuries.* Edinburgh.

Snodgrass, A. (1979) *Archaic Greece.* Cambridge.

Snodgrass, A. (1988) "The Archaeology of the Hero". *Archeologia e Storia Antica*, 10, 19-26. Napoli.

Tamburnino, J. (1909) *De antiquorum Daemonismo.* Religionsgeschichtliche Versuche und Vorarbeiten. Giessen.

Tarán, L. (1965) *Parmenides.* Princeton.

Taylour, Lord W. (1983) *The Myceneans.* London, [1991].

Thomsen, O. (1992) *Ritual and Desire: Catullus 61 and 62 and other ancient documents on wedding and marriage.* Aarhus.

Thomson, G. (1949) *Studies in Ancient Greek Society*, I. New York.

Thornton, A. (1970) *People and Themes in Homer's Odyssey.* London.

Thönges-Stringaris (1965) "Das Griechische Totenmahl", *Mitteilungen des deutschen archäologischen Institut, Athenische Abteilung*, 80. Berlin.

Toepffer, I. (1889) *Attische Genealogie*. Berlin [New York: 1973].

Torresin, G. (1989) *Homer*. Klassikerforeningens oversigter, Aarhus.

Tsantsanoglou, K. (1997) "The First Columns of the Derveni Papyrus", *Studies on the Derveni Papyrus*. Oxford.

Turner, V. (1967) *The Forest of Symbols*. Ithaca, N.Y.

Turner, V. (1969) *The Ritual Process - Structure and Anti-Structure*. London.

Tylor, E.B. (1873) *Primitive Culture*. London.

Ukert, F.A. (1850) "Über Dämonen, Heroen und Genien", *Schriften der Königlich Sächsischen Gesellschaft der Wissenschaften*, 1. Leipzig.

V.d. Mühl, P. (1952) *Kritisches Hypomnema zur Ilias*. Basel.

Van der Waerden, B.L. (1979) *Die Pythagoreer. Religiöse Bruderschaft und Schule der Wissenschaft*. Zürich & München.

Van Gennep, A. (1909) *Les Rites de Passage*. Paris.

Vajda, L. (1964) "Zur phaseologischen Stellung des Schamanismus", *Religions-ethnologie*, C.A. Schmitz (ed.). Frankfurt a.M., 265-95.

Vallet, G. (1985) "Pindare et la Sicile", *Pindare*. Fondation Hardt.

Vernant, J.P. (1965) *Mythe et pensée chez les grecs*. Paris [1990].

Vernant, J.P. (1981) "Death with two faces", *Mortality and Immortality. The Anthropology and Archaeology of Death*, S.C. Humphreys & H. King (eds.). London, 285-91.

Vernant, J.P. (1982) *The Origins of Greek Thought*. London (translated by the writer, from "L'origines de la pensée grecque", Paris 1962.)

Vermeule, E. (1979) *Aspects of Death in Early Greek Art and Poetry*. Berkeley & London.

Wade-Gery, H.T. (1952) *The Poet of the Iliad*. Cambridge.

Walton, F.R. (1952) "Athens, Eleusis and the Homeric Hymn to Demeter", *Harvard Theological Review*, 45, 105-30.

Warden, J. (1971) "Ψυχή in Homeric Death-Descriptions", *Phoenix - Journal of the Classical Association of Canada*, vol. 25, 95-103.

West, M.L. (1966) *Hesiod - Theogony*. Oxford.

West, M.L. (1970) "The Eighth Homeric Hymn and Proclus", *The Classical Quarterly*, 20, 300-4. Oxford.

West, M.L. (1982) "The Orphics of Olbia", *Zeitschrift für Papyrologie und Epigrafik*, 45, 17-29.

West, M.L. (1983) *The Orphic Poems*. Oxford.

West, M.L. (1985) *The Hesiodic Catalogue of Women*. Oxford.

Wiedengren, G. (1969) *Religionsphänomenologie*. Berlin.

Wiesner, J. (1938) *Grab und Jenseits*. Berlin.
Wilamowitz-Moellendorf, U.v. (1884) *Homerische Untersuchungen*. Berlin.
Wilamowitz-Moellendorf, U.v. (1916) *Die Ilias und Homer*. Berlin.
Wilamowitz-Moellendorf, U.v. (1922) *Pindaros*. Berlin.
Wilamowitz-Moellendorf, U.v. (1959) *Der Glaube der Hellenen*, I-II$^{3 ed.}$. Darmstadt [1976].
Wili, W. (1944) "Die Orphischen Mysterien und der Griechische Geist", *Eranos Jahrbuch*, 11, 61-105.
Wundt, W. (1910) "Völkerpsychologie", *Mythus und Religion*, 1. Leipzig.
Zielinski, T. (1934) "La Guerre à l'Outretombe". *Mélanges Bidez*, 2.
Zimmer, H. (1972) *Indische Mythen und Symbole*. Darmstadt.
Zuntz, G. (1971) *Persephone*. Oxford.

Index Locorum

PLATES

Plate 1. Funeral procession. Dipylon krater.

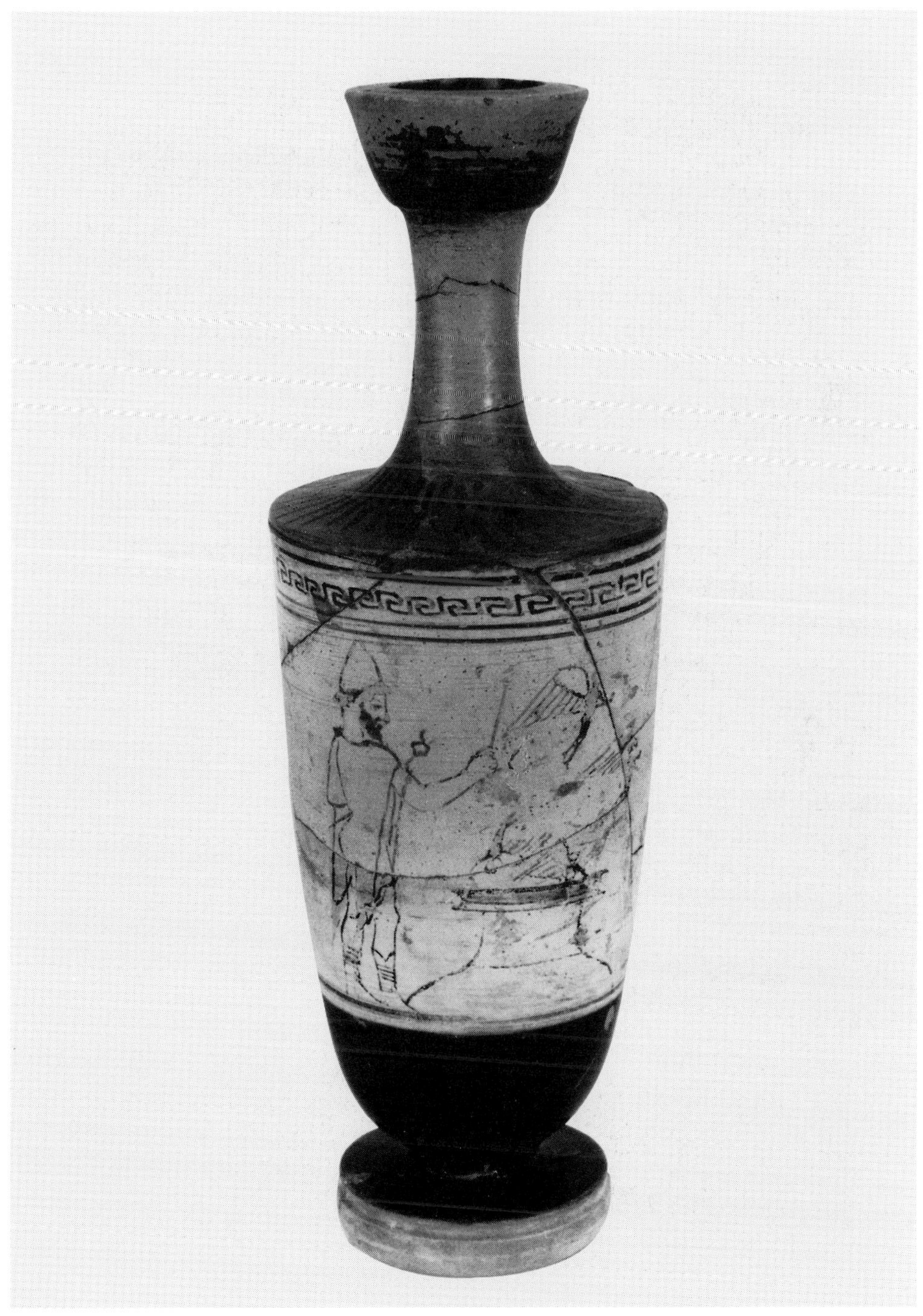

Plate 2. Hermes and the *eidola* at a *Pithos*. Attic white-ground lekythos.

Plate 3a.
Ker and a Fallen Warrior.

Plate 3b. *Keres* at the *Prothesis*. Attic white-ground Lekythos.

Plate 4. Sisyphos in the Underworld. Attic black-figured amphora, late sixth century BC.

Plate 5. The Death of Sarpedon. Attic, red-figured calyx krater.

ΚΑΛΙΣΤΟ
ΜΑΡΣΥΑΣ
ΜΕΜΝΟΝ
ΕΚΤΟΡ
ΘΑΜΥΡΙΣ

Plate 7. Terracotta figurine of Persephone from Kamarina.

Plate 8. Initiation in the Eleusinian Mysteries. The Lovatelli Urn.

Plate 9. Initiation in the Eleusinian Mysteries. Sarchophagus from the Palazzo Spagna in Rome.

Plate 10. Female figure fleeing before the revelation of the cradle. Terracotta relief.

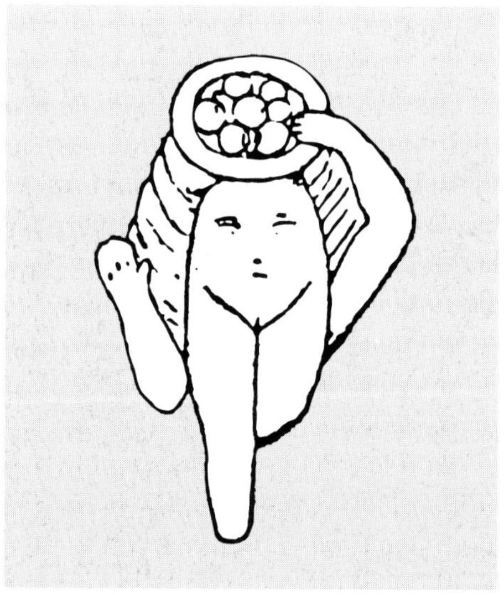

Plate 11. Drawing of Terracotta figurine from Priene.